PORTFOLIO

THE WAL-MART TRIUMPH

Robert Slater, the bestselling author of *Jack Welch and the GE Way*, has probed deeply into the Wal-Mart organization from top to bottom, from Bentonville to China and beyond. His book offers a fresh and fascinating look at this unique company—as it was and as it has become—with an immediacy and insider's feel unrivaled since Sam Walton's own memoir, *Made in America*. Slater was a reporter at *Time* for twenty-one years and has also written acclaimed books about IBM and Cisco.

ROBERT SLATER

THE
WAL-MART
TRIUMPH

Inside the World's #1 Company

★ PORTFOLIO

Previously published as *The Wal-Mart Decade*

PORTFOLIO

Published by the Penguin Group

Penguin Group (USA) Inc., 375 Hudson Street, New York, New York 10014, U.S.A.

Penguin Books Ltd, 80 Strand, London WC2R 0RL, England

Penguin Books Australia Ltd, 250 Camberwell Road, Camberwell, Victoria 3124, Australia

Penguin Books Canada Ltd, 10 Alcorn Avenue, Toronto, Ontario, Canada M4V 3B2

Penguin Books India (P) Ltd, 11 Community Centre, Panchsheel Park,
New Delhi – 110 017, India

Penguin Group (NZ), cnr Airborne and Rosedale Roads, Albany,
Auckland, 1310, New Zealand

Penguin Books (South Africa) (Pty) Ltd, 24 Sturdee Avenue,
Rosebank, Johannesburg 2196, South Africa

Penguin Books Ltd, Registered Offices:
80 Strand, London WC2R 0RL, England

First published in the United States of America by Portfolio,
a member of Penguin Group (USA) 2003
This paperback edition published 2004

10   9   8   7   6   5   4

LIBRARY OF CONGRESS HAS CATALOGUED THE HARDCOVER EDITION AS FOLLOWS:
Slater, Robert, 1943–
The Wal-Mart decade : how a generation of leaders turned Sam Walton's legacy into the world's #1 company / Robert Slater.
p. cm.
Includes bibliographical references and index.
ISBN 1-59184-006-6 (hc.)
ISBN 1-59184-043-0 (pbk.)
1. Wal-Mart (Firm)—History.   2. Discount houses (Retail trade)—United States—History. 3. Walton, Sam, 1918–   4. Businessmen—United States—Biography.   5. Retail trade—United States—Management—Case studies.   6. Success in business—United States—Case studies.   7. Entrepreneurship—United States—Case studies.   8. Leadership—United States—Case studies.   9. Corporations—United States—Growth—Case studies.   I. Title.

HF5465.U64W357 2003
381'.149'0973—dc21   2003040588

Printed in the United States of America
Set in Minion with Helvetica Neue

CONTENTS

THE **WAL-MART** TRIUMPH

INTRODUCTION

The 7,500 Wal-Mart managers, district managers, divisional vice presidents, and various senior and executive vice presidents gathered in January 2004 in the Kansas City, Missouri, Convention Center, screaming joyously over their company's latest financial triumphs. The company was likely to be ranked #1 in revenue on the *Fortune* 500 list for 2004, with projected revenues of $258 billion, amounting to a 12.4 percent increase in growth over the previous year. That would mark the second straight year that Wal-Mart could claim the title of being the largest company in the world. (Earnings rose 13.3 percent to a record $8.9 billion for 2004.)

Although Wal-Mart's founder, the late Sam Walton, had little interest in building a company that grew so powerfully, the next generation of Wal-Mart leaders regarded growth as the company's top priority. And no matter what is happening to the United States economy, no matter how many new competitors enter the field, Wal-Mart continues to grow, and to triumph. The end is not in sight. Both domestically and internationally, Wal-Mart has many more opportunities to grow. That was what I found so intriguing about the company and why I was prompted to write *The Wal-Mart Decade: How a New Generation of Leaders Turned Sam Walton's Legacy into the World's #1 Company.* The hardcover edition was published in June 2003. We now present the paperback edition, newly named *The Wal-Mart Triumph.*

Wal-Mart always had its critics. And in 2004, in the wake of the company's unparalleled, mind-boggling success, those critics have become even more vocal, seizing upon the company's soft spots, exposing faults and flaws to the media, hoping to show that Wal-Mart's climb to the top has been undeserved.

Both of these themes—Wal-Mart's phenomenal growth and the challenges posed to its reputation—were discussed at length at the

Kansas City sessions. One executive after another rose to the stage, and urged the crowd of managers to become an even more aggressive sales force in the coming year. No executive dared say it, but Wal-Mart was finding it much easier to keep its phenomenal growth record intact than to ward off its critics.

In the year since I wrote *The Wal-Mart Decade*, the company has to an even larger extent found itself fighting on two battlefronts: making sure that its millions of customers continued to shop at Wal-Mart; and defending itself against a string of assaults, some political, some legal, some community-driven.

The hardcover edition explored in great depth the remarkable record of financial growth of the new Wal-Mart leaders, who increased annual revenue from $43 billion in 1992, the year Sam Walton died, to $256.3 billion in 2003. Another sign of the leaders' great growth record: as of December 31, 2003, there were 5,268 Wal-Mart stores worldwide, including 3,499 within the United States, and another 1,769 in ten other countries.

In 2003 and the early part of 2004, the company began settling into what seemed likely to be a long-term run as the world's largest enterprise. But, during that same year, Wal-Mart's critics intensified their attacks on the company, serving notice that the battle for Wal-Mart's reputation would be a long and undoubtedly painful one.

The media played its part in the latter part of 2003 in making Wal-Mart even more visible and more controversial. A *Business Week* cover story in October 2003 headlined the question: "Is Wal-Mart Too Powerful?" The subhead read: "Low prices are great. But Wal-Mart's dominance creates problems—for suppliers, workers, communities, and even American culture."

A *New York Times* article on December 8, 2003, headlined this question: "Is Wal-Mart Good for America?" The article noted that Wal-Mart's low-priced formula had apparently led to the bankruptcy of the premium-priced toy company F.A.O. Schwarz, the latest example of what had come to be known as the Wal-Mart effect. That effect was essentially the powerful impact that Wal-Mart exerted over suppliers, forcing them to become more efficient so that

Wal-Mart could pass those gains on to consumers in the form of lower prices.

Wal-Mart grew more visible and controversial in the past year as well because of some major legal skirmishes. Even as Wal-Mart was trying to clear its legal dockets as quickly as possible, there was still more litigation against the company than against any other private institution in the United States, some 6,649 lawsuits as of September 2003. The majority of those cases continued to center on accidents and injuries at the stores. But others were far more contentious and thus far more difficult for Wal-Mart to keep out of the newspapers.

The case that drew Wal-Mart's concern the most was a discrimination lawsuit that, if elevated to a class action, could add 1.5 million plaintiffs and make it the largest suit of its kind. It centered on a charge by six former Wal-Mart employees that the country's largest private employer discriminated against women in pay and promotions.

For a good part of the 1990s, Wal-Mart did little to counter the legal and other attacks against the company other than to deny the veracity of allegations. Then the company began to realize that the attacks on the company could have a serious effect on the company's growth. "Even if we didn't do anything to improve our reputation," said Jay Allen, the senior vice president for corporate affairs, "Wal-Mart will continue to be a profitable, successful company. But in a given market, the question becomes: are we going to have a few stores or truly be a retail leader?" The answer had to do with how successfully Wal-Mart could ward off those attacks on its reputation.

And so in the 2000s, the company decided to launch a major offensive both in public relations and community relations; and in the latter part of 2003 and early 2004 that offensive is continuing to grow. For the first time, Wal-Mart executives were publicly blaming the labor unions as the main source of the attacks against the company. "We are the focus of a number of outside parties, with the unions probably leading the way," Jay Allen asserted. "We're enemy number one to outside parties who don't want us to grow; and they are throwing a lot of resources behind the effort."

Attempting to be proactive and engaged rather than being on the defensive, Wal-Mart executives sought where possible to correct misimpressions about the company and to encourage the media to write about the positive aspects of Wal-Mart. The new proactive strategy did not always have the desired effect. For instance, during the 2003 runup to the presidential primaries, Wal-Mart executives were baffled and furious when two Democratic Party presidential candidates (Richard Gephardt and Howard Dean) declared publicly that Wal-Mart purposely hired part-time labor to avoid having to pay employees health care benefits. Such arguments resonated mightily among voters who had made health care a major issue of the 2004 presidential campaign.

Insisting that the candidates had it all wrong—that indeed 80 percent of Wal-Mart's employees were full-time and were getting full health care benefits—Wal-Mart executives had developed a new taste for taking on its critics. If in the past they let such arguments reach the public without rebuttal, now these executives were taking the campaign directly to the candidates, and directly to the media to point out what Wal-Mart considered to be monumental errors about company policy.

At the Kansas City meeting, Wal-Mart executives acknowledged that the negative attacks on Wal-Mart were unlikely to disappear in the near future. But they vowed that the company planned to tell its story better. For all of the controversy surrounding the retail giant in 2003, in March 2004, *Fortune* magazine still chose Wal-Mart as the most admired company in America for the second year in a row.

The battle for growth remained the top priority for Wal-Mart executives, however, and hence that was the dominant theme at the winter meetings in Kansas City. "Top line sales growth is our most important action item today," Mike Duke, the president and CEO of Wal-Mart Stores, told the crowd. "We're a sales-driven company and we're focused on the customer. Our real focus in 2004 will be top line sales. It's amazing how other things fall in line if you get the top line sales going."

How does the largest company in the world in revenues get its thousands of managers excited about top line sales? Wal-Mart had the answer. It summoned its 15,000 managers to Kansas City over a five-day period; it then sought to get their adrenaline overflowing with enthusiastic speeches, the company cheer, a rock 'n' roll band, and some impressive computer graphics that put Mike Duke's head on top of the body of John Travolta, letting Travolta do the dancing.

The audience roared each time someone mentioned the name of a Wal-Mart business unit. When their bosses yelled out from the stage, "Whose Wal-Mart is it?" the crowd yelled back, "It's my Wal-Mart!"

In case anyone hadn't gotten the message that next year had to be a better sales year than this one, Wal-Mart's senior executives paraded their favorite products on stage and proudly boasted about their low prices and high margins. The products ran the gamut from breath fresheners to raincoats that folded into a tiny size. The executives urged their managers to sell thousands of the products, to ring up millions of dollars of sales—to sell, sell, and sell more.

In writing this introduction for the paperback edition, I want to add a personal note: some reviewers, acknowledging that *The Wal-Mart Decade* was the most comprehensive and detailed description of the company since Sam Walton's memoirs had appeared in 1992, would have preferred that I had been harsher on the company. I am troubled by such comments for they seem to suggest that the only way to write about a major company is to concentrate on its flaws and play down its successes. I chose Wal-Mart as the subject for a book not because I wished to lash out at the company but because I believed there was a very good story to tell: how the new generation of leaders who had taken over from Sam Walton had turned Wal-Mart into a far greater success than Walton had ever dreamed. I would argue that the book does contain lengthy discussion of Wal-Mart's shortcomings, but I chose not to use the strident tones that some Wal-Mart critics prefer. I mention Wal-Mart's shortcomings, not to be muckraking, but as part of explaining how Wal-Mart tries to deal with these assaults.

Robert Slater
January 2004

PART ONE

WAL-MART TODAY

CHAPTER 1

CELEBRATING
IN A BASKETBALL ARENA

June 7, 2002. Thousands of Wal-Mart loyalists storm into the cavernous Bud Walton Arena on this summer morning in Fayetteville, Arkansas. The blaring music, the screaming crowds, the bright lights assault the senses—it is, after all, only six in the morning!

Hard to believe, but when the annual shareholder meetings began more than thirty years earlier, Sam Walton, Wal-Mart's founder, huddled with five other people around a table at a coffee shop next to a company warehouse and speedily dispensed with business.

In stark contrast today, the Wal-Mart gathering lasts six hours. It is, at least for that morning, the greatest show in town. No other company in the world puts on a show for shareholders quite this spectacular. One after another, executives race to the stage, adrenaline pumping, fists waving, and smiles on their faces. Roaring with approval, the crowds pour their hearts and souls into an event that has all the trappings of a pep rally or a political convention. Whoever said that a shareholder meeting had to be stuffy or formal?

Other corporations race through annual shareholder meetings. Why shouldn't they? The way others conduct these meetings, they are too boring for anyone to want them to last more than fifteen minutes. The Wal-Mart attitude is different: If you're going to assemble twenty-thousand Wal-Mart loyalists under one roof, the least you can do is give them a rousing good time. And so Wal-Mart turns its event into a wild weeklong celebration, replete with canoe rides,

3

concerts, fireworks, seminars, visits to a company distribution center, and, lest anyone forget why they had all come together, tours of the home office in Bentonville, a thirty-minute drive to the north.

The Wal-Mart assemblage takes up nearly every seat in the 19,300-seat arena, making this the largest corporate annual meeting in the world. More in keeping with a sporting event than a corporate gathering, the visitors wear every possible combination of company buttons and banners and hats. The red hats and banners identify one Wal-Mart division, the green, another. The reds and greens applaud and scream unendingly, but they save the loudest roars for that golden moment when someone on the stage mentions the name of their division. Then a section of the arena erupts, and you really feel as if someone has just scored the game-winning basket for the home team.

The Wal-Mart audience—"First Lady" Helen Walton and her four children, executives, rank-and-file employees ("associates," in Wal-Mart parlance), the board of directors, shareholders—gathers here on this day with one purpose in mind: to rejoice. Every year they travel—some of them thousands of miles—to take part in this corporate festival with the dual purpose of learning more about the place at which they work and to celebrate the achievements of the past year. Never have they had more to celebrate.

★ ★ ★

It has been just over ten years since Sam Walton died, leaving behind a discount merchandise business that few believed would ever make waves but that has defied the imagination of even the greatest of skeptics. At first there just seemed no way that a backwater retailer like Sam Walton could make a mark. Too many of the big boys in retailing had already established footholds in the big cities, the only places that counted for a retailer. But Sam Walton had two very important things going for him: First, he was perhaps the greatest merchant of his era. He had an uncanny instinct for sensing what products would sell, at what prices they would sell; where to locate stores, and what those stores should look like.

FREE TO DO AS HE PLEASED

And he also had a vision that was both prescient and revolutionary: He became the first mass merchant to focus on the small-town backwaters of America. Initially the skeptics howled derisively, mocking a man with such foolhardy pretensions. The skeptics, as it turned out, helped him enormously, as their dissent served to alert others how foolhardy it was to do retailing anywhere but in the large cities. Had the other large retail chains followed young Walton into those small communities, they probably would have pulverized his burgeoning initiative, since he had so little experience and financial support. But they paid little attention to what he was building, leaving him free to build what he wanted at his own pace. And build he did. At the time of his death, on April 5, 1992, Walton had built Wal-Mart into a $43.8 billion enterprise.

Just as doubters greeted the first Wal-Mart stores with deep skepticism, so after Walton's death new Cassandras predicted that Wal-Mart would disappear or at least slowly atrophy. "The betting in dozens of tiny stores around the country," wrote *Time* magazine somberly two weeks after Sam Walton's death, "is that Wal-Mart will reach its own plateau." Because of his death, "the soul of his corporation will change." The betting may have been based on wishful thinking: How nice it would have been for Wal-Mart's competition if the passing of its founder did indeed mean that the chain of discount stores would atrophy or at least reach that plateau. It seemed a safe bet. With Sam Walton's death, the ownership of the company automatically shifted to his widow and four children. Often such family-run corporations cannot withstand the death of the founder. There was just no reason to assume that Sam Walton's retailing genius was transferable to other family members. Indeed, without its soul, Wal-Mart's demise, however slow, seemed a safe bet.

The Walton family had no desire to see The House That Sam Built wither and die. Besides, Wal-Mart was a gold mine, and there was no telling to what heights it might grow under the right leadership. The Walton family exercised shrewd intelligence in realizing how unwise it would be to tamper with the founder's creation; how unwise to tamper with the transition plans that Sam Walton had set in motion.

And so, although many aspects of Wal-Mart changed in the ensuing decade, the essence of the place, the culture and the business philosophy that Sam Walton had devised, remained. For the Walton family, these were crucial decisions, staying involved in the company and insisting that the Sam Walton Way be forever enshrined as company doctrine. John Walton, Sam's son and in 2002 a Wal-Mart board member, recalled: "We thought it was crucial to all of our futures that there be no question about the family's commitment." For no one could be sure that as the company grew, which seemed inevitable, it would be possible to let the past dictate the future to such a degree.

Some central figures, usually for reasons of ego, do their best to assure that a company cannot function smoothly without them. Call it a death wish. Call it a feeling of insecurity bred by a fear that the company under one's heirs might perform better than it did under the founder. So these central figures simply refuse to create a leadership team to carry on after their death. If they *do* choose the next generation of leaders, company founders often select them in their own image. To do otherwise would be to suggest that the founder's brand of leadership was flawed and needed modification.

To be sure, with the same attention to detail that he had shown his stores, Sam Walton created a transition team that would guarantee his posterity. He painstakingly groomed a new leadership team comprising the Walton heirs and a professional group of managers, a group that he felt confident would insure the survival of his original vision.

But a large measure of Sam Walton's genius was in selecting a leadership team he knew would be unmistakably different in personality and leadership style from his; but that, he was confident, would remain loyal to the main tenets of his business philosophy. In truth, the founder had little choice but to pick successors who differed from him. No one in his midst had his very special qualities, as they would readily admit. What he could have done but chose not to—and this is where his genius came in—was to simply ignore the question of succession. He could have left it to those just below him to hash things out after his death, but he must have understood that such a strategy of indifference might have created a most unwelcome vacuum.

He wanted to make sure that a leadership team was already in place, ready to simply carry on once he left the scene. That is precisely what he did. He did not let himself be bothered that his successors would operate in a different manner from his. He understood that the Wal-Mart of his day, relatively small in comparison with what it might become, had benefited from a leader who could make frequent contact with customers and associates. His low-profile, small-town-oriented Wal-Mart did not require the leadership skills that a much larger, more complex, and more exposed company would.

To his credit, Sam Walton understood that the next generation of Wal-Mart leaders would not be able to run the company with the kind, personal touch that he had; they would have to grapple with all sorts of issues that were avoidable when the company was much smaller. They would have to rely on their colleagues a few rungs below them to develop the personal touch with store managers and employees that had been the signature of Sam Walton.

He thought of himself first and foremost as a merchandiser, as someone who had a knack for creating the kind of store environment that would appeal to the customer. He was chiefly concerned with assuring harmony among store managers, employees, and customers; he had much less time for such organization-wide issues as technology, distribution, and logistics. Those were issues that people in the home office would take care of, and he wanted as little to do with the home office as possible. It was, in one of his favorite phrases, a necessary evil. He worked at the people level, not the administrative one.

And yet he knew that, however he resisted certain changes, if Wal-Mart was going to thrive, it would have to build the apparatus of a large organization requiring leaders with talents beyond merchandising, beyond people skills. He must have understood that some or all of his successors would want to put far more emphasis on growth than he had. He accepted that. He understood that he would have to put in place a leadership team that could develop the company's technologies, broaden its distribution systems, and manage its ever-more-complicated logistics. He recognized that Wal-Mart did not need a hundred more Sam Waltons; it needed a hundred more executives who, even if they could not get to the stores as much as he did, could function in a post-Walton world that would inevitably be more complicated and more challenging.

Not only did the post-Walton leadership team believe in growth; they were perfectly attuned to do all that was required to advance Wal-Mart's growth. Most importantly, they were risk-takers, and it was that leadership trait that separated them from Sam Walton more than anything else. While they showed respect for the way Walton expanded the company, they always noted how grudging he was in approving new initiatives, how he always made them jump through hoops to push this technology or that. To be sure, Walton took risks. He took a risk in believing that customers from small towns would flock to his stores for cheap goods rather than drive miles to stores in the cities. He took a risk by amassing huge debt to build the first Wal-Mart stores. But for Sam Walton, the risks were small compared with those taken by the new leadership team.

It is this leadership team and its remarkable accomplishments during the past decade that is the focus of this book. A core theme throughout these pages is the challenge that the leadership team faced in deciding when and how to implement Sam Walton's vision and when and how to implement its own strategies. All through the decade after Walton's passing, it met that challenge remarkably well. In early June 2002, thousands of Wal-Mart devotees come to the shareholder meeting in Fayetteville to celebrate a glorious reality: Not only had Wal-Mart successfully survived the death of its founder; this new generation of Wal-Mart leaders, molded in Walton's image, fanatically devoted to his culture and business philosophy yet mindful of the new complexities of twenty-first-century corporate life, had created the most powerful company growth engine in the world.

GETTING THROUGH THE FORMALITIES

At precisely 7 A.M., a video entitled "Let's Roll" starts, loudly extolling Wal-Mart and pumping up the crowd. Not that they need pumping up. More speeches follow, with more videos and more charts and more hollering. Two hours later, Rob Walton, eldest son of the founder, who took over as chairman of Wal-Mart two days after his father's passing, gently advises the crowd that it is time for the formalities. He seems to feel guilty for robbing the audience of precious time to scream. Some in the audience groan; a few head for the rest rooms.

The crowd shrugs its collective shoulders at the business part of the meeting. Rumors that NFL quarterbacks and the model and actress Cindy Crawford are waiting in the wings waft through the stadium. Similar rumors a few years earlier had proved correct when the teenage singer Britney Spears appeared at a shareholder-week concert. Maybe this rumor was true too. Craning their necks to get an early peek at any celebrities, the audience squirms in its seats as Rob Walton breezes through the formalities. He too is eager to see the NFL quarterbacks John Elway and Joe Montana, the teenage television stars Mary-Kate and Ashley Olsen, and Cindy Crawford.

Needless to say, these celebrities rarely appear at shareholder meetings, but this is Wal-Mart, the biggest and most powerful retailer in the world. No other company has tentacles in so many facets of everyday life. No other business enterprise can offer a Joe Montana or a Cindy Crawford the entrée into American retail life that this corporate giant can. The audience extends well beyond Fayetteville. Back at the 4,485 Wal-Mart stores, spread throughout the United States including Puerto Rico and nine foreign countries, employees watch webcasts of the shareholder festivities. Wal-Mart looks on the surface very much like a company that has a lock on success for the coming decades.

Yet the current generation of Wal-Mart's leaders knows all too well that success can be fleeting. No Wal-Mart executive wants to sound tentative, unsure of the future, but none wants to sound over-confident either. "There's no feeling," said Rob Walton, "that we've got it right now and we've got to try to keep doing the same thing." These are men brimming over with humility; Sam Walton taught them that: There would be no swelled heads, no inflated egos at Wal-Mart. So as executives acknowledge past success, they refuse to gloat: "We celebrate this success for about ten seconds," cautions Tom Schoewe, the executive vice president and chief financial officer. CEO Lee Scott suggests that while Wall Street and the media are con-scious of Wal-Mart's achievements, the average shopper will not be that impressed: "I've yet to meet a customer who came to a store be-cause we're Number One: If they come it's because of the value we give them."

Perhaps Wal-Mart's new leadership team fears the stagnation that complacency can bring. Or, more likely, they worry that they will not be up to the challenge of running an increasingly complex organiz-ation. They know that they have set themselves a seemingly contra-dictory set of tasks: To keep Wal-Mart humming, they must act both as if Sam Walton were still alive and as if he were not—no easy task. They must balance between deploying Sam Walton's powerful man-agement legacy and meeting the exigencies of a modern corporation. Even though Walton resisted creating an unwieldy, bureaucratic Wal-Mart, this new set of post-Walton leaders finds themselves sit-ting atop a huge, multifaceted organization that has grown far be-yond what anyone expected and far mightier than anyone could have believed.

The new Wal-Mart, with its thousands of stores, its massive em-ployee force, its global flavor, the hundred million visitors pouring into its stores weekly and its bulging revenue, no longer justifies the label of underdog or backwater retailer. And yet so much of the legacy of Sam Walton and of Wal-Mart carries the We-Are-David, They-Are-Goliath mystique, and so much of what the founder wanted of his retail chain was that it retain that sense of smallness that worked so well for it in the early days. Always the new leadership would be expected to pay homage to that mystique, conjuring up a Wal-Mart that had benefited from being faceless and anonymous, almost never making waves. But was there such a thing as paying too much homage to the past? What if embracing the traditions and style of the old Wal-Mart kept the new Wal-Mart in shackles? Or to be blunter, what if putting the growth engine into overdrive meant discarding the mystique, meant setting aside as no longer relevant the old quaint ways of the past?

What parts of the past should be kept? What parts dropped? The executives who formed the new management team will tell you that this was not a difficult decision, that it was the easiest thing in the world to decide on retaining the wonderful management legacy that Sam Walton left behind. Most if not all of that legacy is enshrined in a tightly woven set of business rules that govern the running of the Wal-Mart stores. Calibrating the Walton management legacy to the stores' smooth operation was for the new leadership simply a matter of not fixing something that was not broken—as easy as that. The real challenge for them—and this was more difficult for them to acknowledge—was figuring out how and at what pace to build up a corporate organization that would have to be far more intricate and far more complex than anything Sam Walton would have wanted in order to manage and keep control of the hypergrowth that was defining the character of the new Wal-Mart.

WOULDN'T SAM BE PROUD?

For all the outward signs of solidity and self-confidence at the shareholder meeting on that June morning, there are hints of the tug on the leadership team as it wrestles with the past and the future, as it tries to decide whether and how much of the new Wal-Mart should be defined by the Wal-Mart of Sam Walton.

On the one hand, Sam Walton remains a strong, commanding presence, both because of the genuine affection that every executive feels for him and because his business philosophy continues to have such relevance. And so the new leadership venerates him in speech after speech, dwelling on the theme that today's shareholder meeting fulfills all of the founder's dreams: "Don't you think Sam would be so proud if he could see what we've got here today?" asks Coleman Peterson, executive vice president of the people division. The crowds respond with screaming and applause. Executive after executive recounts a favorite Walton anecdote that highlights the man's business genius. He has been dead ten years, but on this day he's certainly not forgotten. It is as if he were still sitting in the front row, wearing his favorite Wal-Mart baseball cap, nodding his approval, waiting impatiently for his turn to speak.

Yet for all the adoration of the founder, for all the constant referencing of his style and ideas, his image seems to be moving ever so slightly toward the margins. Photographs of the friendly, grandfatherly, white-haired man with the keen, piercing eyes and the knowing smile are largely missing in the arena. Nor is there a video biography of his career highlights. To be sure, when "Miss Helen"— Sam Walton's widow—makes a late entrance, she gets a standing ovation, but then so do the quarterbacks Joe Montana and John Elway. And so does the current crop of senior executives. It is as if the new Wal-Mart management knows that the time is approaching when it will have to make most decisions without asking, "What would Mr. Sam have done?" Thus far the new generation of leaders seems to be doing quite nicely. Proof of that came just fifty-three days before the shareholder meeting.

It was then that *Fortune* magazine reported that Wal-Mart had for the first time topped the *Fortune* 500 list, with 2001 revenue of $219.8 billion, putting it ahead of such corporate titans as Exxon-Mobil ($191.5 billion), General Motors ($177.2 billion), Ford Motor ($162.4 billion), and Enron (yes, *that* Enron, $138.7 billion). Wal-Mart had become the largest company in the United States as measured by revenue, indeed, the largest company in the world.

Fortune's designation was historic: No longer did automobile or oil companies rule the roost. A company without factories and smokestacks, one that took other people's products and sold them inexpensively to a loyal and massive customer base, was now atop the field. Wal-Mart indeed seemed the ultimate service business.

Its business success had little to do with keeping capital assets or labor in check. Unable to sell its wares without building ever-larger stores and staffing them in ever-greater quantities, Wal-Mart was both capital-intensive and labor-intensive. It did not rely on great margins for many of the products it sold; the Wal-Mart food line especially relied on thin margins. Its secret, although there was nothing really very secretive about it, was figuring out how to sell in volume. Willing to make less profit per item, Wal-Mart reduced its margins and thus sold products in greater numbers than its rivals. To lure customers into the stores time and time again, it eschewed the "high-low" policies of others (offering a high price one day on an item, a "sale" or low price on the same item another day). Wal-Mart offered everyday low prices—no sales, no special prices. The result was that products moved off the shelves with lightning speed.

★ ★ ★

It is the new leadership team that can take credit for increasing the financial size of Walton's enterprise nearly fivefold since the founder left the scene. Not surprisingly, it is that team that projects the strongest images at the shareholder meeting, radiating a new self-confidence that it hopes will not trip it up in the near future: CEO Lee Scott, in the job just two and a half years, joining his senior colleagues on stage to lead the throngs in the Wal-Mart cheer; Tom Coughlin, the president and CEO of the Wal-Mart Stores and the Sam's Clubs USA, getting a childlike kick out of introducing the NFL star quarterbacks to the crowd; David Glass, a onetime president and CEO of Wal-Mart and still chairman of the Wal-Mart board's executive committee, trying hard to look Cindy Crawford in the eye as he tries to teach her the Wal-Mart cheer, and finally Rob Walton, playing a more visible role than he normally does, presiding over the meeting, symbolizing the Walton family's carefully-constructed role in sharing power with the professional management team.

With many more stores covering far more of a geographical reach, Wal-Mart is not only a more powerful, influential enterprise than in the founder's day; it is also far more exposed to the outside world than the founder had allowed during his era, far more visible, far more controversial. In short, Sam Walton's boundaries, geographic and otherwise, are not Lee Scott's boundaries. McDonald's has a wider international reach, but Wal-Mart is the largest private employer in the world, with 1.38 million employees. Microsoft has come under the scrutiny of the federal judiciary system, but Wal-Mart is a leading target for lawsuits. Home Depot, Staples, and all the other superstores have spread their brands in far-flung places across the nation, but Wal-Mart has become the greatest symbol of the Big Store, the most visible of the large retail organizations, the one chain, more than any other that arouses passions, mostly positive but some negative, in the communities it enters.

The old Wal-Mart under Walton was a simpler organization. It rarely aroused passions. It deliberately sought to steer clear of the limelight. Wal-Mart exploited the benefits of geographical isolation by methodically building up a large chain of discount stores and not tooting its own horn. Few outside of the southwestern part of the United States, Wal-Mart's original home turf, knew much about it, and that was fine with the people who ran Wal-Mart. The new Wal-Mart emerged from that less visible and controversial past, arousing passions, and confronting a whole set of external forces—in the communities, the unions, and the media—all of which wanted to have a say in the new Wal-Mart.

COMING OF AGE

Although this June day does not mark a true changing of the guard—that occurred a decade earlier with Sam Walton's death—the gathering in the Bud Walton Arena still has much significance. It is, if you will, the coming of age of the current group of post-Walton leaders, the first time that the senior management under Lee Scott, its relatively new CEO, feels that it has a team in place that can take it through the awesome challenges of the next few years.

It is also the first time that this particular leadership team stands before representatives of the entire company since achieving Number One status. That new status comes up here and there in different presentations, but the leaders won't let it become a main theme of the meeting. That top-of-the-heap status is all too new. And even as Wal-Mart was inching toward the top of the *Fortune* 500 list in the last few years, the executives were still trying to get used to being at the controls of a growth engine that seemed to know no bounds. Reaching the heights would take some getting used to. For sure, these executives had gotten used to growth. Year after year in the nineties, the company produced billions of dollars of revenue growth, and no one in the upper echelons was troubled that the founder had been something of a killjoy about growth. They knew that he equated size with complacency, but they simply would not let themselves grow complacent.

With the new leadership gaining more confidence in itself, there was still the growing awareness that with each passing year the men—they were almost entirely men—who had known him personally, had admired him, had become his disciples, were retiring from active assignments. Some of those Walton-bred executives were bidding their farewells that very day: one of them was Don Soderquist, who was retiring as senior vice president of Wal-Mart Stores. Soderquist got a standing ovation when he was called to the stage. The audience loved him, but then everyone at Wal-Mart had always loved the man who since Walton's death had been the most articulate communicator of the company's culture. Soderquist, along with David Glass, had helped run Wal-Mart in Walton's final years.

Glass himself, while still maintaining an office at Wal-Mart, was fading slowly from the scene, now that he had become the owner of a major league baseball team, the Kansas City Royals. But it was not as if the entire flock of disciples was slipping away. Lee Scott and Tom Coughlin had spent years working with Sam Walton, as had a number of their colleagues in senior management. And the place still had a chairman who had grown up at the founder's knee.

★ ★ ★

In *The Wal-Mart Triumph: Inside the World's #1 Company*, we ask—and try to answer—one of the more intriguing questions in American business: How has the subsequent generation of Wal-Mart leadership turned the company into the most successful company in the world despite the departure of its founder Sam Walton a decade earlier.

The book will indicate how the new generation of leadership has parlayed the special profundities of Sam Walton into a core capability: relying on his business philosophy and the culture he created to underpin the strategies that continue to guide the running of Wal-Mart stores. But it will also suggest in what ways the new leadership found Walton's wisdom an inadequate guide for the management of a more visible, exposed, and controversial Wal-Mart.

We will look briefly at Sam Walton and his business philosophy. We will also spend time portraying leading members of the new generation of leadership; men like David Glass, president and COO from 1984 to 1988 and president and CEO 1988 to 2000; the current CEO, Lee Scott; Don Soderquist; and Tom Coughlin, who, as president and CEO of Wal-Mart Stores and Sam's Club USA, has emerged as one of the company's most powerful figures.

We will show how these four men possessed a mix of leadership skills that in some ways were reminiscent of the skills that Sam Walton possessed and in some ways were not. It was this new mix of leadership capabilities and the way the leadership team used those capabilities to make decisions that took Wal-Mart from a small-town retail chain to the largest company in the world.

It was not only the new leadership team that faced a monumental challenge with Sam Walton's passing. Unlike other business heirs, the Walton heirs had decided to maintain a strong connection to

Wal-Mart. Their major challenge was not whether to play a role in the company but what kind of a role to play.

After the founder's death, the family continued to hold 38 percent of the Wal-Mart stock, making it the largest owner of the company. Tying their wealth to the stock meant that the company's success was the measure of their own economic well being. The eldest son, Rob Walton, selected as chairman after his father's death, took on the responsibility to make sure that the family's (that is, the shareholders') interests were upheld.

NO SAM WALTON

The towering gray eminence of Sam Walton continued to shadow the new leadership. Though it seemed clear that cloning him was not the way to go, it was equally obvious that the culture he built would have to be at the forefront of Wal-Mart policies. Walton's successors became more and more aware that the Walton guidelines had relevance for the stores but not for the ever-growing corporate organization that was mushrooming day by day.

Mostly what Sam Walton needed to do to run his business was to make sure that the stores functioned successfully. The new leadership, however, had far larger responsibilities than just the stores, for the more the company grew, the more visible and controversial it became, and the more it required the kind of bureaucratic apparatus that had seemed, quite understandably, so unwelcome and so irrelevant to Sam Walton. In time the new leadership came to recognize that the Sam Walton management legacy applied by and large to the smooth running of the stores. For all the rest, it would have to rely on its own experiences and instincts.

★ ★ ★

As the crowds began dispersing on that June morning in Fayetteville, as the new leadership team began to chat informally with board members, investors, managers, employees, and the media, the team

started to sense that it had acquired, however unwittingly, a new burden: It now presided over the largest corporation in the world, making Wal-Mart's own world no longer so simple. Gone were the days
when shareholder meetings could be held over a coffee house table or
when the founder could survey his chain of stores by flying the skies
in a small plane or when analysts and journalists needed little attention or when it seemed unnecessary to court government officials.

By the summer of 2002, only a Martian would not have heard of
Wal-Mart (and who knows? If the price of real estate on Mars were
cheap enough and enough Martians lived in a certain community . . .),
and very few people were left who had not shopped in one of the
4,485 stores.

The new Wal-Mart management presides over nothing less than a
retail empire, so powerful that even the false rumor of a new store in
a community sends shock waves through the residents:so influential
that politicians have begun writing legislation specifically designed
to curb Wal-Mart: so ubiquitous that the company's logo now rises
over such far-flung places as China, Brazil, Germany, England, and
Mexico.

There is of course a price to be paid for such power, such influence, and such globe-trotting. The price comes in various forms and
from many unexpected places. It is the price that one pays for being
the largest, the most visible, and the most important of anything.
The price, for Wal-Mart, is controversy. The main controversy
stemmed from Wal-Mart's entry into certain communities. Individuals and, later, protest groups sought to keep Wal-Mart out, arguing
that a Wal-Mart store automatically brought economic harm to
small mom-and-pop stores and to a community's downtown areas.
The company countered that there was ample evidence to suggest
that either with or without a Wal-Mart, these stores in downtown
areas would eventually disappear because the stores did not stay
close to their customers. The controversy lingered, creating issues for
Sam Walton's successors that were doing their part to help define the
new Wal-Mart.

★ ★ ★

Walton's admonition to keep the business simple worked well in its day, but of late, Wal-Mart has been anything but simple. It is a company that gets into the newspapers when almost anything out of the ordinary happens, whether it is a deer on the loose in the aisles of a Supercenter or a pregnant woman about to give birth near the cash registers; a rumor that Wal-Mart might be moving into a community or a lawsuit that a disenchanted customer has filed.

Now that Wal-Mart has become the Number One company in size in the world, the company is at an intriguing time in its history, but the signs of how it is dealing with its most difficult challenges are barely visible at the shareholder meeting that morning. The executives seem to relish the idea that the gathering resembles a political convention or a pep rally. They want nothing to disturb the joyous mood. Yet behind the scenes these same executives are deeply engaged in a battle on behalf of the company against an often-faceless array of critics and protesters who want to bring the corporate giant down a peg or two.

The leadership team is confident that it knows how to apply Sam Walton's wisdom so that its stores run efficiently, but it continues to cope with the challenge of presiding over a corporate organization that is so visible, exposed, and controversial. It has become controversial because unfriendly forces have sought to define the company as some kind of corporate monster, uncaring, greedy, and arrogant. In his day, Walton defined the company; no one else offered other definitions either because they did not care or did not dare. He defined Wal-Mart as a place that cared for customers and associates, that wanted only to raise the standard of living of those in its midst. Publicly, the leadership team suggests that its greatest challenges are in finding and training a pool of store managers and corporate executives in sufficient numbers to allow the company to grow as rapidly as it has in the past. But privately, the Wal-Mart leadership team believes that the other challenge—the question of who will define the new Wal-Mart: its leadership team or its critics—is just as daunting as the staffing issue.

In the rest of the book, we will dissect the post-Walton Wal-Mart leadership: we will go behind the scenes to tell the inside story of how the new leadership team is successfully integrating Sam Walton's business philosophy into the new Wal-Mart. We will also show how that team is developing its own management strategies to deal with the complexities of the emerging Wal-Mart empire. Finally, we will look closely at the battle that the new leadership team is waging to define its future rather than let others do it for them.

PART TWO

THE FOUNDER AND HIS LEGACY

CHAPTER 2

THE MAN FROM KINGFISHER

Sam Walton's story began in Depression days in Oklahoma. It was a time when ambition, an eagerness to compete, and a passion for winning gave someone an edge. The young Sam had all those qualities in abundance. From childhood, he loved playing—and winning— the game, whatever the game. At first it was football; eventually it was merchandising. He believed that what distinguished him from others was his passion to compete. He could not imagine failing: he believed that he had a right to win.

The right to play the game, to enter the fray, and, if one had the right talents, to succeed—this was the American Dream. Samuel Moore Walton, born March 29, 1918, in Kingfisher, Oklahoma, certainly had the requisite critical skills and made the most of them. "No one," wrote *Time*, "better personified the vitality of the American Dream in the second half of the twentieth century than Sam Walton."

From an almost irrational self-confidence evolved a decisiveness that made Walton one of the great artists of business execution. His nature, he once said, had always been to press ahead, to want to do things immediately rather than later. Sam assumed that his drive and ambition came from his mother Nancy Lee (Lawrence) Walton, a great motivator who urged him to become the best that he could at whatever he did. His passion to win became an obsession and informed his every action.

From his father, Thomas Gibson Walton, a farm-mortgage bro-
ker, he learned the value of working hard and of being honest; he also
gained an appreciation for the art of negotiating (his father loved to
make deals for anything—cars, farms, houses, cattle, horses, mules.)
But Sam Walton believed that he never quite got the knack of negotiating: "I lack the ability to squeeze the last dollar," a comment loaded
with irony, considering Wal-Mart's reputation for doing just that.

While still a child, Walton moved with his family to one town
after another in Missouri, where he observed Dust Bowl farms. He
promised himself that he would never be poor. Ambition helped him
become an Eagle Scout at the unusually young age of thirteen, a student leader (his high school class voted him "most versatile boy"), a
basketball star, and quarterback of the Hickman High School state
championship football team in Columbia, Missouri.

He never regarded himself as poor, though his family lacked
much disposable income. He was taught to contribute to the house-
hold: From age seven, he sold magazine subscriptions; he had a
paper route from seventh grade to college; he also raised and sold
rabbits and pigeons and milked cows. He learned how hard it was to
make a dollar—and how worthwhile.

TRAINING AT J. C. PENNEY

In the fall of 1936 he enrolled at the University of Missouri, running a paper route throughout his undergraduate days, which earned
him the nickname, Hustler Walton from his fraternity brothers. At
age twenty-two in 1940, he graduated with a degree in economics.
Joining J. C. Penney in Des Moines, Iowa, as a seventy-five-dollar-a-
month trainee, the young man demonstrated a knack for retailing. A
visit by the owner, James Cash Penney, to the Des Moines store left a
positive impression on him, especially after J.C. showed him how to
use the smallest amount of ribbon to tie a package that would still
have it appear attractive.

For three years starting in 1942, young Walton served as a captain
in the United States Army intelligence office. He supervised security

for aircraft plants and POW camps in California and elsewhere. On February 14, 1943, while still in the army, he married Helen Robson of Claremore, Oklahoma. Their first child, a son they called Rob, was born on October 28, 1944; they had three other children: John, Jim, and Alice.

Once the war was over, millions of Americans wanted to build quieter, safer futures and to live in their own homes so they could raise families. The consumer age took hold. It was the right time for Sam Walton to begin a career in retailing.

The twenty-seven-year-old Walton felt ready to run his own store; he borrowed $20,000 from Helen's father to purchase a Ben Franklin store from Butler Brothers in the tiny Delta cotton town of Newport, Arkansas. The store opened on September 1, 1945. Within four years he turned the money-losing store into the top Ben Franklin franchise in Arkansas.

He had no predetermined idea about retailing; his way of learning was to listen to those in the business rather than read retail magazines. From early on he sought a competitive advantage through adept market intelligence, visiting rivals across the street, checking on prices and displays, seeking any information that might help in his own store. Borrowing ideas rather than being creative never bothered him. He was not embarrassed to admit that just about everything he had done in his career he had copied from someone else.

At first he docilely went along with the existing arrangements a store manager used to obtain goods for a store. Butler Brothers told him what merchandise to sell, setting the price he would pay for the goods (including a 25 percent premium) and the price at which he would sell them. He felt constrained; finding a clause in his agreement that allowed him to buy a sizeable percentage of goods from other sources, he urged manufacturers to sell directly to him. Unwilling to irritate the Butlers, some manufacturers turned the young merchant down. But others were more acquiescent; he made night runs in his car, picking up the cheaper goods and putting them in his store first thing in the morning.

In 1949 Walton lost the lease on the building at the Newport store.

He wanted to buy a St. Louis department store, but Helen insisted on living in a small town; accordingly, he bought a Ben Franklin franchise, a five-and-dime variety store, on the western side of the town square in the sleepy backwater town of Bentonville, Arkansas.

He opened the Walton 5 and 10 as a Ben Franklin franchise in March 1951, the forerunner of the Wal-Mart chain that began eleven years later. To Helen Walton, who insisted to her husband that they live only in towns smaller than 10,000 people, Bentonville still seemed like a "sad looking country town." It had fewer then 3,000 people. But the family pitched in to make the store a success. Rob Walton remembered how he often carried boxes to the stock room as part of his chores.

Two years later, in 1953, Sam Walton opened a second store in nearby Fayetteville, where the locals bet that Woolworth's would force him to close within two months. They lost their bet. By 1962 Sam Walton owned and operated sixteen franchise stores in Arkansas, Kansas, and Missouri. He had become one of the largest independent variety store operators in the United States.

Operating the five-and-dimes taught Walton that there was a future for merchandising in small towns. He believed that people in small communities should not have to pay more for merchandise than they would in the large cities. Small-town merchants charged higher prices because of the difficulties of distribution and the merchants' inability to buy as cheaply as the big-city chains.

Walton viewed the small-town populations as an untapped reservoir of consumerism, exploiting the unwillingness of the much larger chains to penetrate these tiny communities. He loved merchandising and knew that it was crucial to provide quality goods at cheap prices; hence he delighted in convincing suppliers to give him the best possible prices so that he could pass the savings on to customers.

The real future, young Walton decided, was in discounting—buying directly from manufacturers and displaying the merchandise in bulk—rather than in five-and-dimes.

He was an eager innovator, introducing self-service into his stores. Rather than have the sales help fetch merchandise, shoppers could select the goods themselves. To get to his far-flung stores, he acquired a plane, an 85-horsepower 1948 Ercoupe and learned to fly it. Passengers remembered him as less skilled than a professional pilot. He liked to swoop down low in search of airports. Once the Federal Aviation Authority got on the radio to warn the young merchant-pilot that he was flying too low. He simply turned the radio off.

★ ★ ★

The year 1962 was a pivotal year for retailing. Such giants as Woolworth's and Sears dominated the scene in the cities, and opening that same year were three new ventures: S. S. Kresge, an 800-store variety chain, opened a discount store in Garden City, Michigan, and called it Kmart. The veteran F. W. Woolworth started its Woolco chain. Dayton Hudson opened its first Target store. (Four decades later, Kmart was bankrupt, Woolco no longer existed, and Target, though profitable, doesn't have Wal-Mart's reach or impact.)

Though he had become the largest Ben Franklin franchiser in the United States and his stores were nowhere near the big cities, Sam Walton felt threatened by these discount stores. He traveled extensively around the country and checked out such discount operations as Ann & Hope, Zayres, Arlans, Korvettes, and Two Guys, concluding that they were the wave of the future. His only concern was that these discounters might set up business in the rural backwaters.

Too small and too poor to take on Woolworth's and Sears head-to-head, Walton continued to focus on rural towns, where the only competition came from local independents and where consumers frequently traveled huge distances to save money. Young Walton had the revolutionary thought of converting Ben Franklin stores into a discount chain that specialized in low prices every day, not only on sale days. Rural consumers could then shop locally, enjoying the same goods at the same cheap prices existing in hard-to-reach places.

THE BIRTH OF WAL-MART

Walton approached the executives of Butler Brothers, the parent company of Ben Franklin, to persuade them that there were great opportunities in discount merchandising; price reductions would be made up for by an increase in sales volume. He wanted to be their guinea pig. But the executives were adamant: They would offer him no franchising possibility, concerned that Sam Walton's discounting plan would halve their 20 to 25 percent profit margins. If Walton wanted to proceed, he would have to do it on his own. He continued to sense that these small towns represented a potential gold mine. His only real competition might come from the small-town merchants, but they offered high prices, lacked retail experience, and operated out of small stores.

It was against this background that Wal-Mart was conceived.

On July 2, 1962, the forty-four-year-old Walton and his younger brother James (Bud) Walton established their own discount store, Wal-Mart Discount City, in Rogers, Arkansas, adjacent to Bentonville. The store was twice the size of the Bentonville store. Sam and Helen co-signed the lease, providing 95 percent of the investment. Though heavily in debt, Sam Walton could at least get on with his dream of pursuing discount retailing. He stocked the store with everything from hardware to ladies' clothes, and though others were not so sure, he was certain that customers would come just for the bargains.

He was mildly encouraged when on opening day a group of executives from the Chicago headquarters of the Ben Franklin stores, dressed in pin-striped suits, marched into the store and coldly asked to see the owner. Wordlessly they ventured to the rear and, finding Walton, issued an ultimatum: "Don't build any more of these Wal-Mart stores." They exited just as coldly, just as silently. At least, thought Sam Walton, someone is nervous about the new Wal-Mart.

Sales were an impressive $975,000 the first year.

Sam Walton's retailing secret lay in offering low prices across the board. Cynics argued that he could not survive on such small margins; he believed that it was the very act of reducing his margins that would induce greater profit. He offered a hypothetical example: "Say I bought an item for 80 cents. I found that by pricing it at $1.00 I could sell three times more of it than by pricing it at $1.20. I might make only half the profit per item, but because I was selling three times as many, the overall profit was much greater." This kind of pricing strategy was, in his view, the very essence of discounting.

To get the cheapest products, Walton became his own distribution system, traveling in his pickup, driving miles to suppliers, and returning to his stores with a loaded truck. Once he had the goods in his stores, he promoted certain products. This item-merchandising, as he called it, set Wal-Mart apart, creating a great competitive advantage. He would pick an item and then call attention to it. He liked to say that it was possible to sell anything if you hung it from the ceiling. Had he left the item in its normal store position, very few would have been sold.

Such tinkering with store items—Sam Walton jokingly called it fiddling and meddling—was in his DNA: "I have always been a maverick who enjoys shaking things up and creating a little anarchy." It meant that he would make mistakes, but he was unfazed, believing that it was all right to be wrong at times, an acceptable cost of trying to improve things. David Glass, who met Walton in 1964 but did not begin working for him until 1976, observed that "he could have owned a carnival and been very successful. He could have been an entertainer. Sam just liked getting out front and doing those kinds of things."

THE SOUL OF AN OPERATOR

From his earliest days he seemed so much more than an ordinary businessman.

He was that rare individual in business, a true merchandiser who operated the business carefully and cautiously, a powerful communicator; his keen eye was able to detect both a good product and a good store location. He had people skills as well as operational skills; above all else, he was most comfortable and incredibly successful at establishing the best possible shopping ambience within his stores. Others had one or more of those skills. No one but Sam Walton possessed them all.

He was, above all, a promoter par excellence, and he admitted it: "I have occasionally heard myself compared to P. T. Barnum because of the way I love to get in front of a crowd and talk something up—an idea, a store, a product, the whole company—whatever I happen to be focused on right then. But underneath that personality, I have always had the soul of an operator, somebody who wants to make things work well, then better, and then the best they possibly can."

But even a love of experimentation and an uncanny sense of promotion did not create great stores overnight. Sam Walton decided to open a second Wal-Mart in nearby Springdale, then Harrison, another neighboring town of Rogers. Opening day in Harrison was a low point in the company's early history, as Sam Walton's attempt to lure customers led to some farcical scenes that have become Wal-Mart legend. In 115-degree temperatures, Walton stacked a truckfull of watermelons on the sidewalk. He also offered donkey rides. The combination of the watermelons and the donkeys proved unwise, to say the least. The watermelons began to pop. The donkeys started to relieve themselves.

The parking lot outside the store took on a most unappealing look and smell. David Glass, then working for Crank Drugs in Springfield, Missouri, arrived for the opening. He described the new Wal-Mart as the worst retail store he had ever seen. Walking through the crowded store, with its eight-foot high ceiling, its 12,000 square feet, he unknowingly tracked the watermelon/donkey cocktail along the floor on his way to greeting Sam Walton for the first time. This Sam Walton seems like a nice fellow, he thought to himself, but he'll never make it as a merchant. Because he liked the store owner, Glass candidly told him what he thought of the store—and suggested that he find something different to do.

If Sam Walton was still finding his way, he also began to realize that what truly mattered were not the threats from Ben Franklin executives nor the unspectacular appearance of the store; what would bring Wal-Mart success was offering the same merchandise as nearby stores did for 20 percent less. It was as simple as that.

But hardly anybody noticed Wal-Mart for quite some time. Within five years, Kmart, with 250 stores to Wal-Mart's 18, had sales of over $800 million to Wal-Mart's $9 million.

Concerned that other retailers would identify small towns as ripe, Walton thought it crucial to build as many stores as he could. He was not a pure expansionist; he simply wanted to protect his turf. Yet while other discounters like Kmart were expanding around the country, Walton could raise only enough funds to build thirty-two stores by 1969. Sales had grown to $30.8 million. Walton was opening on average two stores a year.

Wal-Mart was slowly growing into a chain of discount stores located in the northwest part of Arkansas, then spreading into Oklahoma, Missouri, and Louisiana. It had hundreds of rivals and no discernible national presence. But Walton was unfazed, deciding that he knew how to attract and keep customers, relying on three cardinal beliefs: providing great customer service, showing respect for the individual, and striving for excellence.

In the early 1970s Wall Street analysts predicted that Kmart would crush Sears and dominate retailing in the latter part of the twentieth century. But Kmart's reluctance to look for ways to improve bred the kind of complacency that played into Wal-Mart's hands. Moreover, Sears' neglect of Wal-Mart played a major role in its decline. For his part, Sam Walton monitored his competitors closely: To gain valuable intelligence, upon entering a rival's store, he sometimes took off his trademark baseball cap and donned sunglasses, earning him the sobriquet, "the stealth retailer." When he found an item priced lower than at a Wal-Mart, he phoned the nearest Wal-Mart manager and had him immediately undercut the price.

Even though the new Wal-Mart chain grew, Walton was $2 million in debt by the end of the decade. He had continued to put up stores in order to lower the debt, knowing full well how risky a strategy that was. He did not want to give even partial control to outside investors, but he had no choice if he were going to get rid of his debt. As a last resort, he took the company public in October 1970. That single act erased Sam Walton's debt and set in motion a major store expansion.

By 1979, Wal-Mart, with 276 stores and 21,000 employees, had reached $1 billion in sales, making it the first company to reach that mark in as few as 17 years. Walton was opening on average a hundred stores a year. With so many store openings, some communities began protesting what came to be called "Sprawl-Mart", the arrival of a Wal-Mart and the eventual decline of small-town merchants. Wal-Mart countered by arguing that the decline occurred not because of Wal-Mart but because these stores did not stay current with their customers.

Though both Kmart and Sears were far larger than Wal-Mart, Sam Walton had some things going for him. The upstart Wal-Mart's formula was catching on in the small towns and underserved rural areas: Selling brand-name goods in high volume at low prices lured loyal customers. Responding to the fast, friendly service and the consistently low prices, customers scooped up everything from records to cosmetics, lawn furniture to clothing.

PICKING STORE SITES WHILE AIRBORNE

Walton chose his sites skillfully, piloting his plane over small towns to check out the best possible locations. He took his time. He did not want to waste money on a bad site—or on anything, for that matter.

He was passionate about keeping the costs of the business as low as possible, partially because saving money was in his DNA but also because he knew that to expand his business he would be forced to spend on buildings and payrolls so he had better hold down all other expenses. So he scorned fancy frills; he questioned every proposed expense, convinced that the only worthwhile cost was one that got the customer to buy a product. When colleagues pressed him to invest in a new piece of technology for the stores, he grimaced: He had little faith in newfangled devices; he believed that ultimately they put too much distance between their users and the customers. Nothing, however, irritated him more than an employee's staying at high-priced hotels or eating in expensive restaurants; such frills, he argued, drove costs up and had nothing to do with luring customers to the stores by offering cheap prices. To reinforce these convictions, he drove around in a 1984 red and white Ford pickup truck when he could easily have afforded a driver and a limousine.

He questioned the wisdom of investing in high-tech logistics systems but eventually became convinced that the systems would give Wal-Mart great efficiencies in its distribution arrangements. Taking advantage of Wal-Mart's increasing size, Walton was able to buy goods more cheaply and get them delivered more inexpensively than his rivals.

To him, unions posed a threat because introducing them into his stores would only increase his costs. And so he would not permit anyone to unionize a store, passing word that he would rather close the place than accept unions. But to keep the unions away, he had to make sure that the employees felt that they were being treated fairly. He became one of the first retailers to start a profit-sharing program for rank-and-file workers, not just executives, allowing his employees to invest in company stock and share in company profits. This resulted in hourly workers earning significant sums in stock value. The unions had a hard time competing with that.

In the early 1980s an attempt was made to unionize the distribution center in Searcy, Arkansas. Sam threatened that if the union gained a foothold there, he would take away the profit-sharing plan of the employees; he also warned that he had 500 applicants waiting to take over jobs of those already employed there. The employees voted against the union.

In 1983, at age sixty-three, Sam Walton contracted a rare form of leukemia. He opted for an expensive experimental drug called interferon; by a seeming miracle, the disease went into remission. That year Wal-Mart earned $4.6 billion in revenue. Sam Walton was worth $2 billion.

He promised employees that he would dance a hula at high noon on Wall Street if the company achieved a pretax profit of 8 percent in 1983. (The industry's average had been only 3 percent.) Walton did indeed do the hula to celebrate Wal-Mart's glorious achievement. It was hard to say which was more surprising: the sight of the Wal-Mart founder decked out in a hula skirt, waving his arms like a good Hawaiian, or the national publicity his dance attracted.

In the spring of 1987 *Time* said that Wal-Mart had become the fastest-growing and most influential force in the retailing industry, thanks to Sam Walton's ability to motivate employees and cut expenses. The magazine cited analysts who called it the best-managed company in the United States.

By the end of the 1980s, Wal-Mart, by then in twenty-five states with over 1,400 stores, was one of the country's most successful retailers. Sales had grown to $25.8 billion. The first of the Sam's Clubs appeared in 1983 in Midwest City, Oklahoma; they were no-frills, cash-and-carry discount warehouses designed primarily for small businesses. The first Supercenter, with a complete grocery department plus general merchandise, opened in Washington, Missouri, five years later.

In 1988 Sam Walton began implementing a succession plan, naming David Glass as president and CEO of Wal-Mart. At the end of 1989 Wal-Mart became the first retailer in history to report aftertax profits of $1 billion.

★ ★ ★

Sam Walton thought of business as a simple exercise, so he kept his strategies uncomplicated: buy cheaply, sell cheaply, keep your shelves well stocked, treat your customers with warmth and respect, and pay careful attention to what your rivals are doing right. He was a shrewd manager, constantly fearful of falling behind, worried to death that his rivals would get the best of him by offering lower prices and by making their stores more attractive than his; and so he believed fervently in the value of shaking things up, experimenting, making changes just for the sake of change. He modified store formats and exchanged store managers. Knowing that he would make mistakes, he tried to learn from those mistakes and never looked back.

His goals were always to change the lives of others, not to make a huge personal splash, certainly not to accumulate vast amounts of riches. He had seen poverty firsthand as a child, and it became a personal crusade to lift the standard of living of those most in need of such lifting.

His management style was based on the notion that the less time spent at the home office, the better for him and the better for the organization. He lived to be in the stores, to listen to employees and managers, to give them the benefit of his wisdom, to fix things on the spot if he could. He was in the stores three or four times a week. Certainly in the early years he could get to every store at least once a year. Some stores he could visit a number of times over the year. He found other ways to avoid the home office as well: He loved to hunt and play tennis. He often left the office at 3 to 4 P.M. and spent a few hours hunting. Flying into a town to visit a store, he sometimes radioed ahead for his secretary to arrange a tennis game for him, often within an hour after landing.

The one fixture in his week at the home office was the Saturday morning meeting. He made sure to arrive at 2 to 3 A.M. to prepare for the meeting a few hours hence. During that time he went over weekly sales figures at each store. Usually he presided over the meetings, relating what he had learned during recent store visits. Occasionally he turned those duties over to another executive. He liked to surprise, and he enjoyed keeping everyone at the edge of their seats. Without warning he might call on someone to explain what they did for Wal-Mart. Partly he simply wanted to stay in touch with the staff, but he undoubtedly wanted to make sure that each person was making a direct contribution to the stores and customers.

He was an early riser all week long. On weekdays before he showed up at the home office, he would breakfast at a hotel, then arrive at his desk by 4:30, setting an example for colleagues. (I once had a meeting scheduled for 7 A.M. with Rob Walton; when I commented that it was early for such a meeting, a Walton employee attending the meeting corrected me, suggesting that it was actually late.)

FILLING UP HIS YELLOW PAD

Part investigative journalist, part master spy, Walton paid surprise visits to stores, sometimes creating embarrassment or downright consternation both for himself and for employees. Certainly anyone who had worked at a Wal-Mart for at least a week knew that Sam Walton was the boss, but not everyone recognized him. Once he ran his pickup into the back-end of a Wal-Mart truck while cruising around the parking lot, presumably counting cars, and injured himself. Entering the store, he opened a few packages, apparently towels, to clean off his blood, only to discover that an employee had reported his suspicious actions to a superior. Another time an employee noticed a man wearing a trench coat and thought that he had nothing else on. She approached him, asking, "Hi, Can I help you?" She soon recognized the putative flasher as Sam Walton.

It was hard to keep the man away from his stores or those of rivals. A weary Helen Walton tried to be a good sport on their vacations, noting, however, that "Sam never went by a Kmart that he didn't stop and look at it." When he swept into a Wal-Mart store, Walton greeted employees over the public address system. Hearing his voice, they knew it was time to greet Mr. Sam, as they called him affectionately. Pulling some crackers off a shelf, he got employees to congregate around him at the back of the store. He deliberately chose to meet with employees before getting together with their managers, assuming that they knew the most about what was going on at the stores and certain that they would talk more freely out of the presence of their immediate bosses.

After some back-and-forth banter, he got down to the business of querying them on what products were moving and what were not. He filled his yellow pad with their comments. The managers and employees may not have been aware of it, but Walton was taking the measure of each as he threw out questions to the crowd of employees. He did not hold back. He might ask an employee how a manager—call him Bill—was treating him or her. If the person answered "fine," if Walton sensed any hesitation on the employee's part, he would ask the question slightly differently: "Now come on. Should we keep Bill?" Walton would never expect the employee to urge him to get rid of Bill, but he did have a sense about these things. He could look someone in the eye and have a feeling for whether there was a reason to check Bill out more carefully.

When he was well versed in what the employees thought, Walton went to the managers and prodded them to do the things that were not being done.

Often dressed in a flannel shirt and khaki pants, he liked to stand behind the checkout counter to help clerks approve personal checks or to show up at the loading dock with doughnuts for the crew. He would lead the Wal-Mart cheer at store openings, yelling at the end, "Wal-Mart, we're Number One."

Sam Walton never thought that visiting stores was something extra to do. It was simply the best way to learn what was going on in the business and to get some fresh ideas. He was markedly different from other CEOs in that respect. Most CEOs, especially those running large corporations, paid visits to their company's installations, however far-flung. But those visits were infrequent, and the conversation between CEOs and local staff was often limited by the boss's whirlwind schedule.

THE ADVANTAGES OF QMI

Were the CEO to learn something interesting from the local staff, it was unlikely that the boss could disseminate the findings to senior personnel in person; at best, the CEO might disseminate a written report or send an E-mail. Sam Walton never felt constricted by time. He spent hours in a store. And when he found an interesting problem in a store, he made a note on his yellow pad, knowing that he would have a chance to pass on his findings to Wal-Mart's senior executives in a few days at the Saturday meeting. It was this quick market intelligence (QMI) that caught the eye of many other admiring CEOs. They tried to imitate Sam Walton's management style, but because their temperaments were different and their corporations were overly bureaucratized, they could not quite replicate Walton's QMI.

Walton's was very much a spur-of-the-moment management style. If something came up at the last moment, he had no trouble rearranging his schedule to tackle the issue. He made decisions on the basis of what felt right on a given day, not on the basis of what he had decided weeks or months earlier. That was certainly the case when he picked up the phone one day to ask John Huey, then a reporter for *Fortune*, if he would be interested in helping him write his memoirs. Walton invited the young journalist to Bentonville to discuss the project.

A year or two earlier, Huey had shown up in Bentonville to do some reporting on Wal-Mart and to get a photograph of Walton. For a few weeks Walton ignored Huey's overtures. One day Huey located him at a Chinese restaurant and followed Walton's truck back to the home office. The two men talked briefly, and Walton finally relented.

Now, a year or two later, Walton seemed ready to reward Huey with a prize—cowriting his memoirs—for showing such zeal in the past. Arriving at Walton's office to discuss the project, Huey waited two to three hours before Walton invited him into his office.

Finally, when he opened the door and approached Huey, Walton asked him in a perplexed voice: "What are you doing here?"

A slightly dazed Huey mentioned the memoirs. Walton retorted angrily. "Why should I do a biography?"

They talked for an hour. In the end, Walton agreed to have Huey cowrite the memoirs. *Sam Walton: Made in America* was published in 1992, shortly after Walton's death.

★ ★ ★

Walton had no dreams of becoming the emperor of the retail world. To be sure, he wanted to be the best retailer in the world but not necessarily the largest. He favored the growth of the business, but the growth had to be profitable and could not come at the expense of the stores. He was never a big dreamer. He came from small-town America, and, at least at the outset, it never occurred to him to turn his Wal-Marts loose on the nation at large. When he expanded, he did so cautiously, moving the circle of stores outward bit by bit, beginning in Arkansas, spilling over into Oklahoma and Missouri, then down to Louisiana. To leapfrog into the state of Washington or Texas or Michigan was never part of his thinking. He was similarly cautious about starting a global Wal-Mart. He imagined that if all went well, the stores might one day cross American borders, but that was far off in the future, if at all. Above all, he understood how important it was to keep to his core capabilities. When others, sensing his business acumen, proposed that Wal-Mart enter such fields as manufacturing, for example, he quickly nixed the idea. He knew precisely what the company's strengths were and were not.

Sam Walton's personality was very much small-town, and though he became the wealthiest man in America he clung tenaciously to his country roots, preferring to live more like a commoner than a king. Hence, the Arts & Entertainment cable-television network titled its 1997 biography of Sam Walton, "The Bargain-Basement Billionaire." All that media talk about his wealth made him uncomfortable. He found it intrusive and irrelevant. One magazine wrote that "Sam Walton had more wealth than a warehouse full of sheikhs but traveled like a Bedouin." And while he did not set up a tent Bedouin-style when he traveled, he did not allow himself to travel like a sheikh either. Because he kept the company headquartered in Bentonville, he found it much more appropriate to get around town in a pickup truck with his hunting dogs sharing the front seat with him than to be driven in a limousine, something he could certainly have afforded. He was in many ways a very private person, but he refused to let the media turn him into a hermit. He liked the friendly ways of the small towns too much for that, so his mailbox bore his name, and his phone number was listed in the local directory. The media made a big point of noting that he got his hair cut at the local barber and ate in local restaurants, but that was just Sam Walton's being Sam Walton, the man from Kingfisher. He did not yearn for a magnificent penthouse on Fifth Avenue, nor would he have felt at home in such surroundings.

He cherished his privacy; to him, all that wealth did for him was to drive the media into his backyard. Who needed that? He got increasingly annoyed as the media descended on him, expecting him to spend large chunks of his time explaining who he was and his business secrets. It was all a waste of time as far as he was concerned. He was a doer, not a promoter, so he saw little value in public speaking, granting interviews, exposing himself or the inner workings of Wal-Mart to Wall Street or the media. He didn't think that his personal life was all that interesting, and he didn't want an army of journalists digging in the inner sanctum of his company; it was not good for business. He genuinely feared that competitors could benefit from all that media exposure. He was grateful to live in a tiny spot on the map called Bentonville, Arkansas. At least that kept him and his company a safe distance from the national media.

If he could keep others, especially his competitors, from learning too much about Wal-Mart, he could exercise control over his destiny. If Wal-Mart's secrets became common knowledge, he might feel compelled to match the competition by making drastic changes. Above all else, he was concerned that he might be compelled to grow too fast. That would force him in turn to add the trappings of a large corporate bureaucracy, something he was dead-set against. He refused to turn Wal-Mart into one of those corporate behemoths, the kind headquartered in New York and elsewhere. So he kept the organizational chart streamlined: He made do with a bare-bones public relations operation; he opposed sending lobbyists to Washington, D.C. The legal staff and the human resources unit stayed small.

He was used to direct personal contact with store managers and employees; he railed at the thought of creating corporate layers back at the home office; he did not want an excess of vice presidents. Why would he need such bureaucracy? He felt no need to publicize the company; he did not want to chase after officials in Washington,

D.C., or Wall Street types. As for in-house lawyers, Wal-Mart's legal imbroglios were simply not that complex or frequent to warrant anything more than a skeleton staff. Nor could he fathom why Wal-Mart needed a human resources unit to look after the employees; that was his job. None of these add-on functions appeared to aid the customer directly, and he wanted to keep the company's focus on the customer.

★ ★ ★

In 1991 he received the good news that Wal-Mart for the first time had passed both Sears and Kmart, making it the largest retailer in the United States. That same year, he began to get an ache in his bones, the first sign that he was suffering from bone cancer. While undergoing chemotherapy and radiation, he tried to keep up his routine as much as possible, but it was increasingly difficult. On March 17, 1992, President George Bush traveled to the Wal-Mart home office to present Walton with the Presidential Medal of Freedom, the nation's highest civilian honor. He appeared at the ceremony in a wheelchair. His face reflected the obvious pain and discomfort that he was feeling, but it also reflected the pride he felt at the presence of a president of the United States in the home office. The meeting place held its own poignancy: It was the same auditorium where Walton had presided over so many Saturday morning meetings. Walton later described the event as the highlight of his entire career. The President praised Sam as an "American original." For his part, Walton expressed satisfaction at what Wal-Mart had accomplished and promised that things were just beginning. A few days later, Wal-Mart's founder checked into the University of Arkansas hospital in Little Rock. When he began Wal-Mart thirty years earlier, retailing experts warned that he was too late and that his ideas were not original enough. Yet as his life was ending, he had secured a place for himself in American history for having built the greatest retail empire in the world. He undoubtedly took less pride in a second statistic: He was at the time of his death second only in wealth to the Sultan of Brunei.

★ ★ ★

When Sam Walton died of cancer on April 5, 1992, a week after his seventy-fourth birthday, the local *Benton County Daily Record* headlined the story of his passing, MR. SAM DIED AT AGE 74. It carried a statement from his elder son Rob, noting that no changes were expected in the corporate direction or policy of the company.

Time wrote that the "folksy, frugal retailing dynamo" had gone from a job delivering newspapers in college to becoming the richest man in America. *Time* wrote, "Frustrated with the high prices and operating costs of a variety-store franchise he bought in 1945, Walton started his own discount establishment in 1962 and built his Wal-Mart empire to more than 1,700 outlets in forty plus states—as well as two stores in Mexico—with profits last year of $1.6 billion. His concept, which put many Main Street merchants out of business: strategically locating giant-size general stores that sell brand-name goods at rock-bottom prices."

CHAPTER 3

GIVE ME A SQUIGGLY:
SAM WALTON'S CULTURE

Let's face it, shopping can be drudgery.

To be sure, there are those who love to shop, but there are just as many for whom the experience is a burden.

Sam Walton understood that point better than anyone else in retailing and built an entire company culture around the idea that shopping need not be drudgery.

It can be made easier by salespeople who are eager to help customers. It can be made more pleasant by managers and employees who help and care for one another, keeping the store to high standards of cleanliness, efficiency, and customer service. It can be an adventure, an hour or two of fun even, as employees work hard to be creative, keeping customers of all ages and all types involved and getting enjoyment out of their journeys around the store.

The idea of course was not simply to give customers an enjoyable experience. There was a purpose behind all of this: It was to make them feel so satisfied that they would come back time and again. There were other lures as well, though none as important as the notion of everyday low pricing. Talk to a Wal-Mart customer about why he or she is shopping in the store on that day and the answer inevitably has to do with saving money. Saving money on a Monday or a Wednesday when there were special sales was a nice gimmick but— and this was what Walton understood so well—it was not nearly as much of an enticement as the offer of low prices every day around the clock. That was Wal-Mart's special differentiator, and customers felt that difference every time the checkout person rang up their bills. They felt the difference every day of the week.

SKIPPING THE DRUDGERY

But Walton also understood that everyday low prices, while the greatest come-on, had to be part of a larger package of benefits: The products had to be of a sufficiently high quality, there had to be a wide variety of those products, and they had to be available at all times.

If managers and employees were going to execute properly, if they were going to remove the drudgery from shopping, if every aspect of the store was to function smoothly, someone at the top had to establish guidelines that would provide everyone with a road map. If the guidelines were indeed established and disseminated properly, they would form the backbone of the company's culture. They would have to be communicated to every manager, every employee, time and again. It was no good writing them in memo form and distributing them. People would simply read them and toss the memo aside. (One could view Walton's personal communication skills at a Saturday morning meeting in October 2002. A Wal-Mart employee spoke to the audience about a "smile contest" she was sponsoring. As part of her presentation she showed a video of Walton speaking about the great virtue of smiling at customers and greeting them in a friendly manner. It was clear what a splendid communicator he was. He seemed so—authentic. Everyone else at Wal-Mart in 2002 was doing his or her best to transmit Sam Walton's culture. Well, here was the man himself, and he seemed to speak with such ease and so naturally. It suddenly became evident why in his day he was the main channel for the Wal-Mart culture. No one could replace him, and indeed no one tried.)

For the corporate culture to catch on, the messages had to be communicated personally. Sam Walton got that point. That was one reason why he spent so much time in the stores. He wanted to build and then spread a culture, because only if the messages were transmitted consistently and with great clarity would the organization function effectively. Wal-Mart was small enough in its early days for Walton himself to spread the culture by becoming part teacher, coach, and preacher. Other companies, wishing to spread a culture, ran into trouble precisely because they were too large, too distant, too out of touch, to transmit the messages personally. Wal-Mart had a Sam Walton who was never more at home than in the stores. As a result, Wal-Mart had a culture that worked.

★ ★ ★

The culture established a framework that worked toward creating a joyful, even adventurous atmosphere in the stores. It all began with the employees. They were the ones who would make or break the culture. If they walked around gloomily or sullenly, the drudgery barometer that customers carried within themselves would go through the top. But if they made themselves available to customers, if they put a smile on their faces, if they showed a willingness to help, if, above all else, they seemed enthusiastic about what they were doing, shopping would not seem so bad after all.

Walk through Wal-Mart stores and the overall impression is of employees who are cheerful and eager to please, who are looking for ways to serve the customer. Employees appear to be programmed to be nice to you. "Y'all have a great adventure," said the Wal-Mart greeter at the door of the Supercenter in Bentonville, Arkansas, slapping a visitor on the back who was walking into the store. The visitor cringed at the thought that the greeter might discover that his purpose was just to buy a magazine. No matter, it was his job—and the job of all the other employees in the store that day—to make people feel good being at a Wal-Mart. Sam Walton would have been pleased with him. The greeter was spreading the Wal-Mart culture.

When I began my research for the book, I decided to visit other stores similar to Wal-Marts to see if I could detect a difference between a Wal-Mart and the other stores. At times, as I made a genuine attempt to purchase some merchandise in a Wal-Mart rival, I made a point of searching for a store employee for help. One occasion made an indelible impression on me: I was looking through men's shirts, checking out sizes and prices and having a hard time with both. A few feet from me was a salesperson sorting through a box of men's shirts, presumably getting them ready to put on display. I asked her for help. "Just a minute," she replied. "I'm busy." Her abrupt and unpleasant manner suggested that I was interfering with her day. I asked myself: Where was the culture of this store? What had happened to the guidelines? Surely at some point a boss had instructed this salesperson to be nice, to be helpful to customers.

A MEMO LOCKED IN A DRAWER

After that incident, I had a better sense of why the Wal-Mart culture works as well as it does. There was a Sam Walton and there were other senior executives who hammered away at the ingredients of the culture. I'm sure that the rival store had similar ingredients in some memo locked in a drawer. At Wal-Mart, the people at the top made sure that those messages filtered down to the employees clearly and frequently. At the rival store, memos were written. At Wal-Mart Sam Walton paid a store visit. The difference was clear.

The Wal-Mart culture is thus a set of marching orders that taken together, create what is unique about the company. It is often noted that every retailer has essentially the same things: four walls, the same shelves, the same merchandise, and the same colors. But where retailers differ from one another, where some excel and others fall down most ingloriously, is in the attitude the organization takes toward its customers and its employees. That attitude is the sum and substance of what the Wal-Mart culture is all about. The attitude is all about having clear, consistent messages and making sure that they are executed.

★ ★ ★

Sam Walton had a rule of thumb about how to know whether some task was important for a Wal-Mart executive or employee to perform: Did that task directly affect the customer? If it did, it was worth doing. If it did not, it was not worth spending a penny to do.

To Walton, it was crucial to motivate the employee to show respect for the individual and serve the customer above all else. Accordingly, the culture was designed to turn Wal-Mart employees into friendly, animated people when dealing with the customer. So it was not surprising to find that the company has its own cheer that is joyously shouted at almost every meeting, large or small. Sometimes the store manager leads the cheer. Sometimes, it is Lee Scott. In earlier days, it was Sam Walton.

Once I was touring the large Wal-Mart distribution center in Bentonville. I peered through a glass door into a room where eight employees sat. Suddenly the room exploded with a loud noise. The employees were shouting the cheer. It was my first exposure to it. All I could think of was the scorn that was heaped on IBM for having something as corny as a cheer, but then it dawned on me that perhaps the scorn was directed at IBM for getting its employees to cheer when the company had such a poor bottom line. When you are the company with the largest revenue in the world, you don't have to worry that anyone will put you down for having a cheer.

What I heard coming through that glass door was the following.

The cheerleader: "Give me a W!"

The crowd in response: "W"

It then carries on:

"Give me an A!"

"A"

"Give me an L!"

"L"

"Give me a squiggly!"

Hold on. What is a squiggly?

It is the starlike mark between the Wal and the Mart on all Wal-Mart store signs. When asked to "give me a squiggly," each person eagerly twists his or her body in a downward motion in what has been described as the famous Wal-Mart rump shake. One writer thought it hilarious that "just over one million people are willing to regularly wriggle their rear ends in public at their employer's behest."

WHO'S NUMBER ONE?

Moving beyond the squiggly, the cheer finishes off with "Give me an M" and so forth, culminating in the question: "Who's Number One?" Employees then shout: "The customer. Always!"

In 1977 Sam Walton introduced the cheer to Wal-Mart employees after seeing employees of a South Korean company give a morning cheer along with their calisthenics. He took to the idea, hoping that a cheer would prevent his own employees from walking around with long faces; it might even make them more productive. The cheer had side benefits: It pumped employees up so that they would stay enthusiastic throughout their shift. It made them all feel as if they were part of a much larger entity, since more than 1.3 million employees would utter that cheer at least once a day around the world. Each time I approached the front door of a Wal-Mart in China during a visit there in early November 2002, I encountered fifty or so Wal-Mart employees, dressed in their red shirts and wearing Wal-Mart identification tags around their necks. As I got to the door, they began the Wal-Mart cheer in Chinese. They were thousands of miles from Bentonville, yet they were every bit as caught up in the Wal-Mart culture as their counterparts at the Supercenter across the street from the home office. And they were certainly pumped up. To walk around the store, with their friendly smiles greeting me at each turn, it was not drudgery at all.

It was easier to engender a rousing team spirit in the employees than in the more conservative, laid-back executives. And yet, as I watched the senior executives run up on the stage time after time and lead audiences in the Wal-Mart cheer, they seemed very much at ease and to be enjoying the experience. Lee Scott acknowledged that when he attended his first Wal-Mart meeting in August 1979 and listened as the others gave the cheer, he was bemused: "I wasn't on the front row doing it. I was just coming to a company to do a job and to get paid a certain amount of money." But he eventually joined the shouting: "I want to tell you, the second year, I was participating, and the third year I was on the front row."

Ask anyone to explain the Wal-Mart culture and usually the cheer is the first point mentioned. It's certainly true that the cheer has become the main symbol of the culture, but it's far more than that. It is the great equalizer that Sam Walton had been searching for to create a sense of unity in the masses of managers and employees of Wal-Mart. It is the one thing that every Wal-Mart employee does on a regular basis, whether it is Lee Scott, David Glass, and Tom Coughlin (the management team) or a division manager, a store manager, or an hourly employee. Getting everyone to do the cheer makes it that much easier to get everyone to think about implementing the other parts of the culture. And of course the culture was far more elaborate than a simple cheer.

The culture included a set of guidelines or rules that Sam Walton established for the smooth running of the stores. He had a tightly knit business philosophy, a rarity among most business leaders, and he translated that philosophy into those rules. The aim of the rules, indeed the aim of the culture, was to raise the standard of living of Wal-Mart customers.

THE THREE BASIC BELIEFS

In its most elementary form, the culture consisted of Three Basic Beliefs: 1) respect for the individual; 2) service to the customers; and 3) striving for excellence. But in addition Walton devised a set of ten rules designed to help employees implement the Three Basic Beliefs.

Often during his visits to the stores, he passed on his business philosophy, small pearls of wisdom that he never took the time to write down systematically until he got around to publishing his memoirs in 1992. There he described his Ten Rules of Business:

Commit to your business

Share your profits with all your Associates, and treat them as partners

Motivate your partners

Communicate everything you possibly can to your partners

Appreciate everything your Associates do for the business

Celebrate your success

Listen to everyone in your company

Exceed your customers' expectations

Control your expenses better than your competition

Swim upstream

Rule 1 was "Commit to your business." That meant bringing passion to one's work. Employees who had that passion, who loved their work, would try to do the best they could every day.

Rule 2 was "Share your profits with all your Associates, and treat them as partners." Walton urged managers to encourage employees to become true partners in the company as stakeholders. Offering discounted stock and granting employees stock for their retirement proved to be the best thing he ever did, he said.

Rule 3 was "Motivate your partners." Motivating employees with money and ownership, while important, was not enough. Employees had to feel that they were competing, that someone was keeping score. Motivating also meant switching people's jobs to make sure they didn't get stale. Walton was a great believer in what he called cross-pollination. Most of all, he believed in motivating by keeping everyone guessing about the next step. The worst thing was to become predictable.

Rule 4 was to "Communicate everything you possibly can to your partners." ("Partner" was the term Walton used for anyone working in the store, primarily nonexecutive employees). Keeping employees informed was crucial to getting them to understand the business and care for the business. Withholding information from employees conveyed a lack of trust.

Walton's purpose was to make sure that everyone working in the

stores, from managers to employees, possessed the same information, financial or otherwise. Accordingly, at daily employee meetings,
store managers communicated all sorts of details about the company,
focusing on the store's performance the previous day or week, covering strong or weak sales of products, the performance of various departments, etc. There were limits: For instance, employees were not
told Wal-Mart's plans for new store locations or relocations, but neither were store managers. Walton's theory was that as stakeholders in
the business, employees would work harder if they knew as much as
possible about the company's and the store's performance.

Rule 5 was "Appreciate everything your Associates do for the business." Again, it wasn't enough to supply an employee with a paycheck
or a stock option. Employees needed to be told how important they
were, and they needed to be told that frequently. Words of praise,
Walton liked to say, cost nothing and went a long way to win over
employees.

Rule 6 was "Celebrate your success." Perhaps this was the most important rule of all, so we quote Sam Walton: "Find some humor in
your failures. Don't take yourself so seriously. Loosen up, and everybody around you will loosen up. Have fun. Show enthusiasm—
always. When all else fails, put on a costume and sing a silly song. Then
make everybody else sing with you. Don't do a hula on Wall Street. It's
been done. Think up your own stunt. All of this is more important,
and more fun, than you think, and it really fools the competition.
'Why should we take those cornballs at Wal-Mart seriously?' "

Rule 7 was "Listen to everyone in your company." Walton understood that the people who best know what's going on in the company
are those on the front lines, the employees. He favored listening to
employees and adopting their good ideas.

Rule 8 was "Exceed your customers' expectations." Always give
customers more than they expect. Show them your appreciation;
admit your mistakes; don't make excuses, just apologize. Whatever
happens, stand behind everything you do. Walton could not think of
a more important phrase than the one he put on the first Wal-Mart
sign: "Satisfaction Guaranteed."

Rule 9 was "Control your expenses better than your competition." Nothing gave greater competitive advantage than keeping costs down. By running an efficient operation, one could make numerous mistakes yet still survive.

Rule 10 was "Swim upstream," a particular Walton favorite. In his words: "Go the other way. Ignore the conventional wisdom. If everybody else is doing it one way, there's a good chance you can find your niche by going in exactly the opposite direction. But be prepared for a lot of folks to wave you down and tell you you're headed the wrong way. I guess in all my years, what I heard more often than anything was: a town of less than 50,000 population cannot support a discount store for very long."

★ ★ ★

The Wal-Mart culture became the glue that kept employees enthusiastically loyal and kept the stores striving to meet the high standards set by Sam Walton.

The culture drove home a key point: If you treat your employees and customers properly and if you don't allow yourself to grow complacent, you will thrive. Such seemingly self-evident assertions were clearly not part and parcel of the belief systems of most store owners. In other places, too often the relationship between employer and employee was confrontational, providing great service to customers was alien, and indifference and a lack of creativity ruled the day when it came to the running of a store. But Sam Walton believed that given the proper motivation, store managers and employees would develop the necessary enthusiasm and provide the kind of service that would encourage customers to keep coming back to the stores.

"Sam's philosophy was so basic," said David Glass. "His approach was if you take everybody and make them partners, that will work better than having an employer-employee relationship. If you respect them as an individual, if they can always be heard, whether they're right or wrong, if they share in the good and the bad, in the profitability, and are truly partners, then he believed that's what people want."

Of the three cultural cornerstones—respect for the individual, service to the customer, and striving for excellence—the first—service to the customer—is perhaps the most important.

Everyday low pricing is another key part of the culture. The Wal-Mart pricing philosophy included another concept as well: the roll-back, an ongoing program to lower prices even further when an opportunity presents itself. For example, Wal-Mart may get a special buying opportunity from a supplier whose production costs have gone down for some reason (perhaps a reduction in cost of raw materials), and the supplier and Wal-Mart then pass those savings on to the consumer; or Wal-Mart may just decide on its own to lower the cost of a particular product for an extended period of time. On roll-backs, prices will be "rolled back" a minimum of ninety days; they may also be rolled back indefinitely.

Striving for excellence is the search to improve the running of the stores. Often that meant keeping expenses down. Little counted more to Sam Walton than that. His philosophy was to manage every penny, nickel, and dime; if you did, the dollars would take care of themselves. The more he kept his costs low, the more savings he could pass on to customers. He was convinced that shoppers wanted low prices more than anything else (it was a given that the merchandise had to be of a sufficiently high quality).

He simply didn't want to part with money.

He set the thrifty tone by building a home office that was far more modest than most other corporate headquarters. "Outfitted like a bus station, complete with plastic seats," suggested one reporter. He set an equally modest tone by living in a simple ranch-style home.

Why did Wal-Mart, once it had become successful, have to remain so cheap? Walton suggested that each time the company spent a dollar foolishly, the customer paid. Each time Wal-Mart saved a dollar, it put the company one step ahead of the competition.

Frugality certainly seemed to be in his blood, but there was a practical side to being frugal too. The Wal-Mart organization was nothing if not capital-intensive and labor-intensive. Adding stores meant investing large sums of money for the building and staff. He told everyone that Wal-Mart was scrapping for just a few pennies of profit; the rest was expenses. It was hard to get him to part with money. He chided his secretary for installing a fancier phone when the simpler, cheaper one would have done fine. He winced when asked to hire additional people. As a result, Wal-Mart's operating costs were significantly less than those of its rivals.

★ ★ ★

Walton was proud that Wal-Mart had its own way of doing things. Indeed, being different, bucking the tide, became an important part of the Wal-Mart culture: Swimming upstream, he liked to say, made Wal-Mart strong, lean, and alert.

To be different, one had to be willing to change, sometimes on a dime. "Dad always said you've got to stay flexible," reported his son Jim. "We never went on a family trip nor have we ever heard of a business trip in which the schedule wasn't changed at least once after the trip was under way. Later, we all snickered at some writers who viewed Dad as a grand strategist who intuitively developed complex plans and implemented them with precision. Dad thrived on change, and no decision was ever sacred." He called thriving on such change "divine discontent." The idea, Kevin Turner, who joined the company in 1986 as a cashier, noted "was that we can always do something better. Everything in the culture can change except for the Three Basic Beliefs."

★ ★ ★

Employees were given the responsibility of deciding how to implement the Three Basic Beliefs, which were left deliberately unspecific. Sam Walton *did* get specific when it came to other parts of the culture. For example, he introduced the Sundown Rule, which was his personal version of the old adage "Why put off until tomorrow what you can do today?" The rule was simple: Wal-Mart employees were expected to answer requests by sundown on the day the requests were received. One favorite example: A Wal-Mart pharmacist received a call at home from a store employee one Sunday morning, letting him know that one of his regular customers, a diabetic, had accidentally dropped her insulin down her garbage disposal. Aware that this put the diabetic in serious danger, the pharmacist rushed to the store, opened the pharmacy and filled the customer's insulin prescription. This was the Sundown Rule in action. Customers would judge a store by how caring the employees were and how quickly they responded. So the Sundown Rule was one way of showing great customer service.

Walton introduced the Ten Foot Rule as well. In college he had won a number of campus offices, including president of his senior class, and he attributed his success partly to his habit of speaking to people coming down the sidewalk before they spoke to him. If he knew them, he called them by name, but even when he did not know the person, he was not too shy to say hello. As a result he knew more students than anyone else in the university, and they recognized him. Remembering that experience, Walton insisted that Wal-Mart employees employ the Ten Foot Rule with customers. Any time an employee came within ten feet of a customer, the employee was to look the customer in the eye and ask if he or she required help of any kind. Touring numerous Wal-Mart stores, I found store managers and employees alike routinely observing the Ten Foot Rule; customers genuinely seemed pleased by the attention. Only on rare occasions did a customer seem bemused by the greeting. Once, to the embarrassment of the manager escorting me around the store, he approached an elderly shopper and asked her if she needed any help. She gruffly replied: "No. I'm shopping! Leave me alone!"

CHAPTER 4

AVOID THE LAYERS, AVOID THE FRILLS

What kind of Wal-Mart did Sam Walton want?

Well, we know how he wanted the stores to run. All we have to do is look carefully at the Three Basic Beliefs and the Ten Rules of Business. But what kind of corporate organization did he want? He was not nearly as systematic in spelling out the answer to this question, but to those who worked closely with Walton, it was crystal clear.

The kind of Wal-Mart that Sam Walton wanted to avoid is significant in large measure because his successors at times could not help but implement things he wanted to shun. They were trying to overturn Sam Walton's dictates. They did think that they had a better way to manage Wal-Mart. They believed that had Sam Walton lived longer, he too might have shifted ground and decided to implement some of the same measures.

First and foremost, Walton wanted Wal-Mart to avoid becoming like those large modern conglomerates that were headquartered in places like New York, Chicago, and Boston.

He was a small-town boy and wanted Wal-Mart to remain a small-town organization. He did not think that the business Wal-Mart was in was very complex; all it did was buy and sell merchandise. The only challenge was getting the right merchandise into the stores and at the right price. And so he wanted to keep the business simple. "He didn't want us to become a bureaucratic organization or a professional organization," said Don Soderquist, one of Walton's chief lieutenants, "in the sense that we were looked upon as a New York City operation, with big fancy offices. He wanted us to be functional, not fancy. He was very strong on the idea that we not get too big for our britches." He feared bigness not only for the bureaucracy that it would bring but for the recognition that Wal-Mart would gain. Walton cherished the privacy that being small brought and the distance from his competitors that it gave him. While he wanted to know what his rivals were doing, he wanted Wal-Mart's doors shut to them.

Jack Shewmaker, who retired in 1988 as Wal-Mart's vice chairman and CFO, fondly remembered those days of anonymity. "We were rarely thought of as a company that would rise to the level that Wal-Mart has now. That gave us a lot of opportunity to do things without a lot of scrutiny from the competition." Among the things it did: Long before its major competitors, Wal-Mart installed computers in its stores. Based upon a predictable flow of goods into its stores, it employed distribution techniques that were far more advanced than anything its rivals were doing. It staffed its stores with hourly employees in order to provide the best possible customer service.

IT'S THE STORES, STUPID

He insisted that Wal-Mart remain faithful to its core capabilities. As Wal-Mart expanded, Walton came under increasing pressure to get involved in businesses that had nothing to do with merchandising, such as manufacturing and financial services. But Walton and his colleagues always resisted such temptations. "We committed early on," said David Glass, "that we would never get involved in anything other than the business we were in. We knew how to do what we were doing, so we said this is what we're going to do. That was a good decision on our part." It certainly was. In the 1980s and early 1990s, a major Wal-Mart rival, Kmart, began shifting away from discounting, acquiring stakes in the chains Sports Authority, Office-Max, and Borders bookstores. By 2002, Kmart was in bankruptcy.

As long as Wal-Mart could stay focused on its one core capability, churning out one good store after another, it would do fine. "What we actually believed," added David Glass, "was that we were in a simple business, that you ran a store at a time, and you made it no more complex than that. If you got each store running the right way, you'd have no problems." In a play on the slogan of Bill Clinton's first presidential campaign, Sam Walton might well have said, "It's the stores, stupid."

★ ★ ★

There it was: a road map for Wal-Mart for all time.

Avoid getting too big, don't get arrogant, don't bring attention to yourself, stay simple, and remain faithful to the things you do best. And most important, get involved only in those activities that directly affect customers.

Everything else had to be justified—or scrapped.

"The home office," David Glass observed, "was a necessary evil that you had to have just to do some functions, but all in all, the company was store-based and store-specific." When Wal-Mart planners proposed to Walton that he enlarge the home office beyond what was needed at the time—to prepare for the inevitable growth—he resisted all such proposals. If we do that, he told his planners, it will cost a great deal of money, it will be big and fancy, and we'll just have to fill the empty spaces with people. "We gave up something when we wouldn't go out and build the home office," said Bob L. Martin, a former senior executive at Wal-Mart, "but Sam didn't want to build too far ahead even if it cost us a little bit more later." It probably would have been wiser to enlarge the home office in those early days, Martin believed; it would have been cheaper to build it out all at one time even had it meant not occupying it all at once. But Sam Walton never compromised.

The founder made a point of using the term home office, not corporate headquarters, to avoid anyone thinking that he had ambitions of replicating the magnificent citadels of stone and concrete found in New York and elsewhere. Home office seemed far more fitting for the rural small town of Bentonville.

To get a sense of how little Sam Walton liked bureaucracy, one had only to attend a Saturday morning meeting. He believed that as long as employees and managers had to work in the stores on Saturdays, it was only fair that executives at the home office gather for a few hours on Saturday mornings. At the meetings Walton went over sales figures from the previous week and tried to get to know his colleagues better.

Once he asked everyone from the human resources unit to stand up. The HR people must have felt a rush of joy at being singled out by Sam Walton himself. Surely he was going to praise them for their past labors. He asked each one to identify himself or herself and to explain what it was exactly that they did for Wal-Mart. As each member sought to explain their jobs, some obviously having a hard time, they slowly understood that Walton was not meting out praise; he was trying to make a not so subtle point: It was not entirely clear to him that Wal-Mart even needed a human resources operation. On another occasion, he went after the people in accounting. Walton's message was apparent: When he saw the seeds of bureaucracy being sown, he honed in on those seeds with a vengeance. Woe to the person who sought to build up his or her own fief.

It made sense for Walton to keep the organization simple in the early days. For one thing, it kept expenses down. Indeed, cost savings became one of Wal-Mart's great core capabilities. There was a drawback, of course: His cost-consciousness meant that the organization was slow in making improvements. From the very earliest days, the stores' appearance—how clean they were, how nicely products were displayed, whether the aisles were obstructed—was critical to Wal-Mart's image. But Walton felt that he could not afford to invest the sums required to improve the stores' look. He acknowledged that there was a lack of emphasis on quality. The stores did not look neat and modern; they didn't seem professional. To keep the home office simple made obvious sense to Walton; to skimp on the stores must have broken his heart. But he was determined to keep things simple—everywhere.

Lacking also in those early days were the technological accoutrements that in later years helped Wal-Mart grow enormously and for which Wal-Mart became famous. Walton noted that for the company's first decade (1962–72), the stores did not have systems or ordering programs or even a basic merchandise assortment. Nor did they have computers. When in 1992 he looked back, he realized that a good deal of what he and his colleagues had done had not been executed well at all. But it was much easier in retrospect for him to be self-critical. At the time Walton firmly believed that Wal-Mart should not get ahead of itself; it should spend money only where absolutely necessary; it should hire people only for jobs that were crucial to the support of the stores and the customers. He had to be forced, kicking and screaming, to earmark resources for technological improvements in the stores. It took lengthy discussions to convince him to sign off on certain projects; once the projects were in place, he still wondered openly whether the expense was truly justified. Sam Walton had a sense of pace, of deciding how fast or how slow the organization should grow, and he would not allow anyone to pressure him into speeding up that pace.

STEERING CLEAR OF STRUCTURE

And so while other companies were busy adding division after division, he was keeping the organization very simple at Wal-Mart. He did not want the company to get too big for its britches. He did not want a spotlight beamed on it. He did not want to behave as if it were inevitable that Wal-Mart would soon become a retail empire. The solution for all of this was to steer clear of too much structure.

Getting too structured meant adding all sorts of corporate functions that Walton believed were irrelevant. He saw no reason for the company to toot its own horn, so it certainly did not need a big public relations staff. He thought that everyday low-pricing would lure customers into the stores, so there was no need to develop a large advertising staff.

He had the same distaste for government lobbying. "We never wanted to lobby governments," noted David Glass. "We believed that if we elected legislators and sent them to Washington, we could depend on them to represent us and not have to protect ourselves from them. So we stayed away from that." Lee Scott remembered that "Sam had no use for being involved in government. He had no interest in talking to people in Washington, D.C., about whether a piece of legislation was bad for Wal-Mart. He genuinely believed that even if Wal-Mart spent 20 percent more of its time on these issues, it would not have a different standing; and it might deflect us from what really mattered—satisfying customers and taking care of our people."

In keeping with his conviction that any time spent away from the stores was a waste of his time, Walton saw no reason to journey to faraway places in the United States to promote Wal-Mart to investors: "As companies get larger, with a broader following of investors, it becomes awfully tempting to get into that jet and go up to Detroit or Chicago or New York and speak to the bankers and the people who own your stock. But since we got our stock jump-started in the beginning, I feel like our time is better spent with our people in the stores rather than off selling the company to outsiders. I don't think any amount of public relations experts or speeches in New York or Boston means a darn thing to the value of the stock over the long haul."

His greatest fear was that all of these corporate functions would distract Wal-Mart from its main business. "He would tell us," said Wesley Wright, a former Wal-Mart executive who spent twenty years with the company, " 'our core business is not government affairs or human resources or accounting or legal. Our business is buying and selling products and taking care of customers and associates.' " One senior public relations manager at Wal-Mart began explaining Sam Walton's business philosophies to me then stopped abruptly, as if he realized that he was talking himself out of a job: "I've taken fourteen media calls so far today, and I'll take fourteen more by the end of the day, but Sam would ask, 'What did you really do for the company?' He would never ask that question if I were out working in the stores helping customers."

★ ★ ★

Walton sensed that he had a winning formula. For his beloved stores, he had the culture in place, a set of guidelines that explained to managers how to behave toward employees and explained to employees how to behave toward customers. For the corporate organization, he had an equally forceful set of ideas, geared to the notion that the less complex the organization, the better off the stores would be.

But as he resisted the urge to make the Wal-Mart organization too complex, he encountered a paradox: He certainly wanted Wal-Mart to grow. He was proud of what he had accomplished in the sixties and seventies, and he was eager to put more and more Wal-Marts into American communities. But the more that Wal-Mart grew, the more bureaucratic it would have to become. And if there was one thing that Sam Walton fought throughout his entire career, it was Wal-Mart's becoming too bureaucratic. Entangling Wal-Mart in such bureaucracy would force executives to spend more and more time and energy talking among themselves, holding endless meetings, and firing off memos back and forth within the home office, taking their eyes off the only thing that counted in Walton's mind— the stores. He would not allow Wal-Mart to become a corporate monster.

Size had another drawback for Sam Walton. The larger that Wal-Mart grew, the more attention it would attract from outsiders. The longer he could keep people from getting wind of what was going on in the sleepy backwater of Bentonville, the more chance he had of sliding by the retailing giants of the big cities. "We never did talk about ourselves or do a whole lot of bragging outside the Wal-Mart family," he admitted. And there was good reason for it. He was determined to keep a low profile.

In keeping with that low profile, he refused to bow to pressures to move the home office from Bentonville to some large city. Bentonville was far removed from the urban centers of commerce in the United States, from the media in New York, and from government officials in Washington, D.C. Whatever disadvantage others saw in being so far removed from the centers of American commerce, Walton believed there was good reason to stay put. Sure, there were those who argued that the suppliers would not make the long trip to

Bentonville. They wouldn't endure the discomfort of the plane ride. They would find the planes and the hotels and the food too expensive. But Walton believed that even if suppliers found it a hardship to travel to Bentonville, they would still make the trip.

They would come because it had become impossible for many suppliers to do business without trying to sell to Wal-Mart. Walton was right about that. The suppliers came to Bentonville, at first in small numbers, then in droves. When there were just a few suppliers, they became warm and friendly with Sam Walton himself. They played cards with him, ate meals with him, met his wife. The suppliers who came in the seventies were the pioneers. They stayed at the Holiday Inn and ate the hotel meals, however repetitive they were, because that hotel was the only game in town. Then when they came in larger numbers, hotels were built and the suppliers took over them. When the trips became too tiring, they rented offices. They were careful not to rent fancy offices. The word might get back to the home office, and suddenly Wal-Mart would negotiate even more forcefully. They rented cars, again not the fancy ones.

They arrived at the home office bright and early in the mornings, carrying huge trunks and suitcases, even paper bags. They greeted Wal-Mart buyers in the lobby of the home office with smiles that may sometimes have been false but never seemed to disappear. They bunched together around tables in the tiny offices reserved for buyer-supplier conferences, still wearing their smiles, knowing that they were in for the bargaining session of their lives. They had their own bosses to please; they could not accept too low a price for their goods. But seated across the table were the disciples of Sam Walton, people whose prime goal was to cut costs. And so a miniwar of sorts was fought around these tables. Still the suppliers came to Bentonville. Sam Walton understood all this. He knew they would come and in large numbers. They would *have* to come. Their arrival gave him the chance to eat his cake and to have it too. He kept Wal-Mart far removed from the corporate titans and media in New York and from the politicians in Washington, D.C. And at the same time, he was doing a bang-up business. He liked what he saw. He had gotten this far by keeping Wal-Mart simple. He wanted to keep it that way.

NO OTHER CHOICE

Every once in a while, the pressures on him to alter his vision for Wal-Mart just a tad became too great and he succumbed. It did not happen often. Indeed, the only time it happened in the early days came not so much because he had veered from his vision of keeping Wal-Mart below everyone's radar but because he was getting into heavier and heavier debt and he saw no option but to take the company public. In the past when others urged him to do just that, he said no. Going public meant giving up a certain portion of the ownership; it meant also ceding a certain measure of control to shareholders, some of whom might not agree with Walton's business philosophy, with the pace at which he was building Wal-Mart, or the format he was using in the stores.

It meant having to explain and justify what he was doing to a bunch of strangers. In the past he had only his wife and a few executives to please. Once he went public he would have to open the company's books, he would have to file reports with regulatory agencies in Washington, D.C., he would have to stand before shareholders once a year and explain why the company had done well—or had not done well. The media would feast on his every word and on every number in the company's books. So would the Wall Street analysts and the politicians, and so would his rivals.

The decision to go public in October 1970 was not an easy one for him. On top of all the pros and cons, he had his wife, Helen, to deal with. She gave him grief on the subject. She simply could not accept opening up the company's finances to all sorts of strangers: "When you go public, they can ask all kinds of questions, and the family gets involved. We just became an open book, and I hated it."

In the end, Walton took the bold step. He simply had to get rid of that $2 million debt. It was eating away at him. Thoughts of the Depression and what it was like to be poor vied for space in his mind with a nightmarish scenario in which he suddenly had to make good on the money. He didn't mind the small debts, the ones he used to build the stores. But the debts got larger; and to cover one bank loan, he took a loan from another bank. He reached the point where he was begging bankers to lend him money, and some were turning him down. He was eager to expand the operation, but without an infusion of more cash he could not pay off the debts and pay for the expansion. Not long before he had been forced to abandon building plans on five sites because of his cash shortage. He was weary of owing money to people he knew and tired of begging money from strangers. After the company went public, the Walton family owned 61 percent of it.

A RUDE SHOCK

One way to avoid becoming an open book was to keep the media at bay. Walton tried his best to do just that. Throughout the seventies and early eighties, it was not difficult. The media took little interest in businesses or the people who were running them. And it certainly displayed little interest in a small chain of discount retailers in the Southwest. That of course changed, which prompted Lee Scott to look back longingly to those days when Wal-Mart was by no means the leading retailer, when it was largely unknown and when its "little guy" status had clear advantages: "We were the underdog. People identified with the underdog and thought it was OK to root for the underdog. Those were wonderful, exciting times, to be based in Arkansas and to be able to run our business the way Sam liked, raising people's living standards, the stock doubling over a period of time; to be able to fly under the radar.

"The press corps in New York and Washington, D.C., didn't have a clue what Wal-Mart was. There was no legislation that was written and directed against Wal-Mart. No one was trying to harm Wal-Mart. Sam didn't have to go out and defend our reputation or assure that harmful legislation would not be put in place. None of these things existed."

The trick to keeping the media at bay was to convince editors that there was no real story in Bentonville. If Walton could show the media that he was just another unsophisticated hick from some small, out-of-the-way place in Arkansas who did not need to be taken seriously, he might retain the privacy that was so important to him. But there was one facet to his life that was working against him: that was the amount of money he and his family were accumulating as Wal-Mart went from one success to another. By 1984 the company's sales had grown to $6.4 billion with profits of $270.8 million with 756 stores in twenty states.

Having so much money left him at best ambivalent about its importance. If he was proud to have accumulated so much wealth, he never seemed quite comfortable with it; and nothing illustrated that discomfort more than his preference to drive a pickup truck than to be chauffeured around in a limousine and to continue to live in a modest house in Bentonville. But he soon found out that he could not have it both ways. He could not have all that money and remain out of the spotlight, not unless he was willing to live like a recluse. And nothing would have been less appropriate for the man at Wal-Mart's helm than to disappear completely from public view. The crunch came for him in October 1985 when *Forbes* magazine named him the richest man in America.

It was one of his rudest shocks. He must have thought that the gods had conspired against him, so eager had he been to maintain a low profile for himself and for Wal-Mart. Now he feared that the media would not leave him alone. He suspected that they would descend in mighty numbers, assuming that they could photograph him near a swimming pool, smoking a $100 cigar, while beautiful women danced nearby. As problematic as it had been taking the company public fifteen years earlier, *Forbes*'s designation was far worse for him. At least when the company went public, he pulled himself out of debt. There was no similar upside to the media onslaught that he imagined was about to happen. He had no desire to become a celebrity. He had every reason to keep his competitors from learning the precise details of how Wal-Mart worked.

But, again, as with the decision to go public, he had no choice but to allow the media at least a glimpse into his life and into the inner workings of Wal-Mart. Perhaps, he hoped, the television crews would decide not to make the trip when they found out that the richest man in America lived and worked in Bentonville, Arkansas. No such luck. Living and working in Bentonville made Sam Walton seem more exotic, not less, to the television reporters. Well, if the media was going to show up on his doorstep, Walton would try hard not to feed the stereotypes of rich men. Perhaps in doing so, he could get them to quickly lose interest in his persona. Wasn't wealth commonly identified with tailored suits and beautiful cars in addition to the swimming pools and the beautiful women? Knowing that this was what the TV crews were expecting and hoping to tape, Walton made sure that they found him dressed casually either in his pickup truck or playing with his hound dogs. Though he could no longer keep the media at bay, he could at least send a message to his larger rivals in the big cities: "Don't worry. We're not a threat to you."

It bothered him that the media paid so much attention to him and his wealth and not enough to Wal-Mart, which he thought was the truly great business story that journalists should be covering. Even as he cultivated the image of an unsophisticated small-town fellow, hoping to distance the media from him and his family, he expressed annoyance over its failure to take him and Wal-Mart seriously. He simply did not understand how the media and some Wall Street people too could think that "we were just a bunch of bumpkins selling socks off the back of a truck or that we were some kind of fast-buck artists or stock scammers." When the media wrote about Wal-Mart, he argued, they either got things wrong or ridiculed the company. The media frequently portrayed him, he noted, "as a really cheap, eccentric recluse, sort of a hillbilly who more or less slept with his dogs in spite of having billions of dollars stashed away in a cave." In other words, he wanted everyone to think of him as not serious enough to warrant massive media treatment but serious enough not to be mocked simply because he and his company were based in some American backwater.

Just as he tried to keep the media a safe distance from him, he took the same attitude toward people who wanted to write books about him. Never was his ambivalence toward such authors more in view than when in April 1989 Vance H. Trimble, a Pulitzer Prize–winning reporter began writing a biography of Walton at the same time that Wal-Mart's founder was penning his own memoirs. Upon learning of Trimble's plans, Walton mentioned that he was writing his own book and urged him to drop his project. For some time afterward, Trimble thought that he had won Walton's grudging agreement to be interviewed, only to learn, when the time came, that Walton had gotten cold feet. As it turned out, Trimble's book appeared two years in advance of Walton's memoirs. They had to be postponed until 1992 after he was stricken with bone cancer.

In seeking to avoid the glare of publicity, Walton appeared to conclude that it was not worth letting the slightest ray of light into his life or that of the company's. He was even concerned that publishing his own memoirs would seem an immodest act, because he had learned that displaying one's ego in public was not helpful in building an effective business. Glory-seekers did not really help a business, he believed. He undoubtedly feared that apart from seeming immodest, the publishing of his memoirs would draw more unwanted attention to Wal-Mart.

PART THREE

A NEW WAL-MART, A NEW TEAM

CHAPTER 5

A NEW MANAGEMENT TEAM
FOLLOWS MR. SAM

Throughout the early part of 1992, Sam Walton was largely disengaged from the company. He was dying of cancer. Although the company that he built was about to go through its greatest shock, an aura of calm prevailed. The founder was about to depart, but no one actually believed that Wal-Mart would unravel. A strong team of professional managers was in place. Walton had installed them there himself. These were men who had been through the wars with the founder, men who knew his business philosophy inside out, men who would carry the culture forward.

But even with the likelihood that Wal-Mart would survive and most likely do well after Walton's death, a question remained. Could Wal-Mart be as successful without the founder at the helm?

To be sure, David Glass had been doing a very good job of running the company as Walton was fading from the scene, but Wal-Mart was Sam Walton's baby: He had created it, he had built it into a retail powerhouse, he had set all the cultural tones. What assurance was there that anyone else could run the company and do a good job?

Then there were the unanswered questions concerning the Walton family's future interest in the company.

Would Walton's heirs want to be involved at all in the company? Would they simply want to detach themselves completely from Wal-Mart and cash out?

Might they find some way to be part of the company? If they chose to stay, would they try to emulate Walton's management style? Or would they try to establish their own brand of management?

The answers Walton's successors gave to those questions would determine in large measure the way that Wal-Mart would be run after Sam Walton's departure.

When a company has a strong founder like a Sam Walton, the succeeding generation often decides to select a similar, strong figure, usually from outside the company; or they decide that there is something in their own genes that will enable one of them, the oldest or the most interested perhaps, to step into the founder's slot. Big mistake!

What other family-run businesses frequently fail to do is to turn control over to an existing professional management team. That the Walton heirs chose to do so was critical to assuring a smooth transfer of power. "There was not a big transition," Rob Walton noted. "With some companies, the founding family seems to penetrate the company. This is something that can happen in European countries; they can get first choice on the jobs. But that's never been the case here. Executives or associates in the company never felt a lack of opportunity because family members were in the way."

Family-run businesses suffer various fates when the founder passes from the scene, none of them especially rosy. The founder's leadership skills, vision, and perseverance had driven the company's success. But left to its own devices, exhibiting a good deal of indifference to the business that Dad built, lacking an able heir, the family often runs the business into the ground. All that matters to such families is to cash out as quickly as possible.

The history of family-run companies was littered with the wreckage of heirs who had little or no interest in the business before or after the founder's departure. It was not uncommon for a business, once the founder left the scene, to wither and eventually collapse. Though Wal-Mart was thriving at the time of Sam Walton's death, some thought he was so central to its existence that the company would collapse once he left the scene. "He was such an icon," recalled Kent Marts, the editor of the *Benton County Daily Record* in Bentonville. "He was such a central figure. He was Wal-Mart."

At the time of Sam Walton's death, no one could predict what would happen to Wal-Mart.

Once Walton died, tongues wagged over how the new leadership, now on its own, would behave. No one could say for sure.

★ ★ ★

In public Sam Walton had not provided a specific road map for the next generation of leaders to follow. Indeed, he said little about how he wanted Wal-Mart run after his death, creating the impression that he believed the future would take care of itself. He behaved as if he would always be running Wal-Mart. "When he was involved," said Rob Walton, "it was as if he were going to continue to be involved. He never really gave up. He talked about what we are going to do now, not in the future."

THREE CHOICES

The truth was, however, that in the final months of his life he wrestled for quite some time with the succession issue. The critical question for him was: Who would be the most appropriate person to replace him as chairman after his death? He had essentially three choices before him, and he studied each one carefully:

1. He could have gone outside the company. The advantage was that he could choose from a large pool of talented, experienced executives. The downside, though, was that none of these people could possibly have been as devoted or as knowledgeable about his business philosophy and culture as a number of senior executives at Wal-Mart were. Probably for that reason he exhibited little interest in searching beyond the company.

2. He could have selected a member of the Wal-Mart professional management team, the most likely choice being David Glass. Clearly Walton had been grooming Glass for a key leadership role, and he was presumably ready and willing to step into the founder's shoes. But something appeared to trouble Sam Walton about giving the top spot in the company to someone other than a family member.

3. He could have selected a family member. Rob Walton was the obvious candidate. Rob was the only one of the four Walton children who had played a senior operational role in Wal-Mart over a long period. He had the added advantage in his father's eyes of being able to represent the family's interests and of truly being a company insider.

The father selected his eldest son to take the post of chairman after he died, clearly wanting to have a family member at the top of the corporate hierarchy. Conscious of Rob's strong executive talents, the father must have been pleased that he could select a family member and feel confident that Rob would know what he was doing.

In deciding on Rob as chairman but not asking him to be CEO as well, the father made it clear that the actual running of the company should be left to a nonfamily CEO. A decade after their father's death, his heirs suggest that they had no wish to second-guess their father's judgment. "We had so much confidence in his judgment," said his son John. "Basically we all talked about it, but none of us would have ever thought of trying to counter what he thought was best for all of us."

Why was it important that Rob Walton be chairman? More than anything else, Sam Walton wanted to make sure that the family would stay involved in the company and at a very high level. "Dad felt," said John, "it was going to be important to maintain the strong connection to the family."

Walton made a key succession decision as far back as 1984 when he had the CFO, David Glass, and the vice chairman, Jack Shewmaker, essentially swap jobs: Glass became the president and COO, and Shewmaker gave up running the stores in order to handle the finances. The swap set up a very public succession race, with David Glass the acknowledged front-runner for the CEO post. Walton was indicating that he wanted professional management to run the company day to day. Four years later, in 1988, Walton relinquished the post of CEO to Glass; Shewmaker, the other leading candidate, retired. Don Soderquist was promoted to vice chairman and COO, and Paul Carter was named to succeed Shewmaker as CFO.

Soderquist was clearly a star on the rise. He had joined the company in 1981 as the head of administration and distribution; he eventually—in 2000—became senior vice chairman of Wal-Mart Stores. Because he was so good at getting in front of an audience, because he seemed to have some of Sam Walton's great cheerleading qualities, Soderquist was increasingly entrusted to dispense the cultural verities, just as Walton had done in earlier days. A gentle sort, he tended to be emotional and philosophical, the kind of fellow who might throw his arms around someone. He was less hands-on than Sam Walton, less shy than David Glass; it was no accident that Soderquist so frequently ran the Saturday morning meetings. Like Sam Walton, he was a performer, a cheerleader, something of a preacher.

★ ★ ★

Sam Walton had always wanted his family to remain an important part of the business. He was adamant that his heirs hold on to their stakes in the company. Whatever they decided to do with their lives, he was insistent that they not join the idle rich. "We don't need the money. We don't need to buy a yacht. And thank goodness we never thought we had to go out and buy anything like an island." Walton knew all too well that such appetites, which his family did not have, often wrecked other companies. He was disturbed at families who sold their stock in family-run businesses in dribs and drabs to live well, thus making the company vulnerable to a takeover. He wrote his memoirs, he said, in the hope that his grandchildren and great-grandchildren would read the book and that it would deter them from such behavior.

Walton did not push his children to take on operational roles in the business. He let them know that they were welcome to enter the business, but if they did, they would have to work as hard as he did; they would have to commit to being merchants. And he hoped they would absorb his values.

Yet even as he laid down guidelines on how he hoped his heirs would behave after his death, he would not be able to control them beyond the grave. When the company was his, it was clearly not theirs;

but once he had left the scene, the company would be theirs; and they would be free to decide on their roles—and to depart from those guidelines if they wished.

Judging by the roles that they played in the company while their father was alive, it seemed likely that most of the four Walton children would not want to assume senior management positions within the company. Three of the four had for much of their adulthood pursued lives away from the business.

Only Rob (fifty-eight years old in 2002) had been an active part of the Wal-Mart leadership for much of his career. He joined the company full time in 1978 as senior vice president, director, secretary, and general counsel. Though he had been at his father's side helping to build the business for fourteen years, Rob seemed in some important respects remarkably different from his father: Though they shared a love of the business, Rob showed no great inclination to mingle with employees, as his father loved to do, and he displayed little interest in resolving issues at the store level. He was far more inclined to look at big-picture topics, such as real estate and the international program. Rob was nevertheless the ideal replacement for his father because in the 1990s the company would need someone at the helm who supported Wal-Mart's growth and who had no trouble investing large sums to support that growth.

The other Walton children had much less to do with the company over the years, though they did keep up some degree of involvement.

Alice (fifty-three years old in 2002) briefly worked as a buyer in merchandising for Wal-Mart but left to run an investment firm before settling down on a ranch in Fort Worth, Texas, living a very private life. Jim (fifty-four years old in 2002) has been running Walton Enterprises, the holding company that runs the Arvest set of regional banks, a newspaper, and the family foundation. John (fifty-six years old in 2002) worked as a Wal-Mart pilot for nearly a year (his father was Wal-Mart's first pilot; John its second) then worked as a crop duster before running his own crop-dusting operations and a boat-building enterprise. He then ran an investment company for start-ups and small companies with new technology.

Yet even as the majority of the children carved out their own lives, they felt a special attachment to Wal-Mart. They, along with their widowed mother Helen (eighty-three years old in 2002) owned 38 percent of the stock, an unusually large amount for the dominant stockholder of a publicly traded company. Had any of them so wished, Jim, John, or Alice might even have assumed senior roles in the company upon their father's death.

THE CHILDREN GET IT

But most likely because of their own personal inclinations to stay aloof and because they had great faith in their father's judgment, the Walton heirs gave their stamp of approval to the succession plan their father had put in motion. The professional management team that Sam Walton had put in place would continue as before. The family made it clear that they wanted and expected the team to keep their father's beliefs as the main drivers of the Wal-Mart culture. Lee Scott noted: "The children all get it. That's unusual. So Sam's legacy lives on. His basic philosophies in business live on in the kids."

The children got something else. They got the central fact that the new leadership should rely on Walton's ideas but should not try to imitate him personally. The family wanted David Glass at the helm, managing the company; it wanted Don Soderquist as a kind of partner to Glass, picking up the spiritual leadership vacated through Sam Walton's death. But it wanted no Sam Walton pretenders. Rob Walton knew that he was no Sam Walton. He knew it, and so did all the others in Wal-Mart's new leadership. He had neither the personality nor the inclination to replicate his father. He was a lawyer by profession, certainly not a merchandise man or operations man.

And yet with all that responsibility resting on his shoulders, Rob Walton might have thought it imperative to show that the Walton family was still running things. But he knew that it had been his father's will to turn operational decision-making over to a group of professional managers, and Rob wholeheartedly concurred with that decision. Passing the mantle of leadership to this new group meant, above all else, allowing it to judge when to retain the management legacy of Sam Walton and when to go its own way.

So Rob was very careful not to give the impression that he was trying to step into his father's shoes. He did not take over his father's office; he gave no media interviews, preferring that the management team represent the company in public; and he was in the home office only some of the time. He did not imitate his father's personal style of management by traveling to as many stores as possible. No one would have gotten the impression that he was trying to play the hands-on role his father had played. But he did take an active interest in the business, and two of his priorities were real estate and the international program. The main liaison between the family and the day-to-day Wal-Mart management, Rob Walton made a point of keeping the public spotlight on the leadership team, avoiding media interviews, allowing Lee Scott and the others to represent Wal-Mart to the public.

In permitting David Glass and later Lee Scott to take center stage, the family was not sanctioning the creation of a new Sam Walton at the helm. But it certainly wanted the new Wal-Mart leadership to keep the Sam Walton flame alive throughout the organization. "After Dad was gone," Rob Walton said, "we made a real strong commitment to keeping his name and his philosophy in the top of minds around the company, and, interestingly, it has gotten even stronger over the years. That was David Glass's commitment. And Lee Scott has carried on that commitment. The name Sam Walton is not part of the marketing of Wal-Mart. It is used more for internal purposes; it is more a part of the culture of the company. What we market is everyday low prices, good service, convenience, keeping merchandise in stock."

The new leadership team understood the family's wishes; accordingly, none of them ever tried to become a Sam Walton, either by re-creating his personality or his management style. Indeed, the stress was always on team leadership, not the branding of one key player. Neither David Glass nor Lee Scott attracted the public attention that Sam Walton did. (Scott thought it significant to mention to me that he often walked unrecognized through Wal-Mart stores and did not appear on business magazine covers.)

The post-Walton leadership team entered into an unwritten agreement whereby it shared and divided power among three senior figures, Rob Walton, David Glass, and Don Soderquist; more recently, Rob Walton, Lee Scott, and Tom Coughlin. No one said it better than Scott: "We're not made up of celebrities. It's the way it all comes together that is our strength. And once in a while, one person will pop up and believe that all of this is because of them. And they'll leave and go somewhere else and not do nearly as well as they hoped."

Having decided not to take senior management roles, the family did not want to go to the other extreme either, exhibiting only marginal interest in the company. They sensed that their father wanted them to become his eyes and ears. Accordingly, the Waltons felt an obligation to remain strongly attached to Wal-Mart. "After his death," said John Walton, "it was clear what our role would be. Rob would be chairman, and the family would try to be even more supportive than when Dad was there."

But other than Rob, none of the family would play an operational role in the day-to-day running of the company. Still, the family would be visible and watchful: One of the Walton children other than Rob would always be a board member, and the other two Walton children could at any time they wished attend board meetings (except for executive sessions).

In addition, as a way of keeping fully informed beyond what could be culled from board meetings, the entire family decided to meet three times a year as a family with Wal-Mart the only subject on the agenda. They met over a two- to three-day period, sometimes at Helen Walton's home in Bentonville, sometimes in a hotel. One occasional participant, a nonfamily Wal-Mart executive, told me that the family put in a full workday on each day of the meetings.

What was so unusual about these meetings was that the four Walton children made a point of bringing their children to the meetings, even the teenagers. For the family understood that it had an obligation not only to apprise itself of the latest developments at Wal-Mart;

it also had to prepare the third generation of Waltons for its eventual responsibilities as Wal-Mart owners. The adults felt that it was important not only for them to be educated about Wal-Mart but also to bind the Walton grandchildren to the family business. The idea, in Rob Walton's words, was to lay the groundwork so that these youngsters could "become responsible and constructive shareholders of Wal-Mart."

For the adults and children alike, the gathering was a chance to hear firsthand from senior executives a series of progress reports on projects around the company. This was all part of the role the family saw for itself as safeguarding the interests of shareholders, which of course meant in no small measure safeguarding its own interests as the largest owner of Wal-Mart stock. When the family held one of these gatherings, on August 4, 2002, all but one of the thirteen members of the family were present: the eighty-two-year-old Helen Walton, her four children, and seven of her eight grandchildren (one was ill). The remarkable success of the new leadership team has eased the family's task, as Rob Walton noted: "There aren't many decisions that shareholders have to make about a company that's run successfully." Just how the family takes decisions at these meetings is not discussed. One occasional participant believed that decisions were probably made by consensus rather than by an actual vote.

IRREPLACEABLE

The new leadership team was thus a blend of family and professional management. The family, through Rob Walton, would monitor the management team, led by David Glass and Don Soderquist, which would run the business on a daily basis.

One more indication that the new management would not try to replicate Sam Walton was the near partnership that evolved among the company's top leaders, David Glass and Don Soderquist. Each had his own particular set of leadership skills. They functioned as a team, and often executives said that "David and Don," not just the

CEO, were handling this or that part of the business. Neither had all of Sam Walton's special qualities; that was one more reason why it made sense for them to function in tandem. David Glass was the operations man par excellence. It was his organizing skills, his willingness and ability to tackle the issues that arose on a day-to-day basis in a multibillion-dollar, multifaceted, ever-growing company that allowed Wal-Mart to surge forward so quickly. He had been close to Sam Walton, and he knew the founder's thoughts and business philosophy inside out, but he possessed very few of Walton's great communication skills. Walton knew how to charm; Glass knew how to manage.

Filling in some of Sam Walton's communication and people skills became the task of Don Soderquist. People said that he could have been a preacher had he not chosen to enter the retail business. Like Sam Walton, he took over a room with his stature and his presence; many at Wal-Mart felt a special affection for him as he became the key leader in articulating Sam Walton's values and culture. He joined the company in 1981; seven years later he was promoted to vice chairman and COO when Walton transferred the post of CEO to David Glass. With Sam Walton's passing, he assumed an even more important role as one of the three members of the new leadership team (the other two being David Glass and Rob Walton).

★ ★ ★

When Sam Walton was alive and running Wal-Mart, it was understood that he was the final arbiter on all matters. But once he died, the management team naturally assumed that it would be left to run the company as it saw fit, at least on the daily operational level. Yet here was Rob Walton, the new chairman, occupying an office a few feet away from the senior management team. How much freedom of maneuver would the management team actually have? A great deal, as it turned out. Because Rob Walton was not around all the time and because he deliberately adopted a low profile, he did not get in everyone's hair: "He's not telling you," said a pleased Lee Scott, "that the

Clorox should be four feet from the end of the counter. Rob is not caught up ego-wise in making some big acquisition that might or might not be good for you."

★ ★ ★

With the Walton heirs effectively ceding control of the company to the new leadership team, the burden on the new team was immense. Free to make critical decisions about the running of the company, it nevertheless had to make the right decisions. In the past, Sam Walton did all that. He had done it so well and was so dominant a figure that the team often, at least in the beginning, chose to ask themselves what Sam would have done in this case or that. Deferring to Walton was also the new leadership team's way of saying that it had no pretensions of trying to attain Sam Walton's iconic status.

As the new leadership team felt its way, Wal-Mart's board members expressed genuine concern among themselves that the leadership team might have a hard time following in the footsteps of such an extraordinary figure as Sam Walton.

Could the new leadership team keep its egos in check and simply try to replicate everything that Sam Walton had done? Or might they decide that one way of stamping their own personalities on the company was to trivialize Walton's accomplishments?

These were crucial questions because the way they were answered would have a great deal to do with the future of the company and with the direction it would take. That was why all eyes were on the man who was stepping into the founder's shoes.

★ ★ ★

In 1964, David Glass drove down from Springfield, Missouri, where he had been working at Crank Drugs, to take in the opening of a Wal-Mart in Harrison, Arkansas. It was the first time that Glass had met Sam Walton. Wading through the watermelons and donkey leavings had given Glass a negative impression of the forty-six-year-old Walton and his store. Writing him off, Glass even suggested that Walton try another line of work.

Walton did not write David Glass off. In fact, he kept an eye on him over the next decade, hoping that he could entice him to come and work at Wal-Mart. Finally, in 1976, Sam induced Glass to join the company as chief financial officer. He also had charge of data-processing, systems-development and distribution. Glass climbed up through Wal-Mart's ranks, becoming president and CEO in 1988. As Walton's illness progressed, he took on increasing responsibility for running the company.

LEADERSHIP TRAITS

For the man who stepped into Sam Walton's shoes in 1992, two key questions were: How much should David Glass be himself, and how much should he simply emulate Sam Walton?

It was clear that Sam Walton had leadership characteristics that meshed perfectly with the Wal-Mart of the 1960s and 1970s. It was not at all certain that Wal-Mart would benefit from having new leaders with the same, Walton-like traits.

Walton was above all else a great merchant, certainly one of the best of his generation; he could select a specific item, promote the hell out of it, and price it at just the right level to generate huge sales. He was also a great operations man: keeping expenses in check, able to understand numbers, setting expectations and getting employees to meet or surpass those expectations. As Wesley Wright, a former Wal-Mart senior executive, suggested, "He knew how to make things happen."

Finally, he used his charisma to get people to do things for him. He believed firmly in making his employees feel a sense of ownership toward the business long before other corporate titans adopted such techniques. Using his immense communication skills, he was able to get managers and employees to go the extra step, to act creatively and innovatively.

These were leadership skills that went well with the management of a small company, as Wal-Mart was in its early years. They were the skills that someone eager and willing to get down in the trenches with his employees would need. But they were not necessarily the skills that would mesh with the running of a much larger, a much more complex organization, as Wal-Mart had become.

Would Sam Walton select someone with the same traits that he possessed or would he understand that Wal-Mart was changing, growing, getting more complex and would need someone with traits quite different from his?

Walton was all too aware that he and Glass were different, different in their personalities, in their management styles, in their opinions about what was needed to expand the company and in their thoughts about how quickly the company should grow. But Walton did not let those differences stand in his way of promoting Glass to senior leadership. He undoubtedly saw in Glass—and this was Walton's genius as much as it was Glass's—someone who had the management skills to preserve all that Walton had built and the imagination and guts to take it to new heights.

While the two men were in some interesting ways similar, they were different in much more striking ways. There were similarities to be sure: Both loved the retail business. The big difference was that Walton had a special affinity for merchandising, Glass for food. Because of Walton, Wal-Mart was essentially a merchandising business from 1962 to 1988; because of Glass, it has been a merchandising and food business since 1988.

Both were superb operations men and knew how to get the most out of their employees; both shared a definite distaste for the home office, yearning to get out into the stores as the only way to truly understand the business.

But David Glass was different from Sam Walton. The latter was the extrovert, the teacher, the coach, the great communicator; Glass was quiet and so plainly uncharismatic that journalists likened him to that other small-town Midwesterner, Bob Dole. Walton's wrinkled face made him look grandfatherly and authoritative: Glass's stern looks made him seem, as the media kept noting, inscrutable, but he was simply obeying an impulse to cast a much smaller shadow than his boss, Sam Walton. Glass was more faceless than inscrutable.

Like Sam Walton, Glass considered himself frugal, but the truth is that he was quite prepared to spend money on things that he thought important. Nothing was more important to him than obtaining new technology for Wal-Mart so as to give it a competitive advantage. It was not easy going, for Sam Walton, more often than not, saw technology as only a cost, not an investment in the company's future.

NO FEAR OF GROWTH

Unlike Walton, David Glass had little fear of growth. For the founder, growth meant going into debt, building bureaucracy, increasing the payroll—one expense after another. For David Glass, it was all right to go into debt to roll out more and more Wal-Mart stores. From 1992 to 1995, Glass increased Wal-Mart's long-term debt from $1.7 billion to $8.5 billion, using the cash to build Supercenters, high-tech food distribution centers, and, today, the land for even more Supercenters.

Because he was determined to keep expenses down and because he had no great feel for technology, Sam Walton was at best a cynic and at worst a rejectionist in his attitude toward technology. Though Walton often eventually gave in to the urgings of David Glass and others to install the latest technology, Glass must have felt frustration and disappointment at how difficult it was to move certain projects forward under him. After Walton's death, Glass was free to make far-reaching decisions on technology, and he did just that. He had the foresight to understand that Wal-Mart's growth required warehouse-size distribution centers and high-tech merchandise-tracking wizardry. By 2000, the year Glass stepped down as CEO, Wal-Mart vendors were electronically exchanging invoices, purchasing orders, and other documents with the company. Through satellite communications, all Wal-Mart stores were linked with the home office to replenish and reorder required inventory. People called David Glass a logistics genius. It was a skill that Sam Walton could not have comprehended.

But the most important attribute that Glass possessed was a penchant for risk taking. Certainly Sam Walton had taken risks: placing

Wal-Marts in small towns when so many thought his small-town strategy was mistaken; investing his own money when that was all that was available. Yet there was a difference in the risk taking of Glass and Walton. It was in the magnitude of those risks. Walton was risking millions of dollars; Glass was risking billions. Both men knew that by the early 1990s Wal-Mart had become a remarkable success. Yet Walton worried that the company would get high on that success, causing it to spend money needlessly; Glass was not afraid to keep the Wal-Mart growth engine churning at full speed. To do that he would have to take calculated financial risks. The thought did not bother him.

Glass was ready to take the company forward. Dating back to the time he took over as CEO in 1988, he had already done an outstanding job, increasing sales from $16 billion in 1987 to $43.8 billion in 1992. He had also nearly tripled earnings: from $628 million to nearly $2 billion.

With Walton no longer around, Glass came into his own. The fifty-seven-year old CEO emerged in a *Fortune* survey taken in the fall of 1992 as the most admired CEO of the most admired companies. By 1995, three years after Sam Walton's death, Glass had presided over a Wal-Mart whose sales had more than doubled, to nearly $100 billion. *Fortune* described that as "an unmatched feat in the annals of the *Fortune* 500."

Into the 1990s Glass continued to be Wal-Mart's great risk-taker, staking the company's growth on making a growing network of Supercenters work successfully. Food would become the lure, the rationale went, to get the typical Wal-Mart shopper to come, not once or twice a month, as was the normal practice, but more than twice a week (the typical amount for grocery shoppers).

Because he was so low-key and taciturn, because he let the company grow so aggressively, David Glass did not seem like a growth king. But his record was clear. Soon after Sam Walton died, Glass increased Wal-Mart's spending. In four years there were 260 Supercenters; eight years earlier there had been none. Because those Supercenters were bringing in $13 billion a year in annual revenue,

Glass talked giddily of adding another hundred Supercenters a year. Again there were risks. The food business, a critical anchor of the warehouse-like stores, was a big gamble for Wal-Mart, because its profit margins were smaller than those found in merchandise. But Glass was not afraid of low-margin businesses. He did not seem to be afraid of anything. Glass continued to build the Supercenters even as analysts doubted that Wal-Mart would be able to trump smaller grocers that by virtue of their associations with networks and cooperatives possessed a good deal of purchasing clout. But the competition did not bother Glass: By 2001 Wal-Mart had $56 billion in grocery sales, making it America's Number One food retailer.

Glass agreed that the biggest single difference between his approach and that of Sam Walton's was "that a long time ago I had a strong belief that technology would ultimately drive this business to be the size that it is. I've championed our efforts in technology and the systems and sophistication that we've been able to achieve, everything from the logistics aspects to all the financial aspects of it."

It all seemed so obvious to Glass: In the early years, having a Sam Walton make his way around Wal-Mart stores three or four times a week was a critical capability of the organization. And having a David Glass playing to his strengths in technology and logistics and distribution was as much a core capability in the post-Walton years.

The culture at Wal-Mart celebrates Sam Walton, but it was David Glass who had a global vision that allowed Wal-Mart to grow in ways that few expected. It was Glass who took Wal-Mart out of Middle America and made it a global brand, turning it into one of the largest corporations in the world, rivaling such corporate titans as General Motors, Ford, and General Electric. It was Glass who turned Wal-Mart into one of the greatest growth machines of all time.

CHAPTER 6

A STRATEGY OF GROWTH

The strange truth about Sam Walton is that as large and influential as he had made his chain of stores, he never quite seemed eager to create the Wal-Mart empire. He was ambitious. He was proud of every new Wal-Mart store that opened. He knew that a key measurement of success in his industry was the number of stores that dotted the landscape. Yet all evidence suggests that size was not nearly as important to Walton as the smooth running of each store.

When President George Bush presented Walton with the nation's highest civilian award shortly before the Wal-Mart founder's death in the spring of 1992, Walton spoke briefly at the ceremonies, noting that he was proud of what he had accomplished and that he thought Wal-Mart had just begun.

But what was he talking about? Did he think that the company was just beginning to build a Wal-Mart empire? Or did he simply mean that Wal-Mart was just beginning to produce the best discount stores in the world? He did not say.

In the last few years of Sam Walton's life, he and CEO David Glass had taken the company to new heights. Sam Walton had long hoped to become the nation's top retailer. By the late 1980s he was coming close to getting his wish.

In the decade before 1987, Wal-Mart had been growing at an annual rate of 35 percent, triple the growth rate of the entire retail industry. With sales of $11.9 billion in 1987, it ranked as the fourth-largest American retailer, threatening to replace Number Three J.C. Penney (1986 sales: $14.7 billion) and fast closing in on Kmart ($23.8 billion) and Sears ($44.3 billion).

In that same year of 1987 Wal-Mart was attempting to move beyond its regional base in the Sun Belt to become a truly national enterprise. It had just recently crossed into the Frost Belt states of Wisconsin, Minnesota, and Indiana. Some in the media wondered whether a company with headquarters in an Arkansas town of 9,900 could cater successfully to customers so far from its home office. Wal-Mart's leaders seemed to have no doubts. That was the year the company completed the largest private satellite communications system in the United States. It linked all of the chains' operating units with the home office by two-way voice and data and one-way video communication.

FAST AND FURIOUS

The growth was fast and furious. In 1983 it had opened its first Sam's Club, the warehouse-style stores of 100,000 square feet or more that served as one-stop suppliers for small businesses; that same year greeters started showing up at the front door of all Wal-Marts; *Forbes,* for the eighth straight year, ranked Wal-Mart as Number One among general retailers. Just four years later it had opened fifty-two outlets of Sam's Clubs, and plans were under way for Wal-Mart to start a chain of Supercenters, offering everything from groceries to merchandise in 220,000-square foot emporiums.

In 1989, Wal-Mart, with revenue of $20.6 billion, 1,402 stores and 272,000 employees, wracked up $1.67 billion in profits, making it the most profitable retailer in America, surpassing Kmart. Wal-Mart was now in twenty-six states, having just added Michigan, West Virginia, and Wyoming.

By 1990 it became the largest American retailer, with discount store sales reaching $25.8 billion. By 1991 its sales had increased to

$32.6 billion. Significantly, nineteen stores were opened in California that year and another three in Nevada, marking Wal-Mart's first entry into the Far West.

Meanwhile, Wal-Mart was rewarding long-term investors with one of the highest returns on equity in American business. From 1977 to 1987 its average annual return to investors was 46 percent. Even in the middle of the recession in 1991, it reported a return on equity of more than 32 percent.

Also in 1991, Wal-Mart became the first retailer to post more than $1 billion in annual earnings, netting $1.3 billion. That same year, it opened its first international store, in Mexico City.

In 1992 the stores, which now averaged 75,000 square feet, had spread to forty-five states, and six of the "new concept" Supercenters opened with encouraging results.

Though Sam Walton contended that he thought hard before letting Wal-Mart grow as quickly and dramatically as it did, by the time he died in the spring of 1992 Wal-Mart had become a $43.8 billion business with $1.6 billion in profits. Wal-Mart was opening 150 outlets each year. But it was still very much a rural establishment. The average population of the communities that Wal-Mart served was 15,000.

In April, the month of Sam's death, Wal-Mart, with 371,000 employees, operated 1,714 Wal-Mart stores; and 208 Sam's Clubs in the United States. It had only six Supercenters and eight stores outside the fifty states (in Mexico and Puerto Rico).

A REAL GUSHER

During Wal-Mart's first five years, super growth was neither a major goal nor even a dream at Wal-Mart. But Sam Walton liked the way the first Wal-Marts were performing, so he began thinking about growth. The first seven or eight Wal-Marts had produced great results, and Walton saw no reason to quit. He saw the potential very clearly. The money was coming in, but he needed to get better organized and find a more sensible way to finance the chain's growth.

Wal-Mart's growth in the 1960s was impressive (twenty-four stores were built in the first five years), and Sam Walton loved that time. He thought that for him personally it was the most exciting time: "It was the retail equivalent of a real gusher."

But even this limited expansion proved burdensome when Walton went into $2 million of debt. If the company was going to expand, he needed an infusion of cash to get out of debt. Going public was the answer. Once Wal-Mart began to trade publicly, the infusion of cash arrived, and Wal-Mart's growth began in earnest.

In 1970, Wal-Mart had grown to thirty-two stores with $44 million in revenue. It added nineteen stores over the next two years and twenty-seven over the two after that, so that by 1974 it had seventy-eight stores with revenue of $236 million and over $6.3 million in profits.

Still, it was a small chain, not even among the top hundred retailers in the United States. Accordingly, few noticed its remarkable growth that decade: While its rivals were opening from three to six stores a year, it was averaging fifty store openings annually. Wal-Mart had 125 stores in 1976 with $340 million in revenue, 195 stores two years later with $678 million in revenue, and by 1980, 276 stores with revenue of $1.2 billion. Profitability rose too: from $1.6 million in 1970 to $41.2 million in 1980.

SIGNS OF AMBIVALENCE

While the company kept growing under Sam Walton, he remained ambivalent about how quickly and aggressively Wal-Mart should grow.

Certainly growth was a big part of the Wal-Mart story in the seventies and eighties, even when Sam Walton worried that costs were getting out of line, even when cynics expressed serious doubts about the Wal-Mart magic's traveling well to other parts of the country, closer to the big cities, far from the Southwest.

But the growth that Sam Walton had in mind for Wal-Mart was limited in scope and therein constituted one of the major differences between Walton and his successors. His key strategy had been to introduce decent-size discount stores into the small one-horse towns that everyone else had ignored. Meanwhile, Kmart helped out by being unwilling to enter towns below 50,000; so too did Gibson's, a Texas-based discount chain, which steered clear of towns smaller than 10,000 or so.

One powerful influence on Sam Walton's keeping to a small-town strategy was his wife Helen. She told him two years into their marriage after they had moved sixteen times that she would go with him any place he wanted as long as he did not ask her to live in a big city. She defined a big city as any place larger than 10,000 people. That meant that any town larger than 10,000 was off-limits to the Waltons. Walton accordingly gave his wife credit for insuring that he pursued the small-town strategy that gave Wal-Mart a strong showing in its early days.

The small-town strategy also had the effect of keeping Wal-Mart a regionalized chain, which was fine with Sam Walton. He was no expansionist: "I always wanted to be the best retailer in the world, not necessarily the biggest. I've always been a little bit afraid that big might get in the way of doing a good job."

He was content to build stores in a ring around a city, then wait for the growth to push into the suburbs. He resisted the temptation to leapfrog into the large markets. David Glass recalled that people told them: "You ought to be in California. That would be fantastic." He added, "But for years and years we just simply expanded those circles out by strategically locating DCs [distribution centers]. There was a tremendous flight from the inner cities to suburbs, and so our strategy was to go to Dallas or wherever and build stores in the suburbs; not because we wanted to be in small towns closest to Dallas but because that's where the population growth was."

There seemed nothing appealing to Walton about a Wal-Mart empire. His son John noted that when Sam Walton spoke about growth "he didn't emphasize store count or volume growth. It was always in terms of improving sales per square foot and of where the opportunities were for putting up new stores and serving new customers. He constantly spoke of growth in terms of quality, of the measurable things that contributed to bottom-line growth." His elder brother Rob concurred: "My father was interested in more than just numbers. He was interested in our people and what we stood for as a company."

GETTING TO THE NEXT NUMBER

A vital part of the early strategy was to make sure that before expanding, every store in a region had to be operating properly. Of course Walton wanted to expand the Wal-Mart chain; he admitted to having an "itch" for such growth. He did not want all his eggs in one basket. But his vision did not take him beyond the wider region around his home. "Sam didn't really encumber the organization with big dreams and big strategies," recalled Lee Scott.

Rob Walton pointed out to me that his father constantly worried that too much growth could hamper the smooth running of the existing stores. "Dad would have shut the growth down in two heartbeats, maybe one, if he thought we were losing the ability to control the stores and run them profitably. He was not committed to growth per se but to taking advantage of the opportunity that was there for profitable growth."

Walton kept to a small-town strategy, saturating a market region by spreading his stores out, then filling them in, in part because he had a limited distribution system unlike those of the big boys, such as Kmart. While his rivals were getting bogged down in real estate negotiations, zoning laws, and municipal politics, Walton avoided all that, as he concentrated on the regional approach, relying on the distribution centers, or warehouses, to keep the stores under control. He wanted the DCs within reach of Wal-Mart's district managers and of the home office. Each store had to be within a day's drive of a distribution center.

In time, Walton overcame the doubters who thought that Wal-Mart would be unable to move beyond its regional presence in and around Bentonville. Walton and David Glass understood that the company's growth was simply a function of its capability to supply its stores. So, David Glass told me: "We drew a circle two hundred miles around Bentonville, and we said we can put stores in that circle. We recognized that if you wanted to grow the business rapidly, you would need another distribution center, and so we decided to put up a second one. There was conjecture on the part of Wall Street analysts on whether we could operate these centers away from Bentonville. We built one in Searcy, Arkansas, in 1978. We drew a circle around it and made it work."

With that policy in mind, Walton could look at a map and determine where to put the first store in the region. He would select a site as far as he could from a warehouse and put in a store. Then he would fill in the map of that territory, state by state, county seat by county seat, until he had saturated the market area.

Even as this hub-and-spoke strategy, as Wal-Mart called it, worked beautifully, Walton did not allow himself to think about accelerating growth. He was confident that if he could keep establishing the stores within the framework of the hub-and-spoke plan, the stores would do well, and he would never get ahead of himself.

His only vision in the early days was to provide unbeatable value and the best possible customer service; it was to create an atmosphere in each store that would make customers come back time after time. Certainly he believed firmly that his brand of retailing was superior to the efforts of his chief rivals, but that did not automatically mean that he had imperial pretensions.

UNCHARACTERISTIC FORECAST

The one occasion when Walton appeared to dream those imperial dreams came at the June 1990 shareholder meeting when he suggested that Wal-Mart could well become a $100 billion company by the year 2000. (In its last full year before the meeting Wal-Mart had revenue of $25.8 billion.) He may have been led to make this seemingly preposterous forecast because that very year Wal-Mart had passed Sears to become the world's largest retailer.

Standing on a runway in the middle of the University of Arkansas sports center in Fayetteville—seemingly oblivious of the cancer that would kill him twenty-two months later—Walton challenged the 8,000 shareholders and employees: "Can we do it?"

"Yes, we can," the crowd roared back.

For David Glass, the man who was being directly challenged, Walton's rallying cry appeared "quite a stretch." After all, it had taken nearly three decades for Wal-Mart to even get to its current level of revenue. Two years later, when his memoirs were published, Walton sounded a more cautious note: He was concerned with talk that Wal-Mart was the biggest retailer in the world only because he worried that it might go soft. True, he wrote, Wal-Mart's size meant that vendors and suppliers no longer ignored the company, but size could also lead to Wal-Mart getting bloated or out of touch or slow to react to customers' needs.

He suggested that outside factors, especially Wall Street, were pressuring Wal-Mart to keep growing and growing—implying that had it been up to him, he would have gone slower. To sustain the company's growth, "you constantly have to consider what you're going to be doing five years out. I think that the stock market pressure has driven us to plan further out so that there will be some consistency next year, and the year after—not only to our profitability but to our operating sales, our gross margins, and those sorts of things."

In other words, to keep the Wal-Mart stock up and thus please the shareholders, the company had to keep growing.

★ ★ ★

Sam Walton was cautious about growth, but his successors exhibited none of his concerns. When they commented about growth, they were much more excited. David Glass once observed: "When I came to Wal-Mart we had just finished a year of $340 million in sales and $12 million in profit. Today, that's roughly the output of a few Sam's Clubs." Moreover, Walton's successors were far more open to installing the corporate functions that Wal-Mart required—and Sam Walton had so opposed—to coordinate all that growth.

Growth became a core capability for the new leadership team. Walton's $100 billion forecast made it easier for the post-Walton leadership to feel good about growth and to feel challenged to quadruple revenue in a mere eight years. But they were ambitious enough so that even had Walton not made such a forecast, they would have aggressively sought growth.

To be sure, a number of Wal-Mart growth initiatives were set in motion even while Sam Walton was still alive. The first two Wal-Mart Supercenters appeared in 1988, the first international unit in 1991. But these two main growth efforts—building Supercenters and taking Wal-Mart international—gained real momentum only when Walton's career had effectively ended.

So growth was in at Wal-Mart, and no one could have been happier than the employees, who, by virtue of their stock plans, benefited enormously from the company's robust growth rates in the nineties. At least 650,000 Wal-Mart employees—roughly two-thirds of the company's American workforce—owned shares of stock in Wal-Mart.

★ ★ ★

The new generation of leaders found gold in its Supercenter initiative. The Supercenter idea, developed to meet the growing demand for one-stop shopping, had evolved from a previous unsuccessful Wal-Mart experiment at one-stop shopping: the Hypermart, huge (200,000 square feet) stores that combined supermarkets with general merchandise plus a variety of fast-food and service shops. The first Hypermart was opened in Garland, Texas, in 1987.

The Hypermart experiment failed, in part, Rob Walton said because of "a lack of commitment and focus." The company simply did not earmark enough resources for the effort. "To say they were a struggle," recalled Don Harris, executive vice president for general merchandise, "is an understatement. We had never built stores that size, with 600 employees and more inventory than we could keep up with." Gaining revenue was not a problem; making money was, because, as Harris noted, "We didn't know how to manage a big project like that."

For all the mistakes that were made with the Hypermarts, there was a silver lining: they did attract large numbers of people, leading Wal-Mart's planners to believe that it was not the concept that was at fault but the implementation. "If we just figured out how to run large stores, we ought to make money," suggested Harris.

In designing the new Supercenters, which were not that dissimilar to the Hypermarts, Wal-Mart officials did away with the Hypermart's tall ceilings and huge archways. Again Harris: "The Hypermart buildings were a monstrosity. They were like a circus. They were simply overblown." But what Wal-Mart mostly did away with when the Supercenters were built was an attitude of indifference and a feeling of being overwhelmed.

The first Supercenter, offering, as did the Hypermarts, food and merchandise, opened on March 1, 1988, in Washington, Missouri. (It had opened as a discount store in 1977 and was enlarged from the original.) The store employs 450 and measures 129,900 square feet.

The Supercenter initiative grew slowly, perhaps because of the difficult experience Wal-Mart had with the Hypermarts. But after Walton's successors took over, Supercenters began to open at a lively pace, so that by August 1994 there were a hundred. The one hundredth Supercenter opened in Greeley, Colorado. When it originally opened in 1986 as a discount store, it was Colorado's first Wal-Mart. It was closed and reopened as a Supercenter; in 2002 it employed 500 and had 201,788 square feet of retail space.

By 1996 there were 250 Supercenters; by May 2002, 1,060. Some of these stores were doing over $100 million in business a year. The Supercenters were a vast improvement over the Hypermarts, because they utilized space far more efficiently and were much more cost-effective than the Hypermarts with their high ceilings, huge archways and excessive floor space. Still, because the Supercenters were organized similarly to traditional Wal-Mart stores, at least with respect to the merchandising section, managers were comfortable running them from day one.

Open twenty-four hours a day, Supercenters offered in addition to general merchandise, bakery goods, deli foods, frozen foods, meat and dairy products, and fresh produce. They hosted as well many specialty shops, such as vision centers, Tire & Lube Expresses, Radio Grill restaurants, portrait studios and one-hour photo centers, hair salons, banks, and employment agencies. The giant stores generally ranged from 109,000 to 230,000 square feet, employed some 350, and offered 100,000 different items, 30,000 of them grocery products.

Within the Supercenter concept, Wal-Mart discovered another growth engine—the retail grocery business, which by 2002 had become a $680 billion industry.

At first, Wal-Mart investors seemed only lukewarm to its entry into the food business. Too much competition, too small profit margins—those were the usual complaints. But then food retailers began to mark up their prices faster than their costs rose. Wal-Mart saw a price opening: Rather than garner the usual penny or so of profit per grocery sale, Wal-Mart made do with less. It counted on shoppers' buying the lower-margin food supplies, then wandering over to the merchandising aisles to pick up higher-margin products.

Banking heavily on the retail grocery strategy, Wal-Mart closed hundreds of conventional stores, some not profitable and others just too close to planned Supercenters. Wal-Mart watched with delight as the revenues from its traditional discount stores doubled when those stores were converted into Supercenters.

Aware that it had little experience with perishables and prepared food, Wal-Mart invested heavily in the infrastructure grocers required, building two giant-size distribution centers to handle dry goods and perishables. It put together a field buying staff. Wal-Mart knew that the extra investment would be worth the effort since the added sales volume expected from the grocery side would more than cover those higher operating costs.

Wal-Mart's main competition came from Kmart, but Target was also getting into the Supercenter business. David Glass said at the time that consumers were going to have fun thanks to all the competition.

The results for Wal-Mart were remarkable: By 2001 Wal-Mart (including Supercenters, Sam's Clubs, discount stores, and Neighborhood Markets), achieved a 16 percent market share. That made it the Number One grocer in America. Grocery sales at the Wal-Mart Supercenters were growing at twice the rate of Wal-Mart's nonfood sales. Just as Supercenters and food were powerful growth engines, so too was the international initiative. As many other American corporations had done, Wal-Mart looked overseas in the early 1990s and saw gold.

Rob Walton and David Glass appointed Bob Martin the first head of the international program; he had previously been the company's chief technology officer. They hoped that Martin would create another powerful growth engine for Wal-Mart.

Walton and Glass set a goal: that as much as one-third of Wal-Mart's growth would come from outside the United States over the next five years. That was indeed ambitious. The hope was that half of Wal-Mart's growth would come from food, one-third from international, and the rest from the domestic Wal-Mart stores.

Wal-Mart might have been daunted by the many challenges that have plagued American enterprises: dealing with foreign cultures and languages, wrestling with the laws and mores of foreign countries, and managing the logistics. It might have been overwhelmed by zoning laws that required vertical Wal-Marts; five-story facilities, as in South Korea; basement ones, as in China. It might have thought the challenge to go overseas not worth it because of the financial complexities: the ever-fluctuating foreign currencies, hyperinflation, and devaluations. But it assumed that it could get a handle on all of these challenges.

BULL IN A CHINA SHOP

Adding to the complexities was the likelihood that every Wal-Mart that opened in a foreign country would catch the local media's attention. Because it was Wal-Mart, because its reputation preceded it, the company knew that its arrival in any foreign country would not be quiet. "When Wal-Mart strides into a new market," wrote

Newsweek, "it's as if a bull has got loose in the china shop. Papers scream the news, stocks gyrate, and local retailers start to scramble." It's the Wal-Mart effect, international style.

Despite the obstacles, the new leadership team decided to take the plunge into international waters. It was too good a growth opportunity to miss. Other American companies, often food-oriented, had gone overseas with various degrees of success. Wal-Mart hoped that the appetite for the mix of general merchandising and food made more tempting by everyday low pricing would be the same overseas.

The international market was tempting not because the door was closing to new stores within American boundaries but rather because of a concern that one day the door just might close. The post-Walton leadership made the international program a strategic imperative. Rob Walton explained: "The math was obvious. You didn't want to wake up one morning and say to yourself: 'We finished the U.S. Now we have to go out and get 15 percent growth outside the U.S.' That would have been a dangerous decision." A slow, but steady effort seemed prudent. "Hopefully, we would make our mistakes early and small," said Rob Walton, "and see what the opportunity was like."

From zero sales in the early 1990s, the international program had by 2001 grown to $35 billion in sales. The spectacular growth in the nineties led Walton's successors to take a whole new look at the organization that the founder had so carefully crafted. As they took that new look, the management team sensed that it would have to make some tough decisions that could alter the shape of the organization.

PART FOUR

WAL-MART AS A GROWTH ENGINE

CHAPTER 7

THE MORE COMPLEX
WAL-MART TODAY

There is a favorite game that people at Wal-Mart play.

The game centers on the question, "What would Mr. Sam think?" Almost any decision, large or small, that Wal-Mart executives make can fit into the game.

Journalists play the game too, asking people like David Glass, Don Soderquist, Lee Scott, or Tom Coughlin to speculate on what Sam Walton would have thought of Wal-Mart's vast size, its huge employee base, its remarkable growth in revenue and earnings.

The game never stops.

One way to play the game is to ask: Would Walton have been pleased with, say, Wal-Mart's culture in the nineties?

Invariably, the answer is resoundingly yes. "He would have been very pleased that the culture was transferable," said Don Soderquist. "Of course he would have asked if we were spending too much money." Pausing, then smiling, Soderquist suggested that "he would have asked about the phone bills. He would zero in on what it's costing to run the business. He would want to know, are we keeping expenses down so we can offer low prices to customers, not so we could make more money."

The new leadership team that took over from Sam Walton believed fervently in the founder's business philosophy and in the culture he had spread through the stores—enough to frequently ask, "What would Mr. Sam have done?"

But they differed from him in one very important respect: They knew that if Wal-Mart was going to grow dramatically—as they wanted—they would have to strengthen the corporate side, something the founder had strenuously resisted.

It was not that the team was less cautious than Sam Walton, less prudent, less thrifty. But they thought more about Wal-Mart's future than Walton had, and they understood that to achieve the growth they all wanted, they would have to erect the very kind of multifaceted corporate organization that had been anathema to the founder.

In adopting an aggressive attitude toward growth and in recognizing that the corporation would inevitably have to become more complex, adding more functions, Walton's successors departed substantially from the management style and the business philosophy of the founder. Therefore, when they did make the changes they felt were necessary, they did so slowly and methodically, remembering that the company had been built up by a man who never liked to rush and who questioned the investment of every single penny. They made these changes, feeling a slight discomfort at having been forced to do them.

A DIFFERENT WAL-MART

It was no wonder then that Wal-Mart's new generation of leaders was plainly uncomfortable with the notion that the company had become all that different from the one that Sam Walton built. For it somehow implied that by making changes after the founder's death, the new leaders had veered from the core of Sam Walton's business philosophy. That was not the case. Walton's successors were as true to that core—Sam Walton's culture—as Sam Walton himself was. Where they veered was in the way they approached Wal-Mart's corporate organization.

The new leadership was also uncomfortable with the implication that Wal-Mart became a dynamic, flexible institution only after Sam Walton left the scene. They quickly and correctly remind everyone that Walton himself was a change master, an experimenter, a proponent of shaking things up, the champion of playing a kind of corporate musical chairs with his executives. They also note correctly that some of the company-altering changes that occurred in the nineties had their roots in Walton's era. The international program and the effort to link merchandise with food into one giant-size Supercenter are examples. But the truth is that both initiatives got started in earnest only after the founder's death.

Still, members of the leadership team who worked closely with Walton recoil at the notion that Wal-Mart began to change only in the post-Walton world: "We were always changing the strategies and what we were doing," said Don Soderquist. "[Had Sam lived longer] we would have continued to change, experiment, try new things; and so I think just due to size and growth and opportunity we would have looked differently if Sam had been here for the last ten years."

★ ★ ★

To be sure, in some significant ways, the Wal-Mart of 2002 is very much a reflection of what Sam Walton wanted it to become—or at least to remain. The stores look the same, only bigger. The culture is as vibrant and compelling as it was in Walton's day. The company's signature phrase is still everyday low pricing (EDLP, in Wal-Mart parlance). Greeters still greet. Employees still cheer. The customer is still Number One. And it's still very much a no-frills kind of company. (One question in the trivia quiz in the 1997 annual report asked: "What percentage of sales goes to run the entire general offices, from the chairman of the board to the secretaries?" Answer: "2 percent." In other words, the home office was still a necessary evil, worth only 2 percent of the company's costs.) The jewels in the crown remained the stores, and while senior executives could hardly cover every single store, they continued to pay store visits with the same zeal and scrutiny that the founder once did.

But in many ways Wal-Mart has become quite different from what Sam Walton created and nurtured. Its spectacular growth is responsible for the changes. It is not only larger. It is far more complex.

For his entire career, Sam Walton had resisted turning Wal-Mart into a sprawling bureaucracy. Bob Martin, the man in charge of information technology in the eighties who later headed the international program, recalled Walton's conviction that administrative functions had no real value. "It just wasn't on his yellow pad to develop these things. Sam thought that if you set up a human resources unit, people in that unit would do nothing but talk to each other. He feared that rather than associates talking to store managers, you'd have suggestion boxes flowing up to the human resources unit, and you no longer would have leadership close to the people in the stores." The impulse to create these functions, said Martin, came later from David Glass and Don Soderquist. "If we hadn't put in these functions, the company would have outgrown the people underneath it. You wouldn't have been able to grow, and you wouldn't have been innovative or smart about being competitive."

NO WAY TO STOP GROWTH

For those who had worked closely with Sam Walton, like David Glass, there was no surprise that size would inevitably create bureaucracy: "No one decides we're going to get some bureaucracy. It just happens. As companies grow," and here David Glass seemed to be talking specifically about Wal-Mart, "you fall into that trap, you create additional levels. It used to be you would have a district manager and a regional manager and they reported to whoever ran the company.

"Now a division manager is stuck in there, and you get a director of operations over them, and people have support functions, a personnel director, all kinds of support help. Then you begin to get specialization in the company, which requires structure for the specialization to work. You become less flexible. If you have six levels in the company instead of four, it's harder to make a decision; it takes longer to get it implemented. Those are all the things we tried to guard against and keep from happening to us."

But David Glass sanctioned growth, knowing full well that the company would have to pay the price of becoming more bureaucratic. The concern of the current leaders—and it was Sam Walton's concern as well—was that a more bureaucratized company would make it harder, not easier, to manage the vast, widespread Wal-Mart. And, to be sure, the task for the senior executives was daunting. With so many stores came so many brushfires to put out each day; with so many employees came so many urgent issues that someone had to handle. When crises occurred, the leadership team prided itself on managing things quietly, calmly, thoroughly, and efficiently.

In its early years, Wal-Mart was anything but bureaucratic; it was run personally by Sam Walton and his band of loyal executives. But as the organization grew, the company's organization chart grew concomitantly. The discount stores were at one time called Division I and were organized into regions of about a hundred stores and districts of seven to nine stores within the regions. But Division I split into East and West (known as Division I and Division IA). Later the geography was halved again, and David Glass found five levels between himself and the store managers. This led him to suggest that it was simply not possible to run a retail company of Wal-Mart's size. He admonished his fellow executive not even to try: Rather than look at the big picture, they should simplify the business and try to run one store at a time.

If Glass's point was valid when he made it in the mid-1990s, it was just as valid, if not more so, in 2002 when Wal-Mart was spread over a number of key divisions: one division that embraced both Wal-Mart Stores and Supercenters and included Neighborhood Markets; Sam's Clubs; International; a speciality group division that oversees other important business areas such as Wal-Mart Pharmacy, Wal-Mart Optical, and Tire and Lube Express.

ONE STORE AT A TIME

The leaders are not prone to shouting, not prone to showing great bursts of anger or frustration. It is as if they know how hard it is to keep on top of what is going on in all those stores around the United States and the rest of the world; by staying calm they are showing that they can manage any situation that arises. Time and again, they will say, as David Glass did in our interview, that the only way to manage such a large and complex organization is to think of it not as large and complex but to think of it as simply a series of individual units, that is, the stores. "We run the business a store at a time," said Glass. "How do you run a \$240 billion retail business? I don't have a clue. But I know how to run retail stores. And if you can run enough of them successfully, that might add up to that \$240 billion, but that would be beside the point."

Tom Coughlin, who in 2002 was president and CEO of Wal-Mart Stores and Sam's Clubs, concurred that it was best to run Wal-Mart a store at a time, but he acknowledged that the sheer size of the organization meant that there had to be corporate layers. "We do everything we can to run this as a small company. It's difficult, no question. I get E-mails from stores all day long. You have to act like a small company, so I respond to those things. But we have got to have many of these [corporate functions] that people would consider the bureaucracy that grows in companies. We do a pretty good job of controlling it. It's done in a modest way."

By becoming so large and complex, Wal-Mart makes larger and larger demands on the people who run the place.

Part of the reason had to do with the company's growing at such a rate that it was forced to add layer after layer, until by 2002 it had six full divisions responsible for the Wal-Mart organization.

When Wal-Mart was founded, there were only the store managers and Sam Walton; later, Walton hired a few executives to help him manage the stores. But all through the 1990s, the organization table expanded and added more and more layers to accommodate the company's growth. By 2002 some 4,000 store managers were reporting to 350 district managers.

These district managers, who were responsible for six to eight stores each, reported to thirty-five regional vice presidents.

These "regionals," responsible for thirty to forty stores, have eight to ten district managers reporting to them. The regional vice presidents, in turn, report to six division heads. The division heads report to Tom Coughlin, head of Wal-Mart Stores and Sam's Clubs in the United States.

There are fifty senior vice presidents who report to the twenty executive vice presidents. The executive vice presidents report either to other executive vice presidents or to CEO Lee Scott.

The way the system works, store managers, district managers and regional vice presidents are in close and constant touch.

Store managers know that when they need or want something, they must turn to their district manager. They are likely to see their district manager at least once a week, perhaps more often. District managers, when they face a problem that they cannot solve on their own, will turn to the regionals, who are in the field three days a week and are therefore easily accessible.

Life is toughest in some ways for the regionals. After all, the store managers and district managers get to live in the areas where they work, but the regional vice presidents are expected to live in or around Bentonville so that they can stay in close touch with the home office.

The only exceptions were certain executives who were simply too far from the home office for it to be practical to go back and forth each week.

For regional vice presidents, the general routine was that every Monday each would take one of Wal-Mart's twenty planes to different parts of the United States, visit stores and managers, and return home on Thursday for weekend wrap-up meetings. In a world of cell phones, high-speed computers, and video-conferencing, Wal-Mart still wants senior executives to stay in personal touch every week.

Arriving in the field on Mondays, the regionals often link up with district managers; together they work their way through one store after another, trying to determine what needs fixing. It is not uncommon to find a regional vice president being the first to discover that there are "outs" (empty shelves) in a bread section or that there are too many trailers in the back of the store, causing congestion.

Given Wal-Mart's massive size, not only must power and authority filter down to the regionals and the district managers but those managers must act quickly and decisively. Lee Scott noted: "You have to be less tolerant of people who don't get the culture. You cannot let these issues simmer. It's not healthy for the stores, for the associates. So the district manager and the regional vice presidents have to step in aggressively and resolve these issues."

By Thursday morning the regional vice presidents have returned to Bentonville, where they attend a meeting conducted by Tom Coughlin; district managers listen in by phone.

A WASTE OF TIME

As Wal-Mart grew, especially during the 1980s, the world at large began to take a more active interest in the company. Until then, the media displayed little interest in a small chain of retail stores in the Southwest. But, the company was growing too fast, its stores were moving into too many communities that seemed at times ambivalent or outright hostile toward their arrival, and it was bumping up against too many zoning and real estate regulations that put it in clashes with citizens, lawyers, and protest groups. No, the media could not avoid a Wal-Mart that was—well, making news.

Sam Walton certainly felt that Wal-Mart did not need a media-relations team. He came under pressure to beef up his public-relations team and to promote the company to large investors, but he simply thought all such efforts a waste of time. He successfully kept his own staff from talking to the media or Wall Street analysts. It was only in 1989 that Walton allowed a media-relations unit to be established at Wal-Mart. Until then he saw no need for one; when he finally approved the unit, you could tell that he did so grudgingly: He kept it tiny. It remained small into the early years of the post-Walton era.

Walton was just as indifferent toward having a full-blown human resources unit. In the mid-1980s, when Wesley Wright was promoted to vice president for human resources, the job was hardly glamorous. Wright tried to get out of it; he didn't feel like a human resources kind of guy. Walton tried to soothe him by explaining that all he needed him to do was to find and train people to run the stores. In the end Wright agreed but on the condition that he could switch jobs after two years. Walton told Wright that he wanted to keep the HR function small. Wright accordingly kept his staff small.

But by the 1990s, with Wal-Mart growing so quickly, the new leadership team saw no choice but to bring in someone with a true human resources background to run a proper human resources division. The new person would be expected to deal with all the people issues that were floating to the surface.

AN IMAGINARY CONVERSATION

When he was appointed to the post of executive vice president of the people division in 1994, Coleman Peterson knew that Sam Walton would not have thought much of the idea of a senior executive being in charge of personnel. "When I came here," recalls Peterson, "I imagined having a candid conversation with Sam Walton, had he still been around. He would have said, 'I'm not really sure we need a human resources area. It's the job of each store manager to take care of his or her people.' Sam believed that every time we set up a structure that didn't directly drive sales and earnings, we might be moving managers further away from their total responsibilities."

But for Peterson, those days are gone. "Then you could almost make all your decisions top down." When he arrived at Wal-Mart, among his first tasks was cashier-training. "That's absolutely out of the question today, because Wal-Mart is too large. Cashier-training is far too specific and too far removed from my current role and responsibilities to the organization, which are much more strategic, much more global, really more focused on our being a business."

It took time, but other corporate functions grew or sprouted in the nineties. The legal staff grew slowly; as late as 1999 there were only 30 lawyers working for Wal-Mart, but that number grew to 90 in 2002 with plans to raise it to 120 in the near future.

★ ★ ★

For years Sam Walton had vetoed the creation of a government-relations unit. Tom Coughlin guessed that "he would be turning over in his grave if he knew that we had an office in Washington, D.C. But I think he'd be pleased that we have people there who are highly focused on things that could be detrimental to our business. But it sounds so unusual for us to have this unit. It certainly has an attitude of bigness when you have offices in Washington."

It was the "attitude of bigness" that Wal-Mart did not want to convey to Washington, D.C., or to anyone else in Sam Walton's day. "There was an underlying sentiment at Wal-Mart back then," said one Wal-Mart official, "that we won't bother Washington and they won't bother us. Everyone hoped that would remain the case, but when you're the largest private employer, the largest company, and you have more stores than any other retailer, the likelihood of flying under Washington's radar is not going to happen." So a government-relations unit was finally established in 1999. It went through a "painful birth," in the phrase of one Wal-Mart official: Three years later, in 2002, the unit had only four people working for it. Wal-Mart officials noted that many companies routinely have lobbying offices in Washington, D.C., that are staffed by twenty people or more.

Tom Hyde was appointed executive vice president for legal and corporate affairs in 2001. Since then he has been showing up in Washington on a regular basis, occasionally taking with him a district manager with fifteen stores or so under his or her command. Happily for Wal-Mart, the politicians are always fascinated with their local stores, and they want to talk about their experiences in them. They are usually less interested in the larger corporation. "We're a bunch of suits to them," said Hyde. "Virtually every member of Congress has a Wal-Mart in their district—or wants a Wal-Mart in their district. They get questions from constituents: 'Why don't we have a Wal-Mart?' When we meet, I get one question, and their eyes glaze over. The rest of the time they want to talk with the district manager. They want to know how things work in the stores, where does the stuff come from, how do you decide how many associates to put in stores; how do you decide where to locate stores."

On one occasion in 2001, Hyde was meeting in Washington with officials of the Equal Employment Opportunity Commission. The first thing that one official raised was a complaint he had about the length of the checkout lines at his local Wal-Mart. Hyde dutifully made a note of the man's complaint, and the meeting shifted over to other topics.

The government-relations unit does have a new, important role: That is to stave off anti-Wal-Mart legislation before it can harm the company. Lee Scott says that Wal-Mart does not aggressively try to influence new legislation: "Today we have to be involved [in government]. But we don't try to influence things that would be good for us but bad for the country. We don't pursue laws that would allow us to carve out an advantage because we're big. We focus on the laws that will do harm to us or our customers, so most of our actions are focused on how do we stop this [action] from going through."

If Sam Walton would have been skeptical about the need for Wal-Mart's lobbying in Washington, one can assume he would have felt just as strongly about a Wal-Mart executive's holding forth with international leaders to build goodwill for Wal-Mart stores in various countries. Bob Martin, the first person to run the international effort at Wal-Mart in the early 1990s, firmly believed that Sam Walton would have had a hard time with company officials' meeting and dining with the British prime minister, Tony Blair, or the Argentine president, Carlos Menem, as they did. "That kind of government affairs was not something that Sam at the time saw any strategic value [in]. But today it's mission-critical. You have to do that. Those skill sets probably would have been ones Sam would have struggled with. He would have thought of those of us who met with these leaders: 'Those are people who aren't close to the business. They are not merchants. What did they sell? They sit at fancy dinners and bend their elbows, but are they doing something for our customers?' "

★ ★ ★

Perhaps the one initiative that created the most complexity at Wal-Mart in the 1990s was the international program. Needless to say, life was far simpler for Sam Walton and everyone in the top echelons of

Wal-Mart when there was no international activity. But with the advent of Wal-Mart stores being opened in Mexico, Canada, the United Kingdom, Germany, Argentina, Brazil, China, South Korea, and Japan, the demands on certain executives to travel to those countries and to monitor activities in their stores added considerably to their plates. It certainly added to Lee Scott's: during one brief period in 2002, Scott visited Germany, the United Kingdom, China, Japan, and South Korea, in addition to flying from one American city to another to drop in on domestic Wal-Mart stores: "Just from the travel standpoint [the international program] adds complexity," says Scott.

★ ★ ★

Now that we've introduced the subject of Wal-Mart's increasing complexity, we will provide more details on other aspects of this pivotal subject. We begin with a look at how Wal-Mart's senior executives have modified the application of the culture in light of the company's growing complexity.

Rob Walton: eldest son of Wal-Mart founder Sam Walton. He became chairman of the company soon after the death of his father in 1992 and has remained in the position through early 2003. Courtesy of Wal-Mart Stores, Inc.

Helen Walton: widow of Sam Walton. She had a strong influence on some key decisions that her husband took concerning Wal-Mart, including keeping Wal-Mart focused on small towns rather than big cities. Courtesy of Wal-Mart Stores, Inc.

Don Soderquist: a leader of the new generation of professional managers at Wal-Mart. A close associate of Sam Walton's in the 1980s who retired in 2000, he was an enthusiastic interpreter of the Wal-Mart culture.
Courtesy of Wal-Mart Stores, Inc.

David Glass introduces actress/model Cindy Crawford to the crowd at the 2002 shareholders meeting in Fayetteville, Arkansas. Celebrities like Crawford are often on view at the shareholders' session.
Sharon Weber/Wal-Mart

Wal-Mart CEO Lee Scott (left) *meets with the president of China, Jiang Zeming, in October 2002. Scott described Wal-Mart's activities in China to the Chinese political leader.* Courtesy of Wal-Mart Stores, Inc.

Coleman Peterson: As executive vice president of the People Division, he has wide responsibilities with respect to employees at a time when Wal-Mart is the largest private employer in the world. Courtesy of Wal-Mart Stores, Inc.

David Glass (center) visiting a Wal-Mart store. The man who replaced Sam Walton, Glass promoted the company's growth in the late 1980s and early 1990s, focusing efforts on the development of Supercenters and on the company's burgeoning international program.
Courtesy of Wal-Mart Stores, Inc.

CEO Lee Scott (left) chats with employees at a Wal-Mart store. Courtesy of Wal-Mart Stores, Inc.

Sam Walton talks to Wal-Mart employees. He enjoyed these sessions and spent as much time in the stores as possible. Courtesy of Wal-Mart Stores, Inc.

Helen Walton and John Walton in 1993. In 2003, John Walton was a member of the Wal-Mart board, one of the two Walton family members on the board (the other was Rob Walton). Courtesy of Wal-Mart Stores, Inc.

A Wal-Mart Supercenter in Shenzhen, China. Wal-Mart has twenty-two stores in China. Elinor Slater

NFL veterans appear on the stage at the 2002 Wal-Mart shareholders meeting. At the far left is former star quarterback Johnny Unitas; at the far right is the now-retired quarterback Joe Montana. Sharon Weber/Wal-Mart

Wal-Mart associates give the company cheer at the front door of a store in Shenzhen, China, in November 2003. Elinor Slater

The first Wal-Mart Supercenter opened in March 1988 in Washington, Missouri. The Supercenters, a combination of merchandise and groceries, fueled the company's growth throughout the 1990s and into the 2000s. Courtesy of Wal-Mart Stores, Inc.

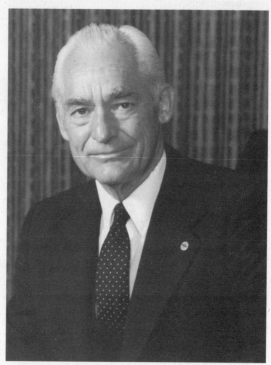

Sam Walton—the founder: A wizard at discount retailing, Walton opened the first Wal-Mart in 1962; by the time of his death in 1992, Wal-Mart was a $43 billion chain. The new generation of leaders used Walton's culture and business philosophy to turn Wal-Mart into the number-one company in terms of revenue in 2002. Courtesy of Wal-Mart Stores, Inc.

The first Wal-Mart store, located in Rogers, Arkansas, circa 1962.
Courtesy of Wal-Mart Stores, Inc.

CHAPTER 8

APPLYING THE CULTURE
A STORE AT A TIME

Sam Walton wanted the customers to feel that they were important. He wanted the customer to have an experience that was different, more satisfying, and more fun than any he or she might have at a Wal-Mart rival. It was this relentless effort to make the customer feel that Wal-Mart employees truly care about the customer that has been the hallmark of the Wal-Mart culture. And it is the culture that makes the organization different.

The signs of it in Wal-Mart stores are still visible, still strong. There are the greeters at the front door; the associates practicing the Ten-Foot Rule. There are also the everyday low prices and the enthusiasm demonstrated by the quick pace of the employees as they move around the stores and the constant smiles on their faces. For Gary Raines, the manager of the Bentonville Supercenter, the culture has to do with how you treat the customers: "If you treat customers like your family, in most towns they become your family, certainly your friends."

A big question for the Walton successors was whether they should stick to the culture Sam Walton developed. The answer was an overwhelming yes. Then the question arose: What's the best way to apply that culture, given that Wal-Mart in the early 1990s had become a very different organization from the one under Sam in the seventies and eighties?

The hypergrowth that Wal-Mart experienced in the nineties

changed many things, none more than the leadership's team ability to apply Sam Walton's culture throughout the organization.

NO TAMPERING WITH THE CULTURE

From the moment they took over, David Glass and his senior colleagues adamantly insisted that they would not tamper with the culture that had worked so well in the past. And they did not. All of the new leadership team had learned the culture directly from Sam Walton. They genuinely believed that it had been that culture that had lifted Wal-Mart's sales to nearly $44 billion in 1992. The culture was not broken; no sane person would try to fix it.

But the new management encountered a very fundamental problem when they began to implement the culture. The problem was the size of Wal-Mart. It was simply too large, too complex, too spread out for them to apply the culture in the same personal, direct way that Sam Walton had done.

David Glass could not have possibly gotten to as large a percentage of the stores as Walton did—there were simply too many by the time he was helping to run things—but once in the stores, Glass could be just as formidable as Walton, just as challenging to managers. Once, on a tour of Wal-Mart stores in upstate New York, he urged a store manager not to get into a price war with the competition over a few items. If you're going to have a price war, he told him, have a big war on a large number of items. Don't be defensive. Wal-Mart's rivals think that we're offensive anyway, so go ahead and offend.

When he goes into stores, Lee Scott tries to focus on how well the culture is being applied, not whether the store is fully stocked—that's the job of the manager. "Are the associates friendly? Are the cashiers thanking people at the checkout? What's the relationship between managers and associates? Do you sense there's a connection?" He can tell how the store is doing in part by whether the employees seek him out, whether they ask him to make sure to visit their department. "If the store is struggling, the associates will turn away from me three aisles before I get to them and head for the backroom. People don't hide their feelings. I can tell if they're not excited about the company."

But Scott is so busy that such store visits are not as frequent as he would like: "I can't get out to stores as much as Sam Walton did. Sam was very fortunate as chairman in that he had David Glass and Jack Shewmaker and then David Glass and Don Soderquist. That allowed Sam to be in stores three or four days a week. But with international and other things we are doing, it doesn't work that way today. Today I have meetings on acquisitions, the transition in Japan. Those are things you can't delegate. You have to participate. So it's a little different."

When faced with this problem, they did not decide to throw all or part of the culture out. Instead they made a calculated decision to figure out how to assure that the same cultural messages that Sam Walton articulated would be spread throughout the organization. They could not simply get into a pickup or a small plane and canvas all of the stores in a year, as Walton had done. But they could calibrate the organization so that to a certain extent they and to a much larger extent other more junior managers shared in the dissemination of those messages.

John Walton, Sam's son and a Wal-Mart board member in 2002, explained: "The culture has evolved, but the core principles are still the same. What has evolved are the means by which we meet those principles. When Dad was there, because he was such a personality, he was able to reinforce those principles daily in his meetings with associates. What the current management team has done so well is to institutionalize those practices in a way that we never had to do when Dad was around; they have found ways in systems and practices to institutionalize the cultural reinforcement that Dad did sort of by the seat of his pants."

By institutionalizing the cultural practices, John Walton clearly meant that the current leadership makes fewer visits to stores but makes sure that the practice of store visits has been institutionalized, that is, decreed to be the responsibility of all Wal-Mart executives.

As the home office took on more and more functions, certain powers that once resided at the top shifted to more junior executives, especially the division and regional managers. It simply made more sense, if only to relieve senior management so that it did not get bogged down.

THE RISK OF SHIFTING POWER

The leadership team understood the implications of their decisions: A certain amount of power would have to be shifted away from them and placed in the hands of the executives closest to the stores—the division managers, the district managers, and the store managers. There was some risk in shifting power so dramatically to the managers below. The more junior executives might not take the task seriously. They might not understand how to implement the culture. They might decide that they had more important things to do with their time. Consistency would be much more difficult to maintain.

Walton's successors were prepared to take that risk. For sharing the responsibility of applying the culture was the only practical, sensible way to replicate, in spirit if not in kind, what Sam Walton had been able to do with such seeming ease.

Other decisions have been far easier to take for the Walton successors: how many stores to build in a year, how much cash to put aside for yearly investment, how many financial resources to allocate to existing projects versus new ones. Compared with the question of how to apply Sam Walton's culture, these issues were straightforward.

But David Glass and his colleagues knew that they had no choice. They had decided from the start that they could ill afford to discard the special business wisdom that had resided in Sam Walton; indeed, they had chosen, without making a formal decision, to turn the Walton culture and his business philosophy into a critical core capability of the organization. Making that decision forced them to ask the toughest question of all: How do we make sure that his wisdom gets to the right places, to the right people?

★ ★ ★

First and foremost, the new leaders made the managers in the field the primary conveyers of the culture. This was what John Walton meant when he said that his father's successors had "institutionalized" the cultural reinforcement that Sam Walton did so naturally.

The shift in power seemed sensible. Regional vice presidents, after all, were in charge of units that brought in billions of dollars of business. The regional vice presidents were the closest versions of Sam Walton that existed within the new Wal-Mart: They visit the stores, spread the Wal-Mart culture, try to gain that quick market intelligence that once would have been written down on Sam Walton's yellow pad.

"The regional vice president has to be closer in skill sets to Sam than they would have been ten to fifteen years ago," said Lee Scott. "The CEO can no longer resolve issues for all 1.3 million people. If you had the same number of issues coming to the top that you had in the earlier days, that would be all you would do. And you'd have a staff of forty to fifty people handling it."

In the past many issues that reached senior management now get handled at lower levels. In the eyes of the management team, there's no other way today to deal with these issues. Moreover, given Wal-Mart's massive size, not only must power and authority filter down to lower management; those managers must act quickly and decisively.

Shifting power to more junior managers did not mean that the senior management had abrogated responsibility for transmitting the company's cultural messages. It remained the task of David Glass and Don Soderquist and later Lee Scott and Tom Coughlin to be the primary communicators of the culture. But they would communicate those messages largely in front of large Wal-Mart audiences, in

Dallas and Kansas City at the biannual meeting of managers, and at the annual shareholder meeting in Fayetteville.

THE FIRST ENABLER

The post-Walton leadership did have an important role to play in spreading the culture, but they wisely chose to spend their time on strengthening the enablers of the culture, rather than on trying to spread the culture to every single employee around the globe.

The first and perhaps the most important enabler that senior management worked on was job retention. It was obviously important for as few people to leave Wal-Mart in the early phases of their employment as possible. For one thing, there was nothing less conducive to inculcating the culture into employees than a high turnover rate in the early phases of employment.

In the mid-1990s, Wal-Mart's annual hourly full-time and part-time turnover rate was from 47 percent to 50 percent. By the late 1990s the annual turnover was a remarkably high 70 percent for hourly full-time and part-time employees—40 percentage points higher than in previous years. The higher rate was attributed to several factors: the introduction and increase in the number of larger Wal-Mart Stores and Supercenters: These stores employed up to as many as 650, compared with the earlier average of 200. The increase in the number of seven-day and twenty-four-hour operations: Managers presiding over stores that were open twenty-four hours a day were finding it increasingly difficult to spend time communicating with employees, especially those who did not work the same shifts as the managers. A steadily competitive labor market: The unemployment rate declined from 7.5% to 4.0% between 1992 and 2000.

Coleman Peterson, the senior vice president of the people division, decided to get aggressive. He set a goal of cutting the turnover by half—down to 35 percent. "I must have needed my head examined. Just to improve by a small amount was so difficult. It was a very tight labor market. Unemployment rates had dropped significantly. It was an employee's rather than an employer's market."

As part of this look at the turnover issue, Peterson discovered an-other serious problem: nearly half (47 percent) of new Wal-Mart hires that left within the first year did so within ninety days; the re-sult was wasted training dollars and inflated recruiting costs. It must have been an enormous challenge to the senior management to pro-mote a key cultural plank—respect for the individual—in the face of such turnover.

Peterson and his team labored hard to identify then remove the causes of these problems. They went to the employees themselves to find out why there was a problem. They relied on two feedback indi-cators: the company's annual grassroots survey, through which the views of over 700,000 employees were obtained, and in-depth inter-views with 100 employees from different parts of the country with varied jobs.

Some employees pointed out that their store had lowered its stan-dards for hiring in the past three to five years. A renewed focus was placed on whom Wal-Mart selected, using interview guides and re-training managers in interviewing and selecting. Another discovery was that 80 percent of orientation occurred in an employee's first five days. The "on-boarding" process or orientation needed fixing. Too much technical information was being condensed into an early pe-riod, without establishing the most important element: the relation-ship between the new hire and his or her supervisory team. Peterson noted: "Too much emphasis had been placed on Wal-Mart's CBL [computer-based learning] without first introducing new associates to our great people culture."

He shifted priorities so that that orientation process attached greater importance to relationship-building and the order in which things were learned. Orientation activities were spread more evenly over the employee's first ninety days. New hire turnover dropped 25 percent in some locations. And the 70 percent overall turnover rate for hourly employees has been cut to slightly less than 50 percent.

★ ★ ★

A second enabler of the culture that senior managers worked hard at was transforming junior executives into culture agents, people who knew what the culture was and how to communicate it to others. In the mid-1990s that became one of Tom Coughlin's prime tasks. He seemed perfect for the job. Almost all of Sam Walton's successors exuded a calmness, almost a gentleness; Tom Coughlin was different. He was big and brash and looked like an aging NFL football tackle. It was no accident that his first job at Wal-Mart in 1979 was vice president of security. His wife was not excited. She kept asking her husband during their first visit to Bentonville why he really wanted to work in a town whose weekly newspaper headlined that day: BENTONVILLE GETS FIRST TRAFFIC LIGHT. Nor was she pleased to learn that Sam Walton had asked Coughlin to see him at 5:30 A.M. To placate her, he made a promise that he would stay at Wal-Mart only for three years. But he stayed way beyond that, gaining a reputation for getting things done, for being blunt and tough-minded. Trying to describe Tom Coughlin, a Wal-Mart official offered this hypothetical: If Coughlin had a bone to pick with someone he was passing in the corridor, rather than invite the man back to his office for a friendly chat he would most likely bear down on him right then and there until he got the answer he wanted.

Tom Coughlin was great at execution.

Toward the end of 1995 Coughlin, the new executive vice president and COO of Wal-Mart Operations, sensed that the five senior vice presidents in charge of Wal-Mart divisions had, in his phrase, gotten away from a strong focus and same-page thinking. They were communicating cultural messages to underlings, but the same message was not always coming from all five executives.

Coughlin brought the division managers together for a set of urgent meetings over a weekend, insisting that they concentrate their efforts on five cultural imperatives, imperatives that Sam Walton talked about all the time:

Stock it.
Price it right.

Show the value.
Take the money.
Teach them.

This was Coughlin's shorthand way of saying that the best way to get a sale was to make sure that the product is in stock; that it has the right price; that you can show the customer why he or she should buy it; that you make sure that, when cashiers take the money, they show aggressive hospitality to assure customers return to the store. "Teach them" referred to specific directives to store and district managers about training for store associates and department managers.

It took time, but Coughlin was pleased to note that eventually these executives organized their approach to the culture around these five imperatives.

Just as he had identified the lack of a clear culture focus among executives, Coughlin around the same time came upon another serious problem with technology that district managers were encountering. He knew that it was simply not possible to "strive for excellence"— one of the three cardinal cultural beliefs espoused by Sam Walton— without managers exhibiting an enthusiastic attitude toward new technology.

The company had invested heavily in high-tech gadgets called Telxons, which were used to track inventory, enabling managers to keep products in stock. It was clear that the gadgets were not being used. Coughlin at first could not understand why employees in the stores had no solid understanding of the new technology. Then as he went up the chain of command, he realized that district managers were setting the tone by refusing to learn how to use the technology.

Coughlin brought the matter to a head by summoning 225 district managers to a winter meeting in Kansas City. After the doors were closed, he asked each of them to take a Telxon 960 and take a simple, basic test on how it worked. Only 24 percent passed. Coughlin said that he was giving the district managers nine days to shape up. When he repeated the test after that interval, he had the feeling that they had done little since but learn how to operate the devices:

Over 99 percent passed this time. One "retired," Coughlin pointed out. From that time on, Coughlin worked with the chief technology officer to make sure that senior people were comfortable with all of the new technology.

Exploiting the Telxons along with a host of other productivity boosters, Wal-Mart was credited with making a significant contribution to America's efficiency gains in the late 1990s. One independent study by McKinsey & Co. said that Wal-Mart's productivity advances represented 25 percent of all productivity improvements within the American economy from 1995 to 1999.

Coughlin offered a good example of how senior management, aware that it could not get into every single store to spread the culture, chose instead to focus on areas of the culture and highlighted them for everyone. The hope was that by word-of-mouth these highlighted experiences would serve as models of behavior for the more than 1.3 million employees.

GET ON THE FLOOR!

On one occasion in the early 1990s, Coughlin decided to emphasize how important he felt it was for store managers to be on the floor, taking care of employees and customers, not in their offices. To Coughlin, this part of the culture—respect for the individual and providing great service to the customer—was all-important. Part of Sam Walton's business philosophy was: If you wanted the people in the stores to take care of the customers, you have to make sure you're taking care of the people in the stores.

In the new Wal-Mart, with its Supercenters and twenty-four-hour-a-day cycles, managers found that they could not afford to spend as much time on the floor as they would like, since they have to manage as many as 600 to 700 employees, hire people, and run training programs for new recruits. With all that, there is ample reason for them to stay in their offices. But Tom Coughlin still did not like the practice, and on one particular occasion, while walking around a Sam's Club, he could not locate the manager. Employees finally said to Coughlin that they rarely saw the manager: He was always in his office. Getting his hands on a hasp and a lock, Coughlin sought out the door to the store manager's office—and locked the poor fellow out of his own office to make him spend more time in the store. The point was taken, and the message of Tom Coughlin's visit to that Sam's Club got out and got out quickly. Since then, Wal-Mart managers spend as little time as possible in the back office.

★ ★ ★

The third enabler was a decision taken by Walton's successors to keep the organization centralized in Bentonville.

Ask any senior executive at Wal-Mart how it was possible to manage the new Wal-Mart with its thousands of stores spread across the United States and across the globe and you receive the remarkable answer: It was not possible.

But then the executive explained, without missing a beat, that at Wal-Mart you did not manage thousands of stores; you managed them one at a time. That was the secret.

In practice, that meant that Wal-Mart's week was arranged in such a way that most of its senior executives, residing in Bentonville or its surroundings, raced into the field on Monday mornings, moved through a number of stores, got an assessment of where there were problems, and reported back to their superiors by the end of the week in meetings on Friday and Saturdays. When they were holding their wrap-up, end-of-the-week meetings back in Bentonville, it was not unusual for a discussion to unfold about the problems of a particular store. That is what executives meant by managing a store at a time.

It was this kind of quick market intelligence that Wal-Mart has become famous for, and it was the key thing about Wal-Mart that so impressed Jack Welch, the former chairman and CEO of GE, when he became familiar with Sam Walton and Wal-Mart's weekly schedule for executives.

Few large companies in America were able to get such quick feedback from their various divisions and units as Wal-Mart did.

What David Glass and, later, Lee Scott understood so well was the benefit to be gained from having senior executives close by the home office at the start and close of each week. It was this system that allowed top management to control which cultural messages needed to be emphasized and communicated at any given time.

SATURDAY MORNINGS

Nothing illustrated the way the leadership teams transmitted the culture better than Wal-Mart's Saturday morning meetings. By keeping everything centralized in Bentonville, the weekly Saturday morning meetings became feasible. Senior executives could join colleagues in more junior positions week in and week out to get a dose of reality (weekly sales in the stores, items that were selling well or not selling well, etc.) and a dose of the culture (not just doing the cheer but hearing the stories of employees who had done something special for a customer).

Originally, under Sam Walton, these get-togethers had little to do with the culture; they were mostly designed to give everyone a chance to learn what the organization had purchased and how much had been invested in those purchases. But a part of those meetings were given over to learning from the mistakes that had been made during the past week. That learning process led Sam Walton to devise his business philosophy and cultural guidelines that remained in force down through the years.

He felt strongly that his executives should attend the Saturday morning meetings in large part because managers and employees in the stores were expected to work on that day; it just wouldn't look right, he argued, for executives to be on the golf course or at a picnic while their colleagues were busy in the stores. Over time Walton realized what a great vehicle the Saturday morning meetings were for creating and nurturing the culture. At those meetings he tried lots of things to get the attention of the audience, including his own rendition of the cheer of the University of Arkansas Razorbacks. The idea was for the meeting to be educational—and fun. Eventually, each

Saturday meeting opened with someone, often Sam Walton himself, leading the Wal-Mart cheer. One Saturday Walton led the audience in calisthenics, another in song. Business celebrities, such as Jack Welch, Larry Bossidy, and Warren Buffett, showed up unannounced and gave talks. So did the comedian Jonathan Winters. Once Walton engaged in a mock boxing match with Sugar Ray Leonard.

On some occasions Walton singled out an employee who was being too derogatory. You never knew how Walton would conduct a meeting; there was always an air of unpredictability. Every once in a while Walton would turn to an executive and order him to run the meeting in his place. No one in the audience dared to fall asleep.

Each Friday morning many of the same people gathered for the weekly merchandising meeting. This gathering was more serious than the goings-on the following day. Problems were aired, and managers were given the following week to sort them out. One Wal-Mart manager told me that a problem at Wal-Mart never lasted more than a week—or at any rate was never supposed to.

Walton believed in lightening up the mood, so the Saturday morning meetings often contained some element of levity—such as the time Wal-Mart's safety director engaged in a persimmon-seed–spitting contest, using the company's general counsel as the official target. Having fun had a lot to do with the Wal-Mart culture: It was supposed to break down barriers between people, and the culture was all about creating links between managers and employees. While he was organizing all that fun, Walton was in fact carefully laboring to make the culture work.

Because confidential sales figures were reported at each Saturday morning, executives were careful to screen who could attend the meetings. Accordingly, outsiders, such as authors of books on Wal-Mart, were rarely allowed to attend. After a number of requests, I finally secured an invitation. I showed up bright and early on an October morning in 2002. The meeting was held in the auditorium in the home office. It sits three hundred or so people and on this day was packed. Purple banners with quotes from Sam Walton adorned the walls. One said: "Swim upstream. Go the other way. Ignore the conventional wisdom." Another one: "Appreciate everything your associates do for the business." On another part of the wall hung the flags of the countries in which Wal-Mart stores were located.

A public relations representative explained to me that there were a number of rules I had to obey. I could not publish any of the financial information I would hear nor could I quote anyone directly. For a while I thought to myself that about the only thing I could report from that meeting was that Lee Scott was wearing a T-shirt and jeans.

I was told that this was "culture Saturday," meaning that the Wal-Mart culture would be given special emphasis on this day. From what I understood about these meetings, however, every one of these weekly meetings could have been called culture Saturday.

SEARCHING FOR THE UNPREDICTABILITY

I was on edge waiting for all that legendary unpredictability at the Saturday meetings to occur. The meeting got off to a very enthusiastic start when a group of Wal-Mart associates in the automotive (lube) section rushed on stage to lead the company cheer. Lee Scott then delivered a twenty-minute survey of world political and economic affairs, noting the good and the bad in the same calm, matter-of-fact voice. He apologized for leaving the meeting early: He wanted to spend time with his wife before boarding a plane that afternoon for a thirteen-hour flight to South Korea (and on to China and Japan—all in six days). He promised to attend next Saturday's meeting, though he thought that he might be a little jet-lagged.

Then the fun part of the meeting began. People in the audience were introduced: someone applying for a job at Wal-Mart; the daughter of a manager; the CFO of Wal-Mart China. Some folks in the audience were singled out and given service awards for working many years at Wal-Mart. One fellow got the award for working in the store-planning division and opening a thousand stores in his career.

★ ★ ★

The fourth enabler was Wal-Mart's open-door policy. Often major corporations trying to strengthen the ties between employees and bosses introduce an open-door policy, offering employees the chance to skip a few layers and take a complaint right to the top of the executive ladder. Often these policies exist in name only: Executives are too busy to honor the pledge to keep their doors open or employees are too frightened to approach a senior executive.

Wal-Mart instituted such a policy and tried to make it work. It wanted the policy to work, because a key part of the Wal-Mart culture was respect for the individual. That was interpreted to mean that the people at the top at Wal-Mart had to show respect for the employees below them. Keeping their doors open was a major step in that direction. It was one of the most important ways that senior management communicated to those below them that they were serious when they said they wanted the Wal-Mart culture spread throughout the organization.

Wal-Mart's leadership does not conceal that a major value of the open-door policy is the weakening of union prospects of penetrating the stores. The theory goes that as long as employees have a way to air their grievances, real or perceived, at the highest levels of the company, there will be no reason to turn to outsiders for help with them.

Sam Walton wrote in his memoirs that he felt he had to make the open-door policy work, because if he was going to fly around the country and tell the employees that he was their partner, he had to at least listen to their complaints. Of course no better open-door policy existed than when Sam Walton visited the stores and employees or managers could get the boss's attention on issues that were important to them. There was no need to circumvent managers, no need to write letters. The boss was just a few feet away. It wasn't even necessary to go through his open door. He was right there at your store.

But as Wal-Mart grew and management layers increased, just trying to find someone more senior than your own manager (against whom you had the complaint) might not have been that easy. Finding that senior person's name and getting the complaint to the person took time and effort and required some courage.

The open-door policy may have been easier under Sam Walton, but it still functioned after his successors took over. Some went to great lengths to test whether it worked.

A PACKAGE FOR THE CEO

Every senior official at Wal-Mart had a favorite open-door anecdote to pass on. For Lee Scott it was the time in 2001 when an employee sent a package that arrived at the CEO's home on a Sunday; it contained a letter and photos that showed evidence of his store's stating that certain items were on sale in violation of Wal-Mart's policy of not having sales except as part of a rollback (which this was not). Scott immediately contacted his senior operations staff, who discovered that everything the employee had written in the letter was true. The practice was terminated immediately. To Scott, it was the ideal example of an employee's utilizing the open-door policy on an issue that the employee most likely felt would get quick attention only if he notified the CEO. Getting the enablers right meant getting the culture to function smoothly at a time when Wal-Mart was growing in all sorts of ways. Steeped as they were in Sam Walton's culture, his successors had a much easier time getting those cultural enablers to function than managing the spectacular growth. However difficult managing that growth was, the new leadership team was determined to keep the growth engine humming. It faced one of its greatest challenges when it sought to take Wal-Mart beyond the seas.

CHAPTER 9

BEYOND THE SEAS:
A NEW OUTLET FOR GROWTH

Just as the Supercenters and the grocery business became engines of growth for Wal-Mart, so too did the quest for business beyond American borders.

There is little to indicate that Sam Walton possessed strong ambitions to take Wal-Mart overseas. He was wrapped up in the domestic growth of the discount chain; for him, going abroad was something for the distant future. He thought much more, his son John said, "of serving specific markets and specific opportunities than he thought in terms of the company expanding—of being in a certain number of countries or continents." His elder son Rob concurred: "He wouldn't have had any interest in putting twenty Wal-Marts into a country," noting that his father cared most about Wal-Mart's American operation, which represented virtually the whole company when he was alive.

When Sam Walton did travel overseas, he certainly imagined the opportunities for Wal-Mart, looking forward to the day, however far away, when the organization was ready to serve international customers. He thought that Wal-Mart could help the standard of living of people around the world just as it had done domestically.

In 1991, on the only occasion that he was involved with an international store, Sam and Rob scouted a site for Wal-Mart's first international operation, a Sam's Club that opened in Mexico City later that year.

Yet the founder winced whenever someone boasted that Wal-Mart
had become the largest retailer in the world. He worried that such
talk would make Wal-Mart go soft. That is why no one can recall
Walton's poring over a map of the world and earmarking certain
countries as suitable for Wal-Marts.

The new leadership team, however, was not intimidated by expanding overseas. To wait too long to get into foreign countries was
to allow competitors to gain a foothold in countries. That would be
giving away an important competitive advantage. And to wait would
still not give Wal-Mart the necessary time to learn the complexities of
international business and to correct its mistakes before others
joined the fray.

★ ★ ★

The challenges and risks of going overseas are immense for an American company. Other than a few restaurant chains—McDonald's
Kentucky Fried Chicken, and Pizza Hut are examples—no important American retailer has successfully penetrated the international
market. In the United States, companies can utilize purchasing
power, reputation, and economies of scale, but these capabilities are
hard to export.

Wal-Mart overcame such difficulties.

IN NINE COUNTRIES

Throughout the nineties, Wal-Mart's international program grew
impressively, playing an increasingly important role in the company's financial picture. From that first effort in Mexico, Wal-Mart
International grew to 1,186 overseas units that employed 300,000
by April 2002. The year before Wal-Mart had over $35 billion in
overseas sales, a 10.5 percent increase over 2000. The 2001 international sales represented nearly 16 percent of Wal-Mart's revenue.
The operating profit for the international program was $1.4 billion
in 2001, a 31.1 percent hike over the year 2000. Wal-Mart was in nine
countries—Mexico, Canada, Argentina, Brazil, the United Kingdom,

Germany, China, South Korea, and Japan. It chose these countries both because they had a large population base and a strong, growing middle-class. (Wal-Mart includes Puerto Rico as part of its foreign operations, although it is part of the United States.)

In just a few years Wal-Mart had become the largest retailer in Mexico and Canada and the third-largest in the United Kingdom. It is also doing nicely in Asia. It has been credited with helping to hold down inflation in Mexico, with improving Britain's cost of living, and with helping to revolutionize the distribution system in China. Though it has purchased only a stake in Seiyu, Japan's fifth-largest retailer, Wal-Mart has shaken up Japanese retailers simply by deciding to compete with them.

But Wal-Mart has much work ahead of it in South America and Europe, where it remains only a minor player. Facing higher labor costs in Europe, tougher unions, and a more paternalistic regulatory environment than the laissez-faire American market, Wal-Mart has confined its European efforts to Britain and Germany. The British experience has been positive; the German one mixed. Wal-Mart not only faced technical constraints—logistics, transportation, and the like—in going overseas. It also had to integrate its corporate culture into its international operations. The culture had become a core capability that contributed heavily to the company's success, and it was unthinkable to build Wal-Marts in overseas markets without exporting the greeters, the cheers, the Sam Walton quotations and photographs, the focus on customers and everyday low pricing, and all the other elements that went into the culture. It was vital to export the culture, Don Soderquist insisted, because Wal-Mart customers were alike regardless of where they lived and shopped: "Over the years many said that we would not be able to serve customers west of the Mississippi, outside of the South, in metropolitan areas or outside of the United States. Frankly, we find the customers want the same things. Regardless of where we are, customers want to be treated well, want to have a good assortment of products to choose from; and they want the merchandise at a great price. The most amazing fact is that our associates around the world embrace and protect this culture that they have built over the last thirty-five years."

NOT ALL WENT SMOOTHLY

Of course the cultural transitions did not always go smoothly. In Argentina, the aisles were too narrow for the unexpectedly large customer traffic; certain cuts of meat that Argentines loved were missing; missing from the jewelry department was the simple gold and silver items that the locals liked. It took some time, but Wal-Mart adjusted: The aisles were widened, the company added specialized cuts of meat, the jewelry line was revised to emphasize simple gold and silver. In Mexico City, Wal-Mart sold tennis balls that because of the high altitude did not bounce properly. It built huge parking lots only to discover that shoppers rode buses. Wal-Mart solved the tennis ball problem and introduced shuttle buses to drop customers off at the front door.

The Mexican operation posed a particular challenge to Wal-Mart. At a certain point its subsidiary, Cifra (now called Wal-Mart de Mexico) decided that it did not need to adopt Wal-Mart's key strategy of everyday low prices, in which all products would be discounted, not just some. It introduced its own strategy of putting only certain items on sale. When Wal-Mart learned of this deviation, it moved swiftly, closing the store for a day and rolling back 6,000 items to the EDLP framework. For a while customers were wary, assuming that the store would revert to its policy of giving substantial discounts on certain items. When there was no reversion, the customers embraced EDLP with the same enthusiasm as their counterparts in Rogers, Arkansas, or the Los Angeles suburbs.

★ ★ ★

Before coming to work at Wal-Mart, Bob Martin was a technology expert at another Arkansas retailer. Twice he had spurned offers to work for Wal-Mart, but finally in 1984 he began an eight-year stint as chief information officer. During that period he was also an execu-

tive vice president and senior vice president. In 1993 David Glass and
Rob Walton asked him to take over as president and CEO of Wal-
Mart's newly created international division. At the time, the interna-
tional operation had only the one Sam's Club in Mexico.

Part of the mandate Glass and Walton gave Martin was to build
the international program into one of Wal-Mart's main growth vehi-
cles, such that the program would contribute one-third of the company's growth within five years, a very ambitious vision. The hope
back then was that half of Wal-Mart's growth would come from food,
one-third from international, and the rest from the domestic Wal-
Mart stores.

Just how ambitious was Martin's mandate? Were Wal-Mart to stay
on course at a 15 percent annual growth rate and were international
to account for one-third of that growth, it would be contributing $10
billion a year.

Martin decided to begin Wal-Mart operations with the Americas,
North and South. Sam's Clubs were organized in Mexico. Wal-Mart
operations aimed at Argentina and Brazil as well. Martin's goal was
for Wal-Mart to become the dominant retailer in North America. A
plan was devised to enter China and Indonesia as starting points for
all of Asia. The hope was to enter Japan as well, despite that country's
strong challenge. That challenge had to do with Japan's being a truly
unique retail market, particularly in terms of consumer tastes on
merchandise and packaging. Japan's relationships between suppliers
and retailers, and its logistics systems also were unique. Martin's
strategy called for getting into Europe, but real estate was difficult to
find. And finding local partners was hard. Wal-Mart was too young,
too unproven.

Martin's ambitious approach led to criticism that he was flag-
planting, that he was simply putting in stores without giving sufficient advanced thought to getting the best locations. But he knew
that there was no way to get strong growth figures from just one or
two overseas operations, especially from the ever-cyclical emerging
markets.

By 1995 the company was still taking early, tentative steps.

Canada was one example. A year earlier Wal-Mart had purchased all 122 Canadian Woolco discount stores. Wal-Mart Canada was not profitable in 1995 except for a small operating profit in the fourth quarter.

It was Wal-Mart's foray into Canada that proved the most significant for the company: It was the first to demonstrate that the company could indeed do well outside the United States, that it could get returns abroad that rivaled its American returns. Not that the operation got off to a roaring start. Indeed, for the first three years (1995–97) Wal-Mart Canada showed losses of such a magnitude that Rob Walton once asked, "Will somebody remind me why we got into this?"

There was hope expressed for the Mexican operation as well, despite recent economic difficulties there. In 1995 Wal-Mart opened three units in Argentina and five in Brazil.

BETTER NEWS

A year later, 1996, the news was much better: Mexico had been profitable in a very difficult economic environment; Canada had generated an operating profit that year, only the second year of Wal-Mart's operation. Wal-Mart began a joint venture with the intention of entering China. Initial results in Argentina and Brazil were encouraging. Operations in Indonesia were about to begin under joint-venture and royalty agreements.

As it turned out, the Indonesia initiative failed; Wal-Mart shut down the whole operation in the mid 1990s, the only Wal-Mart overseas effort to close. Wal-Mart would not have closed up shop solely because of the political climate; it departed Indonesia in the wake of business disagreements with its local partner, though the specter of political unrest did harm the venture.

By 1997 Wal-Mart had international sales of over $5 billion. The international division was profitable that year, with Canada and Puerto Rico showing excellent results. Only three years after Wal-Mart acquired the Canadian Woolco Stores, it had become Canada's highest-volume discount retailer. It broke even for the first time.

Sales had tripled. Profits exceeded Wal-Mart's estimates, and market share kept on growing. Wal-Mart's joint venture in Mexico made it the country's largest retailer.

David Glass was ready to pronounce the international effort a success, noting that with over three hundred locations and over 50,000 employees, Wal-Mart International had become a truly brand name, with worldwide appeal that resembled that of Coca-Cola and McDonald's. Again, in 1997, the international division was profitable, serving five million customers weekly.

On December 30, 1997, Wal-Mart completed the acquisition of twenty-one hypermarkets in Germany, marking its first entry into Europe, one of the largest consumer markets in the world.

In 1998 Wal-Mart acquired a controlling interest in Mexico's largest retailer, Cifra, which operated stores throughout the country, ranging from the largest chain of sit-down restaurants to a softlines (apparel, home furnishings, fabric) department store. Start-up operations in Argentina and Brazil were progressing.

International sales growth was impressive between 1995 and 1999:

1995: $1.5 billion
1996: $3.7 billion
1997: $5 billion
1998: $7.5 billion

Wal-Mart had more than six hundred stores in seven countries with another fifty to sixty planned for 1999. Operating profits from the international division were $24 million in 1997. They reached $262 million in 1998.

By 1999, the fifth year of international operations, it was generating $12.2 billion in revenue and $551 million in operating profit. It added seventy-four units in Germany and acquired four units in South Korea; it also added thirty-six units to the countries where it already had operations.

Wal-Mart Canada had gained an amazing 30 percent share of Canadian department store sales; its rivals Eaton's, Zellers and the

Bay were falling behind fast. Wal-Mart was credited with forcing the entire Canadian retail industry to abandon its old habits.

The Canadian media was smitten by Wal-Mart's low pricing, its capability of stripping costs from the supply chain. "The company's distribution system is regarded as the most efficient in the world," said *McLean's* in a March 1, 1999, article. The smooth flow of goods caught the media's attention as well. The *McLean's* article reported that suppliers' deliveries to Wal-Mart distribution centers had to arrive within fifteen to thirty minutes of scheduling or the suppliers faced fines. It also noted that Wal-Mart was using its enormous power to attain price concessions from suppliers.

★ ★ ★

In June 1999, Bob Martin stepped down as head of the international division. He had built it into a $17 billion operation.

Replacing him was John Menzer, who had joined Wal-Mart four years earlier as the new CFO. "The international division was very much a start-up in Wal-Mart," Menzer recalled of the time he took over. "We were viewed as something that had potential, but international was still such a small part of the overall business."

According to Menzer, although Wal-Mart had been successfully established in a number of countries, "we were bouncing around a little bit and trying a number of different things," from acquisitions to joint ventures to "greenfield" development (building a business from the ground up, from a base of zero, as Wal-Mart essentially did in South America).

AN END TO FLAG-PLANTING

Menzer sought to take a more disciplined approach. He had done some research and found that a rule of thumb existed for entering new overseas markets: It took three years to become profitable, five years to get an acceptable return.

Accordingly, Menzer adopted a less opportunistic strategy, a more cautious one, taking his time to do the proper research. At any given time he was checking out at least ten acquisition prospects, taking long, deep breaths before taking a plunge. Other American enterprises, like IBM and Intel, had required years to make their international programs work in various countries. Wal-Mart hoped to turn the corner in each country in three to five years. Menzer was torn between the high expectations that Wall Street had for Wal-Mart and his rule of thumb. He cautioned patience. "We are on our way to becoming a global company, but we're not there. We're just starting to think globally."

* * *

Unquestionably Wal-Mart's most difficult experience overseas has been Germany, with 80 million people and the largest economy in Europe. Wal-Mart had high hopes of bringing off another international success when in December 1997 it purchased the German Wertkauf group of twenty-one stores and a year later added seventy-four Interspar hypermarkets, one-stop shopping facilities similar to Wal-Mart's Supercenters. The Wertkauf stores did $1.2 billion in business in 1998.

Wal-Mart spent months remodeling: widening aisles, improving the lighting, adding checkout counters, hiring additional staff and guiding them through the corporate culture. Only on August 31, 1999, did it open its flagship Supercenter in Dortmund.

At first it appeared that Germans, who were used to cramped stores and discourteous sales help, not to mention long checkout waits, were responding positively to the friendly and informed employees and the lower prices. But with thinner profit margins, higher labor costs, and smaller stores, Wal-Mart found the competition much tougher than anything it normally confronted abroad. Its German supermarkets were clearing 1 percent or less in net profits, compared with 6 to 8 percent in British ones.

The odds seemed against Wal-Mart. Germany already had a considerable number of discounters, among them Aldi, a countrywide

chain of no-frills, no-service stores that had price-sensitive consumers. Margins were low; costs high. Labor laws and tough unions
made wage-cutting difficult.

The German shopping style did little to accommodate the Wal-
Mart culture. Stores closed Saturday afternoons and reopened only
on Monday morning; in the United States Wal-Mart routinely did a
big chunk of its weekly business on Sundays. German customers were
used to bagging their own groceries, adversely affecting Wal-Mart's
vaunted productivity: When the Germans did the bagging, it slowed
down the checkout lines. Wal-Mart's troubles grew after German consumers failed to warm to the company's everyday low price approach.

Not that Wal-Mart did not try to adapt to German ways. It offered baked soft pretzels and the open-faced sandwiches with
sausage and butter that are called wurstbrot. The pictures on the
Wal-Mart brand of pet food were changed: A terrier replaced the
founder's English setter. Customers were given the option of packing
their purchases. Wal-Mart greeters spoke more quietly, out of respect for Germans. Greeters learned not to approach customers but
simply wait on the side.

Officially, Wal-Mart sought to put a good face on the cultural
challenges. Its spokespersons insisted that the company had made a
major change in the German shopping culture by opening its stores
two hours earlier than the nine o'clock standard. They also noted
that though Germans had at first been alarmed to find greeters talking to them when they entered the stores, the Wal-Mart culture had
eventually established a strong foothold.

Still, tough zoning laws made it next to impossible to build new
stores. Only in 2001 did Wal-Mart finally open two stores built from
scratch. Enlarging stores was slowed down by German red tape.
Newsweek quoted analysts who suggested that Wal-Mart was losing
$100 million a year by 2002.

John Menzer conceded that Germany represented Wal-Mart's
biggest challenge, "because we are trying to put in our distribution,
technology and operating expertise in a market that is slow to
change—slow to adapt to technology and distribution."

In 2002, Wal-Mart opened two new stores, one in Bergkamen and another in Gross-Gerau. It planned to open a new Supercenter in Berlin and a new distribution center in Bingen in 2003.

Privately, senior Wal-Mart executives acknowledged that the Wal-Mart effort in Germany was going slower than hoped. Inculcating employees with the corporate culture was simply not enough. Teaching them the Wal-Mart cheer was not enough to overcome all the other obstacles.

Lee Scott, appearing on CNBC in March 2002, acknowledged that Wal-Mart had encountered difficulty in Germany but blamed it on neither the German economy nor the German people. He blamed it on Wal-Mart stores. "We got confused on what's important, and so we went out and we remodeled stores—and spent a lot of money doing things that wasn't what the customers wanted from us."

He was pleased to report that there had been a dramatic improvement in the German Wal-Mart financial situation. He predicted eventual success in Germany. "We'll be successful because we reprioritized what our efforts are and understanding that market, understanding the German consumer and understanding Wal-Mart stores."

★ ★ ★

By 2000 Wal-Mart's leadership had scaled back its original assessment of how much growth its international division might contribute to the company's overall growth. Rob Walton suggested that over the next five years, 60 percent of Wal-Mart's growth in sales and earnings would come from Wal-Mart stores and Supercenters domestically, another 10 percent from Sam's Clubs, and the remaining 30 percent from Wal-Mart International.

★ ★ ★

Wal-Mart has had much better luck with its acquisition in the United Kingdom. Unlike in Germany, Wal-Mart was able to take over a profitable chain with a brand name. Wal-Mart had kept an eye on ASDA for some time before seeking to purchase it, for, as Rob

Walton noted: "They had a great management team, a similar culture, and their philosophy on retailing was almost identical to ours."

ASDA truly had a similar culture of price rollbacks and people greeters, "permanently low prices forever" and even "Smiley" faces. The reason was not hard to fathom: ASDA has been imitating Wal-Mart's store culture for many years. It even called its employees "colleagues," which was close to "associates." Everyone wore a badge and called each other by first name. And it always felt that it was the underdog (like Wal-Mart in its early days).

Before the prospect of purchasing ASDA came along, Wal-Mart had no specific plans to enter the United Kingdom. It was only when another company offered to purchase ASDA early in the spring of 2000 that Wal-Mart made its move, spending ten days to finalize its own deal with the British supermarket chain.

DEAL OF THE YEAR

To enter the United Kingdom, Wal-Mart paid $10.8 billion to acquire the 232-store supermarket chain. The ASDA deal in June 2000 was Wal-Mart's largest purchase to that date. In 1998 ASDA had $14 billion in sales.

Mergers & Acquisitions magazine named the transaction the Cross-Border Deal of the Year for 1999.

What Wal-Mart executives liked so much about the ASDA acquisition were the apparent synergies between the two new partners: Wal-Mart felt that it would learn a great deal from ASDA about selling food—and it did; ASDA, on the other hand, believed that it would be able to get important advice from Wal-Mart about merchandising—and it did.

At first there were fears that Wal-Mart's arrival in the United Kingdom might adversely affect the two large British chains, Tesco and Sainsbury's. And indeed, the two chains had to reduce margins to try to compete with Wal-Mart's everyday low prices. In 2001, though ASDA trailed far behind Tesco and Sainsbury's in revenue, its revenue growth was twice the market average. So Tesco and Sains-bury's had reason to be worried about Wal-Mart.

The average Wal-Mart Supercenter is 180,000 square feet and does about 30 percent of its sales in groceries. In sharp contrast, the average ASDA store has only 65,000 square feet and does 60 percent of sales in groceries. But though Supercenters are three times larger, some ASDA stores can do as much in sales as the average Supercenter.

ASDA's sales per square foot are the highest in Wal-Mart, accord-ing to Menzer. That is partly because ASDA has a much larger food business and because the United Kingdom has far fewer grocery stores per capita.

Since the Wal-Mart merger, ASDA's monthly comparable store sales have risen 11 percent.

In 2000, Wal-Mart officials noted that there were plans to spend more than $100 million over the next five years to open fifty stores in the new 25,000-square-foot ASDA "fresh" format, which stressed fresh foods and prepared meals. Two new ASDA Supercenters—modeled after the Wal-Mart ones—were also in the planning stages.

* * *

Wal-Mart had spent four years studying the Japanese retail market, concluding that it should avoid building stores from the ground up. It decided that its best option was to search for a local Japanese part-ner to run the Wal-Mart business. Accordingly, in 2002, Wal-Mart paid $46.5 million for a 6.1 percent interest in Seiyu Ltd., Japan's fourth-largest supermarket. Wal-Mart retained an option to buy the other two-thirds by 2007. Seiyu's shares rose 60 percent on the news of Wal-Mart's investment. The stock price of most other Japanese re-tailers plummeted.

Analysts breathed a sign of relief to learn that Wal-Mart had taken a small stake in a Japanese company rather than maximizing its up-front risk by trying to build Wal-Marts from scratch in Japan.

The media believed that Japan, like Germany, would be slow to adapt to the Wal-Mart culture. After all, other Western companies, like OfficeMax, Costco and Carrefour, had not met with early success in their Japanese forays. There was good reason: The Japanese economy was suffering. Consumers were not easy to attract, and Japanese distribution networks were antiquated.

On December 12, 2002, Wal-Mart announced that it planned to raise its stake in Seiyu to over 34 percent. It was exercising in full the first in a series of options it had received earlier that year.

Wal-Mart hopes to help Seiyu become Japan's price leader. But reducing prices by streamlining its operations and supply chain is a new concept for Japan, and American analysts were not sure that Seiyu would be able to cut costs as much as was needed to offer lower prices.

★ ★ ★

The international experience was teaching Wal-Mart that it had great impact around the world. Wal-Mart's executives had been skeptical that the domestic operation could replicate itself easily and neatly when taken abroad. But as its international program grew into a far-flung, financially-successful operation, those officials began to recognize that the company had something going for it that was potentially very significant. Wal-Mart had much to learn, not the least of which was to find the right mix of American and local leadership in each country. Some of the learning had to do with finding out what was the best way to approach an entire country.

Wal-Mart had to deal with city councils and zoning boards within the United States, but a much more delicate kind of diplomacy was required for its international ventures. Its senior officials could not simply seek a meeting with the prime minister of a country and ask for permission to put in fifty stores or even a thousand. Prime ministers did not usually make such decisions. But developing a warm, friendly relationship with the head of a government was important for a company like Wal-Mart: It carried great weight with local Chinese or Brazilian officials when a Wal-Mart official could say, "I had a wonderful meeting with your president yesterday." When he met with the president of China in October 2002, Lee Scott did not ask for approval for Wal-Mart to build more stores in China. But having given the president a detailed report on Wal-Mart's operations and programs for future development, he could enable his Chinese Wal-Mart colleagues to tell local officials that the president was aware of and appreciated what Wal-Mart was doing in China.

★ ★ ★

Once established in those countries, Wal-Mart had to learn quickly what local customers' tastes were, it had to learn how to bring products to the stores economically, and it had to know how to deal with suppliers in each country and make them feel they were an important part of the operation.

But there were great benefits too to the international operation and not just financial ones. Learning opportunities existed: New stores, established in foreign countries, had to innovate in order to compete; sometimes they had to rely on their own intuition rather than past practices. The result was that Wal-Mart's domestic operation found that it could learn a great deal from its overseas stores.

Among the ideas that Wal-Mart was importing from its international stores were:

—The gravity wall: a Brazilian concept, in which fixtures are fed from behind an interior wall, enabling employees to stock fast-moving merchandise—such as sodas, diapers, paper goods, without getting in the customer's way.
—Selling shoes: Wal-Mart's American stores picked up on the Canadian shoe program and its new way of presenting shoes by leaving them in the boxes and displaying them by style rather than size. The Canadian "best practice" was being tested in the United States; it had already been adopted in some other Wal-Mart stores abroad.
—Selling bike racks: Also from Canada, the drawer-style bike rack enables customers to look at and handle bikes more easily.
—Displaying wine: from Mexico, a "best practice" called wine racking, a new version of fixtures for displaying and selling wine.

—Food layout: also from Mexico, a food assortment and layout for the Mexican food area in Wal-Mart American stores based on that in the Mexican stores.

—Selling apparel: from the United Kingdom, George Clothing— a line of fashion apparel that was developed there and began selling in Wal-Mart stores in the United States and elsewhere.

★ ★ ★

The key for Wal-Mart International, as for its domestic operations, was the emphasis it placed on learning from its mistakes. In charge of the company was a group of risk-takers who knew that it was worth taking risks only if everyone figured out when something went wrong why it went wrong.

When mistakes were made in Germany and Mexico, the Wal-Mart staff in those countries tried to learn why those mistakes had been made. Within a short time, Wal-Mart became the largest retailer in those countries.

Wal-Mart still faced many challenges on the international front. If it were going to expand, it would have to select the right countries at the right time. There was a feeling among senior Wal-Mart officials that a relatively small number of countries were ripe for American retailing, perhaps twenty in all. Wal-Mart was already in nearly half of them.

Wal-Mart's long-term strategies for its international program was to leverage the program to make the company truly global. That meant finding global players to lead the different international operations. It meant building global distribution and transportation systems. It meant developing close links between the American side of Wal-Mart and the international side. This would all take time, but it seemed likely to be Wal-Mart's future.

CHAPTER 10

LIVE SNAKES AND TURTLE RACES:
WAL-MART IN CHINA

Of the new strategies that Sam Walton's successors came up with, none was more important than growth; and few other enablers of growth have been as successful as the international program. The success is all the more startling given the limitless possibilities of collision and conflict between the Wal-Mart culture and the national culture in each country.

Of all of Wal-Mart's international operations, none illustrates that potential for collision and conflict as much as Wal-Mart China.

Back in the fifties and sixties few Americans would have dreamed that a half century later the largest discount retailer in America would be setting up stores in China. Yet as China opened itself to the rest of the world in the late 1970s and early 1980s, it was no longer surprising that Wal-Marts were taking root in the midst of 1.3 billion Chinese.

In many ways China seemed the one place in the world where it would be impossible for the Wal-Mart culture to flourish. English was hardly spoken, even at the official level; China had been closed off from the West for so long. How could Americans do business in China?

For the traveler to China in 2002, it was clear that this was a wonderful time for Wal-Mart to be entering the Chinese market. The country had been opening its arms to Western investment over the previous decade, with the result that a Chinese middle class was emerging; for the first time that emerging middle class could be enticed to visit Wal-Mart stores with their everyday low prices, their immaculately clean (by anyone's standards) interiors, and their friendly attitude toward the customer.

It was also a marvelous time for Wal-Mart to set up shop in China, because none of its American rivals had done so. Whatever the reasons were for the rivals staying out—and there were a number of them—Wal-Mart would, just by establishing a handful of stores, gain a competitive advantage that would presumably serve it well down through the years.

CHINESE ON THE BUSES

Finally, a Wal-Mart store offered many Chinese consumers their first opportunity to shop for food that they could safely eat. Until hypermarkets such as Wal-Mart arrived, many Chinese bought their food in the open air wet markets, as the Chinese call them. After buying bad food in the wet markets and boarding a bus, Chinese were sometimes spotted throwing up out the window. By being one of the first of the hypermarket retailers in China to offer packaged meat, Wal-Mart truly offered the Chinese a choice between the primitive wet markets and a highly sanitary hypermarket.

★ ★ ★

Time and again, Wal-Mart managers who served as escorts to visitors in the stores emphasized that they offered only clean food. It seemed an odd point to make to an American used to supermarkets that offer fresh food on a routine basis, but then one has only to think of the Chinese on those buses.

The wet markets, which can hardly be called clean by Western standards, are in narrow alleyways crammed with kiosks. Masses of people look for bargains as they try not to bump into one another. Often the floors are covered with water, making them slippery and dangerous for people, especially elderly women, to walk on.

To sense Wal-Mart's appeal for the Chinese shopper, think of those wide aisles, spotless floors, attractive displays, and everyday low prices. Shopping in the wet markets might save a Chinese shopper money on various items, but shopping in a Wal-Mart would save the shopper a good deal of money on numerous items—and, perhaps most important, the experience of moving around a Wal-Mart was sure to be less irritating, less nerve-wracking, and less discomforting.

Still, the Chinese have been shopping in wet markets for years; it is what they are used to. Even with the emergence of the new Chinese middle class, it will take some time before huge numbers of Chinese become aware of a Wal-Mart in their midst. But meanwhile the numbers of those shopping and buying in the Chinese Wal-Marts is impressive.

Parts of a Wal-Mart in China look like any other merchandise/ food store; parts do not.

The Wal-Mart Supercenter in Shenzhen, which opened on April 20, 2000, has 498 employees and twenty thousand products, 95 percent of which are Chinese (The other 5 percent come from the United States.)

Fruits and vegetables are the most popular department. Electronics and men's clothes do well too. The Shenzhen Supercenter promoted men's leather shoes for $6 a pair and sold fifteen hundred in one week. On October 1, 2002, sixty thousand people visited the store.

And of course, as with all Wal-Marts around the world, the Chinese stores are trying to give the customer some real fun ("retailtainment," in Wal-Mart parlance). There were activities all the time, such as karaoke contests with 10,000 people attending, a Special Olympics event (a soccer match for mentally retarded children), a marathon race, a watermelon-eating contest, fashion shows, and a cake-making contest.

For Chinese shoppers, the exotic products are those common in the United States: a wide variety of breads and cakes attractively wrapped in plastic, meat and fish parts in environmentally friendly packages, and one-person meals ready for home preparation. But to an American shopper, many items standard for the Chinese are exotic. Let's start with the live fish in large tanks, which sell for 75 cents.

Shoppers choose their own fish, which is killed on the spot: At the Supercenter, more than 5,000 fish are sold on a Saturday. Many animals are sold live: eels, snakes, frogs, sea cucumbers. One example of the juxtaposition of American and Chinese grocery products was the eel that was being sold adjacent to boxes of minipizza. Elsewhere in the store, one could watch in fascination as turtles raced—more like walked—in some kind of competition. Were the losers sold for turtle soup?

★ ★ ★

The motivation for Wal-Mart to make it big in China is obvious. An economy that has been growing in leaps and bounds this past decade and its huge population—1.3 billion—represents an incredibly large market. Even the 15 to 20 percent of the population that lives in urban centers means a huge number of potential customers on any given day.

For the time being, Wal-Mart China has located its stores in large cities. The small-town strategy that worked so well for Sam Walton in the early days of Wal-Mart has had no place in China. If Wal-Mart were going to work in China, it had to entice the middle class to shop in its stores, and the middle class lived in the cities. There was certainly enough population in them to keep Wal-Mart going: forty-four of China's cities had a population of at least a million. Because most Chinese do not drive cars, Wal-Mart China depends upon walk-in shoppers; that is in sharp contrast with American Wal-Marts with their huge parking lots, required for a nation of car drivers.

Eventually Joe Hatfield, the president of Wal-Mart Asia, wants to see Wal-Marts put up in small communities in China. But that will take some time.

THREE THOUSAND WAL-MARTS IN CHINA

Such potential shoppers have made the Wal-Mart operation in China very ambitious indeed. Wal-Mart's management in China knows that it is on to something potentially big, and is dreaming big dreams. There is none of the caution that Sam Walton felt in his early days about expanding Wal-Mart. These are people who, while they know they are in on the ground floor, believe that the kind of competitive advantage they enjoy will help them turn the Chinese effort into one of Wal-Mart's biggest operations. That is why when David Glass visited China in the 1990s and told Hatfield that China was the only country on earth that had the potential to produce another $100 billion in sales by itself, no one on the China staff blinked.

There is no evidence to believe that Sam Walton in his earliest days thought that there could be thousands of Wal-Marts dotted around America, but with the operation in China a mere six years old, the potential—indeed the opportunity—is so substantial that it is not out of the question that Wal-Mart China could have as many as 3,000 stores some day. The challenge looks enormous: These people have had to start from scratch. There were no distribution centers. There are still very few stores—twenty-two as of November 2002.

But Wal-Mart China has an advantage that even Sam Walton did not have. When Walton began building Wal-Marts in the early 1960s, he had no distribution centers, and the stores that he put together did not look nearly as good as the Chinese ones do. When he laced the Southwest region of America with Wal-Marts, there was no technology to speak of, certainly not the kind that exists in the year 2002. Yet Wal-Mart stores in China in 2002 were using the most advanced segments of the company's technology, including Telxons, Retail Link, and Linerusher. Experiments had been conducted to test the self-checkout counters. Retail Link is an Internet-based resource that provides suppliers with a full range of information on their business dealings with Wal-Mart, updated on a daily basis. Suppliers can download purchase orders directly, check the status of invoices, and determine the quantity of products sold at each Wal-Mart as recently as the previous day. Linerusher is a program designed to speed up checkout lines, using a device that scans products in a shopping cart while the customer is in line.

Perhaps most important is the self-confidence bubbling over among the Wal-Mart China leadership that comes from knowing that they belong to a company that overcame great adversity in its early days. It was in August 1996 that Wal-Mart China made its debut with a Supercenter and a Sam's Club in Shenzhen. In case there is any question about whether the Chinese would shop at a Wal-Mart, there is this amazing statistic to ponder: On the very first Saturday the Supercenter opened, 80,000 Chinese walked through the door.

Wal-Mart established its Chinese headquarters in Shenzhen, one of five special economic zones the Chinese had set up where Western companies would experience an easier time with China's red tape.

When you walk into a Wal-Mart in China, the first impression is that it looks a lot like an American Wal-Mart. The store is big. The aisles are wide. A good deal of thought appears to have been put into the display of the products. There is no feeling of the products being crowded together. Prices are written in bold black letters on signs that make you feel as if you're wandering around an American Wal-Mart.

But the Chinese are going to shop at a Wal-Mart only in part because the place looks like and has the great advantages of an American Wal-Mart. They are going to shop there only if they can buy the things they are used to buying in the wet market in this new modern environment—at cheaper prices than in the wet market. So Wal-Mart officials visit the wet markets three times a day to check on prices. They want to make sure that their prices are always lower.

John Menzer, who runs the international division for Wal-Mart, told me that he believes the stores in China are among the best in the whole organization; he would stack them up against any in America. This seemed an odd statement for him to make, given how much effort had been put into the American stores.

But then one arrives in China.

And soon after it is possible to understand Menzer's point. Of course what gets Menzer so excited is the great potential that exists for Wal-Mart in China. He is all too aware of how much there is to overcome; how difficult it is to move merchandise from one place to another in China; how the roads have to be improved; how the government, which he said had been very supportive, has to modify its rules even more to allow Wal-Mart to expand.

But he loves the stores and loves the people staffing them—and with good reason.

★ ★ ★

The Wal-Mart experience in China began as early as 1992 and 1993, when Rob Walton, joined by Wal-Mart real-estate personnel, made several advance visits. Wal-Mart's format of trying to lower the cost of living for its customers seemed a natural fit in China.

The Thailand-based CP Group, which had hired Al Johnson, a former vice chairman of Wal-Mart, as a consultant, approached Wal-Mart with an idea. They were opening three Value Clubs in Hong Kong and were also hoping to gain entry into Mainland China. Joe Hatfield, who was executive vice president of merchandising for the Sam's Clubs at the time, and Bob Martin joined Rob Walton and visited the Value Clubs.

Early in the summer of 1994, Wal-Mart began negotiations with CP, and a joint venture was established for entry into both Hong Kong and China proper.

Hatfield decided that a great opportunity existed, and he was prepared to come to Asia to live and to establish Wal-Mart China, hoping to build a full-fledged Wal-Mart China organization. A few weeks later Hatfield relocated to Hong Kong.

His plan to build Wal-Mart stores in China faced numerous obstacles. The largest was the government regulation that permitted foreign retailing only in certain Chinese cities. "Probably the biggest issue," Hatfield told me, "was learning and understanding how to deal with all the regulations and all the approval processes."

When it began its operation in 1996, Wal-Mart was permitted to set up business in only eleven Chinese cities—Shenzhen being one of them—and was limited to three stores per city. The others included all the major cities, including Beijing and Shanghai, plus the five economic zones. Given that Wal-Mart requires mass distribution as part of its business model, if it were to set up only the three stores in Shenzhen and three more in Beijing, it would be impossible to get the necessary economies of scale that it could get from a much larger number of stores.

On June 25, 1999, the regulations were broadened so that the number of approved cities for establishing Chinese-foreign retail joint ventures rose from eleven to thirty-seven plus the province of Hainan.

Hatfield and Cassian Cheung, the president of Wal-Mart China, explained that the three-stores-in-a-city rule was still in effect even after the government expanded the list to thirty-seven cities. Going beyond the three stores in each city required what the Chinese called an exception, and those were difficult to get.

Getting the required permission for each store required getting in touch with officials at the national, city, provincial, and district levels, a process that required numerous meetings with government officials and feasibility studies; that process once took eighteen to twenty-four months but has since been cut to three to six months.

Hatfield and his Chinese colleagues believed that with the economic boom in China, the regulations would most likely be liberalized. He was not overly worried about the three-stores-to-a-city restriction. Taking a long-term view, he was confident that as the regulations loosened, Wal-Mart would be able to build the needed infrastructure that would support whatever growth became possible in China.

When China joined the World Trade Organization on December 11, 2001, it became obligated to waive many limitations on market access, including geographic and quantitative restrictions on foreign retailers, within three years of China's admission to WTO. That means that foreign retailers, such as Wal-Mart, would in all likelihood be able to open stores in any city in addition to the currently allowed thirty-seven cities and Hainan province. The government regulations certainly seemed daunting, but they were nothing compared with the challenge of integrating the Wal-Mart culture into its stores in China.

For Hatfield and his senior Chinese staff, the challenge was to integrate Wal-Mart's values and expectations into employees who when they worked for state-run enterprises had been promised permanent employment and who were not used to having to work on more than one task in their jobs. The state-run enterprises offered almost no training and certainly no incentives to do a good job. The employee was expected to figure out how to do that one task on his or her own. Coming to work at Wal-Mart was an eye-opener for George Zhao, a native of Mianyang, who in November 2002 at age thirty-seven became the manager of a Supercenter in Shenzhen.

He remembered working as a manager at a state-run enterprise. "If an employee made a mistake, they fired him on the spot. At Wal-Mart there is more of a human touch. We have the open-door policy and a coaching process." One Wal-Mart employee was lagging in his work, Zhao said, but thanks to the coaching process, he improved and has become a deputy store manager. "In the state-run company he would have been fired," said Zhao.

The part of the culture that held the greatest appeal for Chinese shoppers was everyday low pricing. The Wal-Mart China staff had to be careful not to sell an item below cost—that was illegal. It could get an exception only with proper documentation.

One unusual selling point for Wal-Mart in China was the fixed prices it offered. Unlike the wet market, where bargaining is the rule, the price you saw on those signs in the stores was what you paid.

Another selling point at Wal-Mart was the authenticity of its products. Sometimes in China people purchased an item only to find that when they opened the box at home, they had not gotten exactly what they thought they had bought. Joe Hatfield noted that "every electronic item that we sell we take out of the box and set up and show the customers how to operate it. And we guarantee the product; they can return it without a receipt within thirty days." Most of Wal-Mart's competitors in China allowed customers to return goods within only seven to fifteen days.

So refreshing was this new way of doing business that Wal-Mart won awards from the Chinese Government for having authentic products at set prices.

To give the customer an ever-greater sense of security and to impose a sense of personal responsibility on the store, Wal-Mart employees developed a plan: When a customer purchased a large appliance or electronic item, the store employee who sold the item would, after testing, put a sticker with the store's telephone number and his or her name on it so that the customer knew whom to call if a problem occurred.

Within the first week of the customer's purchasing the appliance, a Wal-Mart employee would call the customer to ask if the product was working all right. Other overseas Wal-Mart operations have expressed interest in Wal-Mart China's "best practice" home delivery plan. Inculcating the Wal-Mart culture into the Chinese employees required finding a group of leaders who were passionate about their work. At the top of the corporate ladder were Americans: Hatfield and another ten or so in business development, construction, loss prevention, merchandising, and Supercenter management. The rest were Chinese. By November 2002 there were nearly 12,000 Chinese employees in the twenty-two Wal-Mart stores. The goal was to replace the Americans at the top with Chinese leadership; as Hatfield noted: "This is going to be a Chinese-run company some day."

To Hatfield, Wal-Mart China has succeeded because of that critical Wal-Mart cultural belief: respect for the individual. State-run enterprises, reflecting a highly structured society, did not permit employees to talk with managers. Cassian Cheung remembered what a revolution it was for employees when they were told that they should feel free to talk directly with their bosses. "We have had to get our associates to buy into this policy without thinking that the management is trying to trick them," said Cheung. Striving for equality between the manager and the employees, Hatfield decided to limit himself to wearing one of two suits, one of three ties, and one of three white shirts to work on weekdays and one of three sports shirts on the more casual Saturdays. He adopted this style after realizing that his Chinese employees had very small wardrobes; he did not want to come across as someone who could afford a great many clothes. Hatfield noted proudly that he was simply demonstrating respect for the individual.

Getting the Chinese employees to talk to the bosses sometimes produced overkill. At one Saturday morning meeting, he asked for someone to get up and talk about the merchandise. He made it clear he would welcome such comments. He got silence in return. No one was brave enough to speak directly to the American boss. A few months later, he repeated the same request, but this time a young man rose and began speaking—and speaking and speaking. He would not stop. Hatfield wanted to turn the young man off; but how could he interrupt him after having encouraged him? Finally, Hatfield realized that he had no choice. "We had to shut him up after he talked for two hours."

SERVICE TO THE CUSTOMER—CHINESE STYLE

Another cultural belief that Wal-Mart expected its Chinese employees to learn was service to the customer. To appreciate how difficult it was for Wal-Mart to teach this concept, it's worth keeping in mind that Chinese employees and customers sometimes engaged in fisticuffs over the question of who was ahead of whom in a checkout line. Wal-Mart China instituted a rule that any employee caught in a dustup with a customer would be immediately dismissed.

One of the biggest differences for an employee in working in a state-run enterprise and for Wal-Mart was in the amount of training received. The state-run enterprises left a new employee to his or her own devices; new Wal-Mart employees received extensive training both to learn their jobs and to absorb the company's culture.

Wal-Mart employees received training on how to keep rambunctious customers from getting into fights, on picking up trash, on smiling at customers, on cleaning floors according to Western standards. What made all those instructions hard for employees to absorb was that in previous jobs they had only one task to perform; once they learned that, there was little else to learn. At Wal-Mart, employees were expected to pitch in with whatever tasks required handling on any given day.

And so training became a critical issue at Wal-Mart.

There were grooming classes for starting employees: They were trained to shampoo their hair and be aware of their appearance. They were provided with uniforms, so that they would not have to use their own limited wardrobes. They received a comfortable pair of shoes as well.

★ ★ ★

Wal-Mart also had to adjust to subtle differences between its typical customs and practices and those commonly practiced in China. For example, Chinese employees had grown up in a social and business environment that routinely sanctioned gift-giving to thank and show respect for people, including vendors and government officials. Wal-Mart's culture strictly forbade such gestures.

Through straightforward communication and a growing understanding of one another, Hatfield said, Wal-Mart and the Chinese government have been able to reach a common ground in this area that respects and remains true to the culture of both Wal-Mart and China. Now, when Lee Scott or another key executive visits China and meets with senior government officials, gift exchanges are done out of respect to Chinese leaders and their long-standing culture. However, gift exchanges between Wal-Mart and their vendors are still just as forbidden in China as they are anywhere else in the world.

"We had to make some adjustments and work through some challenges in the early days, but in the long run it always seems to work out," Hatfield said. "The real issue here is integrity, not gifts. Wal-Mart is a company founded on integrity and is still just as committed to it today as we were when Sam Walton was alive. We make sure that the people we work with in China share that commitment. So in the end it wasn't that hard for us to find common ground on this issue."

All those high standards—not just of integrity but also of the appearance of the stores and the nature of the products—made Wal-Mart a model for the Chinese retail industry. Joe Hatfield was proud of that. His ability to bring the Wal-Mart culture to Wal-Mart stores in China won him kudos back in Bentonville as well. At the winter manager meetings in Kansas City in 2001, he was presented with

Wal-Mart's Entrepreneur of the Year award, given by the Walton family to the person who best represents the ideals that Sam Walton nurtured within the company, specifically respect for the individual, customer service, and striving for excellence.

★ ★ ★

Hatfield had success on the financial front as well: The twenty-two Chinese Wal-Mart were showing, collectively, an operating profit.

One of Hatfield's great abilities was motivating the Chinese staff. He loved telling the story of the young man who had been in charge of candy in one of the stores. He buttonholed Hatfield one day and told him that he had figured out how to place his candy in a smaller space. He recommended to Hatfield that in the space that had been saved other items be put to drive sales. Hatfield loved that story because the man rose to become a store manager for Wal-Mart China.

Hatfield was pleased with the entrepreneurial spirit he found among the Chinese managers and employees. One in particular had caught his eye. He made sure to put me in touch with Irene Du, the 39-year-old Shanghai-born manager of the Sam's Club in Shenzhen. When she applied to work at Wal-Mart in December 1995 she had no idea what the company did; she thought it was a logistics or a warehouse operation. She had certainly never heard of Sam Walton before.

She was hired as a supervisor at the Sam's Club. Once she began working at Wal-Mart, she was immediately struck by the emphasis on customer service and by the amount of training Wal-Mart supplied. She had worked in state-owned companies and recalled how little training everyone received. "If you are not performing, no one will help you. They tell you what the goal is, and it's up to you to figure out how to achieve the goal. If you don't achieve it, no one cares."

She sympathized with how challenging it was for Wal-Mart to train the Chinese staff to express themselves openly if they had a problem: "Chinese are more conservative. We have a different culture. We don't believe in approaching the boss directly. We believe in hierarchy. We just wouldn't go into the store manager's office."

Her average day is spent managing the 596 associates who work in her store and visiting competitors to check on prices. She frequently bumps into Wal-Mart employees who on their days off are also checking out the competition.

Irene Du was promoted to deputy department manager in March 1997 and department manager in December of that year. In November 1998 she became deputy store manager, then store manager in July 2000.

She has visited the United States twice, in 1999, then in 2001, when she was given the Wal-Mart Hero's Award at the shareholder meeting. She was indeed a hero in Wal-Mart eyes.

Her Sam's Club brought in more than $100 million in sales in 2001. On January 21, 2001, she broke the record for the highest volume of sales at any Wal-Mart in a single day: in excess of $1.5 million. The previous year, on February 2, 2000, she had set the record, doing more than $1 million in sales.

★ ★ ★

As the Chinese adventure rolled along, as Wal-Mart's remarkable growth continued to astound Wall Street, the media, and the company's happy shareholders, another management change was taking place: A new man was taking over. The era of Sam Walton was receding into the past. Soon the era of David Glass did the same. It was time for a new CEO to take center stage.

PART FIVE

WHO DEFINES WAL-MART?

CHAPTER 11

MR. LOGISTICS TAKES OVER

Throughout the year 2002, Lee Scott was running the largest company in the world in terms of revenue. He was the head of the largest private employer in the world. The company he presided over sold more food than anyone else. More than a hundred million people passed each week through the stores that he oversaw.

By virtue of Wal-Mart's arrival at the top of the mountain, Lee Scott certainly must rank as one of the most important, powerful, and influential CEOs of the day. But—and here's the paradox—he's certainly not one of the most visible. By his own account, he can walk into most Wal-Marts around the world and go unrecognized. Sam Walton couldn't do that.

Lee Scott seems comfortable keeping a low profile, partly, one imagines, because he wants to make sure that Sam Walton remains, even in death, the most important personality in the Wal-Mart organization. There seems to be an unwritten agreement among the new leadership team, inspired no doubt by Rob Walton, that Walton's image burn more brightly than that of any of his successors.

Sam Walton and Lee Scott both seemed to be the right leaders at the right time. That has a good deal to do with their contrasting personalities.

Wal-Mart needed a cheerleader, a business-savvy, hands-on kind of fellow at its start and into the seventies and eighties.

It had less need for a cheerleader in the nineties, more for leaders

163

like David Glass and Lee Scott, both of whom had skills and knowledge in logistics and transportation.

★ ★ ★

Most of all, Wal-Mart in the past decade had no great need to project another icon onto the business scene; it needed a Lee Scott to preside over a leadership team that could wrestle with the present-day complexities brought by the new Wal-Mart empire.

Lee Scott carries his near-anonymity with aplomb, eager to give the impression that he's not entirely comfortable wearing the crown that Sam Walton wore for so many years, eager to convey that it will take him time to get used to being the leader of the largest company in the world.

Lee Scott took over as CEO from David Glass in January 2000. When we met for the first time in June 2002 for a brief discussion, he had been in the job only 18 months. He pointed out at our first formal interview two months later that we were sitting in the office once occupied by Sam Walton, and he confessed that he found himself occupying it overwhelming: The office evoked for him the times when Walton would summon him to chew him out about something. It was not only sitting in the founder's chair that he found daunting; it was possessing so much power and influence over the company.

Before becoming CEO, when Scott took part in a Wal-Mart meeting he would trade ideas breezily with colleagues; some were adopted; some were not. As the CEO, he learned to his surprise that colleagues were taking his thoughts much more seriously: "When I got promoted to CEO, I did not become significantly brighter. But I learned quickly that offering what was previously a nondangerous opinion can be perceived, if you're not careful, as a command. And you are no smarter. You have no new insight. But you have more power. So I've been very careful—and I now say it quite a bit—what I'm about to say is not a directive, it's only for discussion."

Lee Scott's low profile and his early unease at having so much power comes, one assumes, from a long-standing conviction that he would never rise to the CEO post. He knew all too well that the person chosen to succeed David Glass, whenever he retired, was likely to be one of the renaissance men, men who possessed skills that made them knowledgeable not only in general merchandising and food but also in operations and logistics and communications. Scott was a logistics man, perhaps the best Wal-Mart ever had, but was that enough to qualify for CEO?

★ ★ ★

David Glass recruited Lee Scott to Wal-Mart.

Born in 1949 in Joplin, Missouri, Scott had grown up in the small Kansas town of Baxter Springs, where his father ran a gas station and his mother taught music at the elementary school. By age 21, he was married and a father; he worked for a tire-mold manufacturer to pay his way through Pittsburgh State University in Kansas where he majored in business administration, graduating in 1971.

When Yellow Freight System, a large Kansas-based trucking company, refused his bid to enter its management training program, young Scott asked a family friend to intercede. As a result, in 1977, at age twenty-eight, he joined the company as a terminal manager in Springdale, Arkansas.

His neighbor, Glenn Habern, a Wal-Mart manager, told David Glass, then an executive vice president at Wal-Mart, that Scott might be worth hiring. As it turned out, Yellow Freight felt that Wal-Mart owed it $7,000 in additional storage costs for failing to accept a delivery on time. Determined to collect the money, Scott drove to Bentonville and confronted Glass.

Insisting that Wal-Mart owed nothing, Glass was nevertheless struck by Scott's abilities and offered him a job with Wal-Mart.

Scott looked at Glass as it if to say, "You've got to be kidding me." He then told Glass: "I may not be the smartest person who ever came into this office, but I will not leave the fastest-growing trucking company in America and go to work for a guy who can't pay a $7,000 bill."

WHAT'S RIGHT FOR THE COMPANY

Two years later, Lee Scott had moved to Springfield, Missouri, and was working for Queen City Warehouse, another company in the freight and transportation business. Glass contacted Scott, asking him to become director of the Wal-Mart truck fleet. This time, Scott was amenable. But upon arriving at the new job, he listened with great surprise as David Glass declared that Scott would have to be only assistant director for some time. Swallowing his ego, Scott told Glass, "If it's right for the company, let's do that."

Burying one's ego helped one go far at Wal-Mart. Lee Scott was off to a good start. He did not, however, have a particularly warm opening meeting with Sam Walton. On his first day at work, Scott was summoned to Walton's office for an interview. Scott got the impression that if the interview did not go well, he might not have a job.

Scott sat down in Walton's office while the chairman propped himself against a table.

"How old are you?"

Scott was not expecting that kind of question right off the bat.

"I'm thirty."

"Do you think you can do this job?"

"Yes, sir," said Scott.

Walton gazed into Scott's eyes for a long moment and said, "I reckon you can," signaling that the meeting was over.

The meeting was short and abrupt, but at least Scott could be grateful that his new job was intact—for the time being.

Taking up the job of assistant director of the trucking fleet, Scott quickly got on the wrong side of Wal-Mart's truck drivers when he threatened to fire anyone violating company rules. He thought that displaying such personal initiative would win him points with the top brass.

So when a driver failed to make a delivery on time, Scott fired him. The driver complained directly to Sam Walton about the upstart who was wielding too much power. Walton rehired the man on the spot. (Ultimately, Scott's judgment about the errant truck driver was on the mark: He was fired and rehired two more times; finally the fourth time, he was fired, again, and left for good.)

Meanwhile, drivers complained to Sam Walton that Scott was constantly issuing ultimatums and threats to get them to obey the rules. Walton summoned Scott to his office, suggesting that he had been overly harsh to the drivers, considering that only 5 percent of them of them had committed infractions.

Walton had enough good sense and charm to get Scott and the truck drivers to make peace. He did not wish to fire Scott, nor did he want Scott to fire a truck driver too quickly. The solution, Walton told Scott, was to listen carefully to the drivers' complaints before taking impulsive action against them. Walton ordered him to shake hands with every driver and thank them for having the courage to use the Wal-Mart open-door policy.

At times, Walton and Scott would have strong disagreements about this issue or that, but Scott came to prize the relationship he developed with the founder. Scott learned to assess Walton's moods by the name he used for him: He was "Scott" when he had a beef with him, but "Levius" (a Southern name for Lee) when things were all right.

★ ★ ★

In 1995 Wal-Mart entered its fiftieth state, Vermont. It had 675,000 employees; 1,995 stores, 276 of them overseas; 239 Supercenters; and 433 Sam's Clubs.

But the company was going through a sales slump, and its stock (adjusted for splits) fell to below $10 a share. Accusations were hurled at David Glass: He was not up to running Wal-Mart. The place had not been the same since Walton died. The title of an article in *Fortune* published on April 29, 1996, "Can Wal-Mart Get Back the Magic?" said it all.

A disappointing 1995 Christmas season caused Wal-Mart's earnings per share to fall below their 1994 level, the first time that they had dropped since Wal-Mart went public in 1970. The company's fourth quarter for 1995 (ending January 1996) was a low point: Wal-Mart was forced to announce its first quarterly earnings decline after ninety-nine straight increases. Glass did not try to conceal that the company had felt a sense of loss with Sam Walton's death, and he conceded that Wal-Mart may have undertaken so many new initiatives that supervising the existing stores had become more difficult. That was shorthand for "Wal-Mart was growing too quickly."

Glass penned a letter to shareholders, explaining why a company with such seemingly good financial results had not had a great year. In 1995 Wal-Mart had record sales of $93.6 billion and record earnings of $2.7 billion; making it the fourth-largest company in the United States and twelfth-largest in the world; it was the thirteenth-most profitable company in America. "Although this was an acceptable year by most standards, it was not a Wal-Mart year. We are not compared with other retailers or other companies, but with our prior results." It had indeed not been a Wal-Mart year: Net sales increased 13 percent, compared with 22 percent in 1995, and comparative store sales increased by only 4 percent, compared with 7 percent in 1994.

A DIAGNOSIS

Fortune offered a diagnosis of what was ailing Wal-Mart: "This is a company built on magnificent simplicity—the idea was to deliver big-city discounting to small-town America—yet Wal-Mart today . . . is diversified, unpredictable, and very difficult to manage. Its core business appears mature; its chain of Sam's Club stores is flagging; and its future, says the CEO, lies in food retailing, a brutally competitive arena." The magazine added that Wal-Mart's followers were losing faith in the company. Market cap under Sam Walton had grown to $59.3 billion but had subsequently been pared by $7.7 billion.

The Wal-Mart speed bump would never happen again, Glass vowed. To jump-start the company Glass made a number of personnel changes including putting Lee Scott into a new post.

Scott had worked in the company's logistics and transportation area for his first sixteen years with Wal-Mart. He served as director of transportation, vice president of distribution, and senior vice president of logistics. In 1993 he was promoted to executive vice president of logistics.

Then in October 1995, while he was on a logistics scouting trip in Paris, he got a fax asking him to phone Bentonville at 7 A.M. Arkansas time.

He phoned David Glass, Rob Walton, and Don Soderquist from a Paris pay phone, wondering what was going on. They asked him to step into a new job the following Monday. He would remain an executive vice president, but he would move over to be in charge of merchandise and sales for the Wal-Mart Stores division.

Scott was not being touted as a possible successor to Glass. The little scuttlebutt that existed focused on a man named Bill Fields, who had been in charge of Wal-Mart's main operations and was considered the company's star manager in operations and merchandising. Born and bred in Bentonville, he was one of the company's closest links to the Sam Walton era. Walton hired him after he graduated from the University of Arkansas. Some said he was like a surrogate son to the founder.

Scott's star rose when he was selected to be in charge of merchandise and sales, although it seemed odd at first that he, a logistics specialist, would be selected for a merchandising slot. David Glass wanted to play a little musical chairs with his executives to see if that would help Wal-Mart over its bad patch.

★ ★ ★

At the same time (late 1995) that Scott was taking up his new duties as executive vice president for merchandising and sales, Tom Coughlin was starting a new job as well: executive vice president and COO of Wal-Mart Stores division (USA). Before joining Wal-Mart, he had worked at R. H. Macy's west coast division and at Cook United. He graduated from California State University with a bachelor's degree in political science.

Coughlin, who joined the company in 1978, had a reputation for getting results. This was the same Tom Coughlin who had locked a store manager out of his office upon finding out that the man spent too little time on the floor. The result was that that manager spent more time on the floor. Before then, when Coughlin was vice president of loss prevention, he offered employees up to two hundred dollars a year for help in reducing theft and unknown losses. He got results.

Coughlin has held a number of other posts at Wal-Mart: vice president of human resources, executive vice president of Sam's club operations, and executive vice president of specialty groups.

As his star rose in the company, Coughlin became a candidate to succeed David Glass whenever he vacated the CEO post. Another candidate was Bob Martin, who had run technology in the 1980s and who successfully built through the 1990s the international program.

★ ★ ★

The succession race got more interesting in the spring of 1996 when the front-runner, Bill Fields, suddenly announced that he was leaving the company to become the head of Blockbuster Entertainment.

The two most likely candidates to succeed Glass, Lee Scott and Tom Coughlin, had two of the most important jobs in the company. Both would be watched closely, and a contest between them seemed inevitable. But with the company going through tough times, rather than compete against one another, Scott and Coughlin decided to work together.

Self-effacing, eager to listen, visiting stores frequently in the Sam Walton tradition, Scott sought advice from merchandise managers and vendors. In the process he discovered that Wal-Mart had been accumulating far too much merchandise. Store personnel were having a hard time displaying what was current. When they did, the merchandise appeared dark and dingy. What customers mostly saw were markdowns in obvious contrast with the cultural anchor of everyday low pricing.

Over the next two years, Scott slashed $2 billion in inventory. He also asked suppliers to be more creative, in one case urging an apparel maker supplying jeans to pay more attention to fashion trends, resulting in a tripling of sales for that supplier. He sought to improve margins by altering the mix of merchandise and stepping up Wal-Mart's rollback program. He impressed colleagues by staying open to new ideas.

Meanwhile, Tom Coughlin attacked the problem of increased inventories in another way: by getting store managers to use technology more smartly. He wanted the stores to get more accurate readings on stock and to have buyers get a better sense of how much inventory to purchase. It was Coughlin who when he discovered early in 1997 that his store managers could not use the hand-held computers known as Telxons, whipped them into shape, with the result that inventories were cut and the company saved large amounts of money.

BOUNCING BACK

The company bounced back quickly. With sales in 1996 of $104.8 billion, Wal-Mart became the first retail company to top $100 billion in sales in a single year. It was the fourth-largest company in the United States and twelfth-largest in the world. Also that year Wal-Mart became the largest private employer in the United States, with 680,000 employees. It also had 115,000 employees outside the United States. The company replaced Woolworth on the Dow Jones Industrial Average. Wal-Mart had 1,960 stores in the United States, 344 Supercenters, 436 Sam's Clubs, and 314 international stores for a total of 3,054. It was serving more than 90 million customers a week.

The improvement continued: In 1997 sales grew to $117.9 billion and profits to $3.5 billion. Inventories rose by only 4 percent, resulting in a saving of $1.4 billion. The following year sales rose to $137.5 billion and earnings to $4.4 billion.

In 1998 Scott was promoted from executive vice president of merchandising to president and CEO of the Wal-Mart stores. That was the first indication that he was the likely successor to David Glass. In 1999 Scott was named vice chairman and COO of Wal-Mart stores—a further indication that he would likely be the next Wal-Mart CEO. Bob Martin retired in June 1999; some believed that he had made that decision at least in part because of the likelihood that Scott, not he, would be the next CEO.

Scott succeeded Don Soderquist, who became senior vice chairman. Tom Coughlin became President and CEO of the Wal-Mart stores division.

In 1999 Wal-Mart grew by 20 percent, to $164 billion in revenue. Its profits jumped to nearly $5.4 billion, fifteenth-highest in the United States that year.

There had been no announcements that Scott would succeed Glass until the actual one in January 2000 that Scott would take over as CEO and president.

The changing of the guard at Wal-Mart was greeted with little fanfare. Few thought that Scott would conduct business very differently from David Glass. Their offices were next to each other, so they merely exchanged quarters. Scott moved into the same corner office that Sam Walton had occupied, the one in which he had chewed out the young logistics man.

Wal-Mart board members, conscious that other companies suffered through messy, rancorous transitions, were cheered by how well the Glass-Scott transition went, "absolutely the smoothest, most positive succession I've seen," in the words of one of them. Investors took the announcement in stride: The stock dropped only 12 cents, to $65 a share, on the New York Stock Exchange. Few new CEOS ever walked into a company that was doing as well as Wal-Mart.

When the *Fortune* 500 list was started in 1955, Wal-Mart did not even exist. But in the year 2000 Wal-Mart was the second-largest company in America—only General Motors was larger. And unless some unexpected merger occurred among the top enterprises, Wal-Mart appeared likely to become Number One on the list in 2001.

The new leadership team consisted of chairman Rob Walton, CEO Lee Scott, and the head of stores, Tom Coughlin. Don Soderquist planned to retire in the summer of 2000.

David Glass remained around, though no longer in the top post;

he became the head of the executive committee of the board, responsible for implementing policy decisions of the board and acting on its behalf between meetings. Glass had other interests: he was the owner, chairman, and CEO of the Kansas City Royals major league baseball franchise.

FULL THROTTLE

With Wal-Mart's engines running at full throttle, Lee Scott did not have to worry about whether the company would grow—that was obvious. The international program was moving ahead nicely: Wal-Mart had just acquired ASDA in the United Kingdom. The Supercenter effort had gained great momentum. In the food industry, Wal-Mart was gaining an edge on some very tough competition.

Lee Scott's challenge—and he knew it—was to apply the culture and preside over the ever-more-complex organization without trying to be another Sam Walton. (It was understood by both the family and others on the management team that no one could be Sam Walton, nor should anyone try.) Jay Allen, the senior vice president for corporate affairs, recalled: "David [Glass] and Lee talked about how Lee shouldn't try to be like Sam, because there is only one Sam Walton."

As he settled into the CEO slot, Scott was conscious that he had been chosen to lead Wal-Mart not because he resembled Sam Walton but because he brought a particular set of leadership skills that were required at the time.

He had no interest in tampering with the Walton-inspired culture. It had worked well during the Sam Walton era, and it would serve nicely in the twenty-first century. Under David Glass there had been changes in how the culture had been applied, changes that were the result of Wal-Mart's immense size. Glass had visited Wal-Mart stores, keeping up the tradition that Sam Walton had begun, and Scott wanted to make such visits as well. But both Glass and Scott knew that Wal-Mart had become far too complicated and diffuse for the CEO to visit stores as often as Walton had. As Glass had done,

Scott would concentrate on the enablers of the culture, making sure that he and his senior colleagues pressed the various managers in the field to spearhead the dissemination of the cultural messages.

It was not surprising that Scott's leadership traits were more in keeping with the immense size of Wal-Mart. He knew that he could not be everywhere and could not do everything. His leadership style, he liked to say, was "more leadership by erosion than by direction. With the quality of people we have, it doesn't make a lot of sense to bring them in and say do x and y, but I have opinions, and so I will surface something they ought to think about. Sometimes they don't agree. After four or five times, they will usually say we're going to test this, just so we don't have to talk about it anymore."

Wal-Mart senior executives suggest that there is indeed nothing dogmatic or assertive about Lee Scott's management style. He does not sit in his office, come to a decision, and then communicate it to his colleagues. He is far more apt to rub shoulders with other executives, pass on his latest thoughts about something, and seek their advice before making a decision. He is, above all, a good listener, his colleagues say. It was a management trait that Scott used to good advantage when, selected to be the man in charge of merchandise in the mid-1990s, he was sorely lacking in knowledge about that side of the business; and it is a trait that he relies upon as CEO. He likes to manage by walking around, making the rounds of the offices of his senior executives (six of them report directly to him), paying surprise visits to people in the home office and the nearby Wal-Mart buildings. And he enjoys the give and take that goes on at Saturday morning meetings. He likes presiding over the meetings and asks colleagues to substitute for him far less than Sam Walton or David Glass did. Addressing an audience, he speaks softly but authoritatively, rarely showing emotion. He liked to lighten moments with humor, as he did when he noted to an audience when referring to the current spate of corporate scandals that the trouble was you didn't know whom you might wind up rooming with in jail.

He makes a point of visiting Wal-Mart stores once a week. "I find out where there are thunderstorms," he once said, "and I visit stores somewhere else." During the store visits, he wants to know how well managers and employees are practicing the culture. He leaves operational details to the managers. He knows that though Sam Walton in his day gave it a good try, it is impossible in the year 2002 for the CEO of Wal-Mart to manage every issue. During a store visit he will not scold a manager for being out of a certain product, but if checkout employees fail to say, "Thank you for shopping at Wal-Mart" after ringing up the bill, he will point out to the person that he or she has just pulled a cultural blooper—in front of the CEO.

★ ★ ★

Lee Scott's special skill set was in logistics. He had come up through the trucking ranks. He had a sense of what made Wal-Mart function at the macro level—not looking at the interior of the stores only but taking into account such crucial segments of the business as transportation, distribution, and technology. He believed that its superior handling of inventory was one of Wal-Mart's most important differentiators. But in public he talked about customer service and everyday low pricing as the critical factors of success, just as Sam Walton would have.

Scott's largest priority was to get Wal-Mart to pick up speed (though it was noted that few had ever attacked the company for being slow in the past). He wanted, as he said at the time, to get the company to stretch. "You could clearly see that the company was going to grow. But if you only had a small group of people who were making decisions for the company, you were going to bottleneck the company and keep it from growing at the rate that the opportunities provided."

So when Scott talked about stretching, he meant, among other things, upgrading the leadership team, getting various parts of it to learn about areas not under their specific aegis. He wanted to be able to get the leadership team conversant in a whole set of areas, not just their one specific area, so that he could get their input and their feedback. The idea was to prepare a few members of the team for even greater leadership roles in the future.

A REASON TO CELEBRATE

A high-water mark for Scott came on June 7, 2002, when Wal-Mart's shareholders met at the Bud Walton Arena at the University of Arkansas in Fayetteville. He was feeling good that morning.

He sat in the front row of the arena, a huge smile on his face, caught up in the enthusiasm of the crowd. When it was his turn to lead the Wal-Mart cheer from the stage, he did that little twist of the body that everyone does to mark the squiggly. He did not want to let himself get too giddy. He told me that a year earlier the shareholder meeting was decidedly more subdued, because Wal-Mart had not had that great a year. It was as if he were warning himself not to get too carried away.

But it was hard for him not to celebrate.

Just six weeks before—on April 15, 2002—Wal-Mart topped the *Fortune* 500 list of the largest American corporations for the first time. Scott had been CEO for two years and three months when *Fortune* hit the newsstands with the news.

Scott had every right to be giddy. He and the new Wal-Mart leadership team had accomplished the kind of breakaway growth that Sam Walton had never experienced. Back in 1997 sales had gone over the $100 billion mark for the first time. Four years later, in 2001, sales reached $219.8 billion. In short, it had taken Wal-Mart thirty-five years to reach $1 billion in sales. It had taken the company only another four years to double that remarkable figure.

Profits have grown at nearly the same remarkable rate. Net income in 2002 was $6.67 billion, up from $3.056 billion in 1996.

And the place just keeps getting bigger and bigger. Since 1997 Wal-Mart has added 1,360 stores, with average sales at those stores amounting to $41.9 million.

David Glass had kept the vow he made when Wal-Mart was going through a slump in the mid-1990s: Since January 1996 Wal-Mart had produced continuous quarters of increased growth.

★ ★ ★

And so the leadership team was in place. The company had never done better. It was turning in one record growth year after another. All seemed to be in place for years of remarkable progress to come. But there were gray shadows in the organization. They had been lingering just below the surface, and Lee Scott certainly felt that he would be judged by how much Wal-Mart grew. But it was increasingly clear that he would be judged as well by how well he dealt with his greatest challenge—the company's increasingly controversial reputation.

CHAPTER 12

A MATTER OF REPUTATION: TAKING THE GLOVES OFF

Trying to understand the present-day Wal-Mart in all its complexity proved a daunting exercise for me in the early part of my research. It was so big, more than 1.3 million employees, over 4,000 stores, spread out over America and nine other countries. How could one get a grasp on this place, I kept asking myself? Under Sam Walton, Wal-Mart was easy enough to describe and understand. All you had to do was put together a list of the founder's favorite business sayings and give a history of the place. But under the new leadership team— first headed by David Glass; then in more recent years by Lee Scott— it was not so simple. In earlier days Wal-Mart had no trouble defining itself, nor for that matter did it have a problem with having others trying to define it.

Yet this was precisely what was going on in the nineties, and no one said it better than Scott when we chatted in his office on October 3, 2002. He noted that he has been critical that "we've let someone else define our reputation."

I've kept that sentence in mind throughout the writing of this book, for he was helping me to understand that Wal-Mart was faced with perhaps the most important challenge of its history.

We are not talking about the reputation the stores have gained for looking the way they do, nor are we talking about its reputation for the quality of its products. We are referring to the reputation it has acquired and the controversy that has grown up surrounding its moves into communities and the way it handles its employees.

Few talked with me about these aspects of Wal-Mart's reputation, because of a long-standing tradition of Wal-Mart of not speaking publicly about the numerous assaults on the company down through the years. But there was also a feeling in the Wal-Mart ranks that these were far too sensitive topics for any but a few selected Wal-Mart leaders to discuss with an author. Whenever the subject was discussed in a media interview, Wal-Mart's spokespeople dashed off a few sentences and tried to hurry on to the next subject.

So although the company's controversial reputation was clearly on the minds of Wal-Mart's senior executives, none addressed the issue in public in any kind of depth for much of the nineties. And yet throughout that period, the subject was discussed, debated, argued about, and given a great deal of thought at board meetings and among senior executives.

In a nutshell, as Lee Scott suggested above, the issue came down to who was going to set the tone and who was going to define how people thought of the company.

Would it be Wal-Mart?

Or would it be its critics?

Unquestionably, these were the questions that crept into discussions more and more. "The real complexity at Wal-Mart that's difficult for us to deal with," said Scott, "is the outside world's desire to influence us or to absolutely change us."

The senior leadership at Wal-Mart knew that at some point it would have to get its arms around the issue. But it chose to take its time, uncertain what steps to take. Wal-Mart could afford to take its time: The media focused on what critics of the company were saying but never took the story to a higher level, never sought to find out what Wal-Mart was thinking or planning to do about the controversies. For the media it was easier, more colorful, and more provocative to write stories that effectively constituted a growing assault on the company. Therefore what was going on inside the company seemed fertile ground to plow in putting together a portrait of a company that by almost any measure was doing remarkably well but behind the scenes was wrestling, in a sense, with its soul.

★ ★ ★

For many years, one never heard the word "reputation" mentioned in Wal-Mart discussions.

In Sam Walton's day, the problems that the company faced in its relations with the external world were tiny compared with what they became. Fewer stores, fewer employees, and fewer customers—all of that meant fewer complaints from outsiders. Walton knew what a luxury it was to fly under the radar screen of the external world: "The more successful you become, the more suspicious they become of you. If you ever become a large-scale success, it's Katie bar the door. Suddenly, you make a very convenient villain, because everybody seems to love shooting at who's on top."

THE UNDERDOG

Walton accordingly promoted the idea that the company was too small and inconsequential for outsiders to bother with or take an interest in. Such a strategy made a good deal of sense, as Jay Allen, the senior vice president for corporate affairs, recalled: "From the standpoint of the business, from a competitive standpoint, it was better not having people know everything you're doing."

To get the point vividly across, Sam Walton subtly promoted the idea that Wal-Mart was the underdog. And for some time the strategy worked. This little outfit in Bentonville was the darling of Wall Street. It enjoyed a marvelous reputation, if only because people knew little about the place, and what they knew, they liked. Picking on Sam Walton and Wal-Mart was not done in the early days, for, as Don Soderquist noted: "You would have been a fool to pick on Sam because of his wonderful, wonderful reputation. To shoot darts at him or his company, people wouldn't have tolerated it. People would have said: 'You are out of your mind. Get out.'"

For as long as the media and the protest groups ignored Wal-Mart, the company could keep a low profile.

But it was not possible to ignore the outside world forever. When the media began to pay more attention to Walton and Wal-Mart, the founder cleverly went on the offensive, making sure to bolster the media's preconceived notion that Wal-Mart was a small, marginal retail player. Even as Walton gained fame in the mid-1980s as the wealthiest man in the United States, he shrewdly used the new media attention to give the impression that Wal-Mart was not at all mainstream or important. He sometimes complained that the media focused too much on him and not on the company, but the truth was that he preferred the spotlight not to shine on Wal-Mart either.

Jay Allen put it well when he said that "Wal-Mart had this image, and it was wrapped up in Sam, like he was this unsophisticated guy driving around in a beat-up pickup truck who was lucky enough to be in the right place at the right time. Any student of Wal-Mart knows that Sam was fortunate, but he was not lucky. What he did was brilliant in a very common sense sort of way. He knew what he was doing. Clearly, he was one of the most innovative and visionary business leaders of the twentieth century."

MOTHERHOOD AND APPLE PIE

David Glass remembered that Wal-Mart was a great success story, "sort of like motherhood and apple pie. The investment community loved us. The customers in particular loved our stores; we grew rapidly. The stock appreciated, so we seemed to have the best of all worlds until we began to achieve a significant size where we actually made a difference."

When members of the new leadership team reflected back to the Walton era, the period indeed seemed sublime: "We were able to run our business focused on what Sam Walton liked. Sam didn't have to go out and defend our reputation or assure that no harmful legislation was put in place."

Even if Scott can rhapsodize about a past without blemishes, controversies did occur. One source of friction had to do with the effort to unionize employees. Walton genuinely believed that it was critical to take good care of employees, not doing so was a major cause for his rivals' getting into trouble, he believed. But Wal-Mart jobs were low paying, making the stores ripe for union organization. To Walton, unions would get in the way of the strong, direct relationship he wanted to build with employees. Wal-Mart found that weak performance by store managers tended to cause unions to try to make inroads with Wal-Mart employees. So strong store leadership was an obvious way to immunize the company from the unions.

Acknowledging that he had once been cheap toward employees, he initiated a series of benefits with the obvious intention of keeping the unions at bay. With Wal-Mart's stock rising steadily, its profit-sharing plan turned numerous low-paid employees into wealthy people.

Sam Walton's struggles with the unions were sufficiently dramatic to warrant news coverage. But the union efforts and Walton's success in keeping the unions at bay came at a time when the media treated such dramas with a big yawn. (As of 2002, no Wal-Mart store has been completely unionized. The only union success came at a Wal-Mart in Jacksonville, Texas, where the United Food and Commercial Workers managed to organize one department.)

Even with such eruptions, Wal-Mart could cruise under the radar in the eighties. But it was not able to do so for much longer.

★ ★ ★

If there was a turning point, a point when complaints and protests were elevated to a new level, when minor sources of friction turned into full-blown controversies, it was some time after Sam Walton's death in the spring of 1992. Then, in Jay Allen's eyes, all bets were off. No longer did the media feel compelled to rally round Sam Walton and Wal-Mart. No longer did it only write stories about how great the company was. "It was almost like the gloves were off in terms of public external image, external forces. If you look back at the media coverage up to 1992, it was very positive. Either it was about Sam or all that he was about or about Wal-Mart, this upstart but well-run company catching Sears and Kmart."

THE STRUGGLE BEGINS

The problems for Wal-Mart developed slowly, almost imperceptibly at first. For a brief time after the founder's departure, Wal-Mart seemed able to hold on to a certain faceless anonymity. "Though we were a $43 billion company when Sam passed away," observed Lee Scott, "we were still able to avoid much notice; we were seen as the underdog, as a small-time company. We were the people from Bentonville, Arkansas, who had a pretty good company." Scott noted that people felt Wal-Mart would fall apart, that is, would stop growing, when it hit $1 billion in revenue; the same claim was made when it hit $100 billion. "We had detractors but not a great number. But we knew that we were going to struggle at some point."

The struggle developed in part because critics of Wal-Mart felt that it was contributing to urban sprawl and destroying the basis of small communities. The complaint almost always centered on the power that the company allegedly had to force the small mom-and-pop stores of small communities to close once a Wal-Mart arrived in town. Wal-Mart was blamed not only for the closure of those stores but also for turning the downtown areas of small communities into ghost towns. The charge put Wal-Mart on the defensive. But the critics back then were small in numbers and tended to focus on their local communities without trying to turn a local issue into a national one. Fragmented and thus weak, these critics were too inchoate to bring their issues to national attention. But by the early 1990s, groups began coalescing, communicating with one another over the Internet and telephone, offering information and support.

Most importantly, the critics finally started getting through to the media. The idea that Wal-Mart might be flawed here and there got the media's attention. To Don Soderquist, the motivation for attacking Wal-Mart was crystal clear: "As with all people who are successful, [Abraham] Lincoln said, you don't pull yourself up by putting people down, but in [our] society, we tend to do that. The big guys can't be that good; let's find something wrong with them."

Finding something wrong with the big guys was bound to resonate with the media, which was just beginning to take a new look at Corporate America. It was not that the media chose to single Wal-Mart out for scrutiny. It was more that the media was waking up in the late 1980s and early 1990s and realizing that the business world in general needed far more coverage.

It was not the media's job to analyze whether the assaults on Wal-Mart were motivated by individuals and groups with hostile intentions toward the company. Its job was to decide whether there was a story worth printing. As the assaults mounted, they warranted news coverage. But to Wal-Mart executives, the increasing criticism had mostly to do with the inability of its rivals to successfully compete against Wal-Mart and the resulting frustration they felt. "With success," said Scott, "has come the baggage of people who find us difficult to compete with. They then reach out to try to stop us in some way that they can't accomplish through straightforward competition. When we run our program correctly, we really are a good competitor. So people look at zoning and our level of compliance. Some have tried to change zoning laws so they don't have to compete with us. In the past, good intentions and good efforts were seen as very important whereas today people are cynical. We get a lot more press today than we did in our history, and it's likely to get worse rather than better."

Jay Allen added: "Like in any battle, your opponents will attack you where they see you as vulnerable. We've seen many of our opponents come after us governmentally and in the media, in those places where they see us as more vulnerable."

The venom that its rivals felt toward Wal-Mart grew, and Wal-Mart often found itself assailed for wanting to enter a new community. "I don't know how things happened," David Glass said, "but you suddenly become a target rather than everybody's favorite. We were very naive going into that, because from the very beginning we'd always tried to do the right thing. We got involved in the communities. We gave back to them. We supported the appropriate community charities. We tried to do all the right things. Our motivation was not from a p.r. standpoint. But we genuinely believed that if we did the right thing, good things would happen to us. Lots was written about Wal-Mart going into small towns and putting mom-and-pops out of business. When we suddenly became a target it took us a while to realize that that this was an ongoing situation.

"Really only a few people tried to write the real story that said the states of Louisiana and Colorado did a study indicating the failure of small mom-and-pop stores in towns without a Wal-Mart was far greater than in towns with one; that we added to economic growth and viability in the communities we served. The reason that mom-and-pops failed was because they wanted to close their stores at 5 P.M. and didn't want to be open on weekends, and they didn't want to modernize them and didn't want to make investments. But it was fashionable to say Wal-Mart puts people out of business. Everyone picks up on that. The media picks up on those things. We realized we were going to be a target."

★ ★ ★

Wal-Mart became the target in the early 1990s when residents of Greenfield, Massachusetts (population: 18,000), went into battle against the retailer for planning to put up a store in their town. Wal-Mart offered to finance some badly needed road improvements and because the site was formerly an Indian campground, it even offered to pay for an archaeological dig.

Community leaders in Greenfield had already given Wal-Mart their support for the necessary zoning change from industrial to commercial, but it still required approval by a community vote. Members of the community took a look at the artist's sketch and quickly mobilized. The campaign included a barrage of bumper stickers, lawn signs, and newspaper ads that suggested that the planned Wal-Mart would be so large that three baseball stadiums the size of Boston's Fenway Park could fit on the site.

The Greenfield protesters were part of a new grassroots movement across America that had been silent until the early 1990s. Fighting major retailers like Wal-Mart to keep them from moving into their neighborhoods had once seemed an impossible challenge, but protesters eventually rose up against what they perceived to be the likely fallout from a big store's arrival: more traffic, more air pollution, and the slow demise of hometown retailers.

In late October 1993 Greenfield's population voted to keep Wal-Mart from building a store by turning down the proposed rezoning measure. Sixty percent of the residents voted. Proponents of the site were angry; they felt that the protest group had deprived residents of the opportunity to purchase goods and services more inexpensively, and they had also looked forward to the economic boost that Wal-Mart would have provided to the community, especially the jobs that would have been created.

At the time a Wal-Mart spokesman was quoted as saying that for every Greenfield, there were literally scores of other communities that would give their eyetooth for a Wal-Mart.

The events of Greenfield received much media treatment. *Time* ran a long story titled, "They're Up Against the Wal: Communities are fighting to keep out mega-retailers like Wal-Mart," in its issue of November 1, 1993.

★ ★ ★

During the nineties, when Wal-Mart had thousands of stores and hundred of employees per store and the media was increasingly interested in the company, its controversies became magnified. Events in stores that would have been passed up by the media when Sam Walton was in charge began to receive not just local but national or even international media coverage. It might be a woman giving birth in a store, a deer running loose through the aisles, or a shooting on a Wal-Mart site. The shooting would have made the local news even in the eighties, but the other two stories might not have warranted any coverage at all. Now everything that happened at a Wal-Mart was fair game for the media.

The more Wal-Mart grew and the more financial success it had, the more the media paid attention to it. And the media's attention was naturally at its height when the story concerned a point of friction between the company and a customer or between the company and its employees. When a number of employees complained that they had been forced to work overtime without extra pay, the media turned that into a big story. When some believed that Wal-Mart had too few women managers and a lawsuit resulted, it was news. When some accused Wal-Mart, which is self-insured, of paying too little on workers' compensation claims, the media followed the story closely.

A NEW AND PERPLEXING ISSUE

The gloves had come off.

While all this was taking place, Walton's successors were doing very little to ascertain whether they even had a reputation problem. Their initial reaction was to act as if there was no such problem. They behaved that way with good reason: Confronting the issue of Wal-Mart's reputation was never part of the training that David Glass and Lee Scott got at Wal-Mart. The culture had nothing to say about how to deal with the outside world because, to all intents and purposes, the outside world had presented no real challenge to Sam Walton. Walton's view that it was best to keep a low profile, to focus on the stores, and to deal with the outside world as little as possible was widely accepted.

★ ★ ★

Then the equivalent of an earthquake rocked Wal-Mart's world.

It struck eight and a half months after Sam Walton's death.

On December 22, 1992, NBC's *Dateline* aired a program about Wal-Mart. Its roots dated back to Sam Walton's time. Jane Pauley, the anchor, wrote to Walton, noting that Wal-Mart deserved to be treated better in the media since it was doing so well financially. She was ready to do an upbeat piece on Wal-Mart for *Dateline*. Ever cautious about the media, not overly eager to get Wal-Mart on national television, Walton sat on the idea for a while. He eventually agreed to the project, but by the time he gave his assent, the leadership of the company had effectively passed to David Glass.

With Walton and Glass giving their approval to the project, NBC was allowed to film inside Wal-Mart stores and to interview David Glass. Jane Pauley continued to assure Wal-Mart officials that the program would be positive.

The program opened that evening with an announcer saying: "A major *Dateline* investigation—'Bring It Home to the USA'—the marketing campaign of Wal-Mart stores. Their ads promote 'Made in the USA.' Their shelves announce it, and their employees love it, but how does it square with this? Children in Bangladesh working up to twenty hours a day making clothes for Wal-Mart. Brian Ross goes undercover. First, are cheap imports Wal-Mart's secret of success?"

Jane Pauley then declared: "One retailer that for over a decade has been soaring like an American eagle. It is a fitting comparison, because Wal-Mart is practically becoming an institution, as American as apple pie." Then her fellow anchor, Stone Philips, chimed in that *Dateline* had conducted a two-month investigation that would show that Wal-Mart's carefully styled image promoting American goods and the American worker had a side that people were not aware of.

The program tried to show a contrast between what Wal-Mart said and did and the reality. It began by showing Wal-Mart employees giving the cheer. Ross credited Wal-Mart's employees with "a kind of zeal and competitive spirit rarely seen in American business" and noted that Wal-Mart was bigger than Sears or Kmart and was in fact the largest retailer in the world.

Then came the zinger: "all with red and blue promises of low prices and, even better, what appears to be products made in the USA." In using that marketing campaign and showcasing it on television commercials, Wal-Mart had achieved, *Dateline* said, "a marketing masterstroke." Only it was, Ross said, too good to be true, and Wal-Mart was pulling a fast one on the American public: It was not true that Wal-Mart bought American whenever it could; it was actually importing merchandise of all kinds, and the places where these goods were being made did not show up on Wal-Mart commercials. "There are some secrets of Wal-Mart's success that Wal-Mart would prefer to be kept secret."

Ross then recounted how he had traveled to what he called an "Asian sweatshop" in Bangladesh that he said was full of children making Wal-Mart clothes. David Glass then appeared saying that "we can make merchandise in this country as efficiently and productively for every bit the value as they can anywhere in the world." Glass explained that Sam Walton had started the Buy America campaign in 1985, and in the seven years of its existence, Wal-Mart had converted over $6 billion of merchandise that would have been done overseas to domestic manufacturing.

Ross then showed a tape in which, using a hidden camera, he had filmed a number of departments in Wal-Marts where Buy USA signs hung over clothes that had labels indicating that they had been made overseas; they included winter jackets for children made in Bangladesh. Ross asked Glass to explain.

Glass suggested that "that would have been a mistake at the store level" then said that someone would be foolish to put such garments on a rack under a Made in America sign "and believe you could fool people." Wal-Mart did not do a lot of business in Bangladesh, Glass insisted, to which Ross countered that he was told that on a regular basis young children were employed to make clothes for Wal-Mart there. Glass responded: "To my knowledge we don't buy from any vendor that uses child labor."

Ross then showed a tape of what he alleged was a Bangladesh factory with three floors full of children, some as young as nine and ten, making clothes for Wal-Mart. The children were paid $12 to $20 a month or 5 to 8 cents an hour. Sometimes they were kept well past midnight in order to fulfill the day's quotas.

Glass reiterated that Wal-Mart made a "concentrated effort not to buy merchandise from manufacturers where it was made by child labor." Ross said that the Bangladesh factory manager said he had been doing business with Wal-Mart buyers for more than a year.

When Ross told Glass of a fire at the same factory that took many lives, the Wal-Mart CEO replied: "There are tragic things that happen all over the world."

Ross: "That's all you want to say about it?"

Glass: "Excuse me, I don't know what else I would say about it."

With that, a Wal-Mart vice president came on the set and announced that the interview was over. The camera kept rolling. Ross was told that any further questions would have to be submitted in writing. Glass then walked out of the room. *Fortune* noted that it was the kind of drama reporters live for. Wal-Mart could have easily lived without it.

Two weeks later Glass asked NBC to return. He now had a good deal to say about the investigation.

When Ross did, Glass told him that he had been unprepared to answer questions about the Bangladesh issue at their first interview. He was now prepared. He had sent someone to Bangladesh who found no evidence of child labor, he noted, and added: "So I think the stories of children being locked in and exploited are certainly something we've not been able to verify."

Ross acted stupefied: "Your man was there and saw no children?"

Glass: "No. You and I might define children differently. Of course, in Bangladesh a twelve-year-old should not be working."

Ross: "But they are. We saw them."

Glass: "We have not been able to substantiate that."

Ross showed Glass a tape of another Bangladesh factory where, he said, were "more of the twelve-year-old children Wal-Mart says it could not find." Ross asked Glass whether he believed these pictures.

Glass: "Why should I not believe that?"

Ross: "These pictures of young children don't contradict the assurances you received?"

Glass: "The pictures you showed me mean nothing to me. I'm not sure where they were or who they were. They could have been of anything."

Ross: "They're not of anything."

Glass: "I'm comfortable with what we've done."

Dateline accused Wal-Mart of further dishonesty in connection with "Bring It Home to the USA," alleging that Sweaters USA in Siler City, North Carolina, had to close after Wal-Mart shifted orders overseas to get a somewhat cheaper product. Glass retorted that Wal-Mart had stopped dealing with the factory because the product was incorrectly styled and therefore did not sell. Price was not at issue.

WIDESPREAD SUPPORT

As devastating as the program appeared to be to Wal-Mart, David Glass noted soon afterward that the company was getting widespread support. It came, however, mostly from within Wal-Mart's own ranks. Some one hundred thousand employees had sent signatures of support to his office. NBC received the largest reaction of any *Dateline* show to that date: Seven thousand calls and letters came in, mostly from Wal-Mart staff assailing the network for airing the program. Wal-Mart's fear—the fear of any company on the receiving end of such negative media coverage—was that it would hurt business. But judging by Wal-Mart sales that month, the program did not cause harm: Sales were up 10 percent in stores open at least a year and 25 percent overall, ahead of all others in the industry by a large margin. In the year after the program was aired, Wal-Mart increased its annual revenue by $15 billion.

A decade after the *Dateline* program, Wal-Mart officials described it as an ambush that left them feeling betrayed. Referring to the program in a 2002 interview, David Glass tried to suggest that it was past and forgotten, but he still seemed bitter—with good reason. He had had to take the full brunt of the nasty allegations, knowing how ill-prepared he was to counter NBC's shrewd and detailed investigation. While negative stories had appeared before, mostly in print, this marked the first time that a national news operation had targeted Wal-Mart for alleged abuses, and senior executives at Wal-Mart sensed that the days of avoiding the media's glare were over.

The program had an important effect on Wal-Mart. The effect was gradual, but it eventually took hold. A simple fact of life could no longer be denied: The company had become visible, exposed, and controversial.

It was a painful learning experience, as David Glass told me a decade after the program: "Then," he recalled sadly, "we sort of got blindsided about things that we didn't know about it. We were naive. We hadn't been attacked before. Sam and I always said that if you do the right thing and if you have integrity, everything you do in business will work out all right. You don't have to spend a lot of time doing p.r. work or being active in Washington. Our business is to buy and sell merchandise to customers, and we'll ignore all the outside distractions. That will take care of itself if we do the right thing."

Now it was clear that doing the right things or at least trying to was not enough. It was not possible to ignore the outside distractions, because they were not going to go away. But recognizing the depth of the problem did not mean that Wal-Mart was ready to come forward with a solution. Senior executives knew one thing: The company had to think very, very carefully about the *Dateline* experience and all that it meant.

CHAPTER 13

A STRATEGY FOR THE TWENTY-FIRST CENTURY: THE NEW OPENNESS

If a company can be said to lose its innocence, Wal-Mart certainly did with the airing of the *Dateline* program. As the dust began to settle, as the bruises and cuts, still distasteful mementos of the ambush, began to heal, Wal-Mart's upper echelons decided to hunker down. It chose to treat the experience as a powerful lesson of why a company like Wal-Mart should cooperate with the media as little as possible.

Yet the *Dateline* program was a brutal reminder that the media would not leave Wal-Mart alone. So when board members and senior executives started to analyze what had gone wrong, there was anger and frustration of course, but mostly there was confusion and uncertainty about how to rehabilitate Wal-Mart's media reputation. In time, two conflicting schools of thought emerged, their sharply opposing views keeping the company from tackling the issue head-on in the short term.

The hardliners, who were convinced that Wal-Mart could ill afford any further *Dateline* exposes, would have preferred simply turning off the lights in the public relations department and affixing a "Closed" sign permanently on the door. The feeling on this side was summed up by board members who argued, "We were tricked by the *Dateline* program. It won't happen again." Other more moderate voices doubted that shutting down Wal-Mart's public relations operation would keep the media at bay. The moderates believed that *Dateline* had certainly not been Wal-Mart's finest hour, but withdrawing into a shell hardly seemed realistic in a period when the media was becoming increasingly aggressive in its coverage of business, including the retail industry. If Wal-Mart had been "maybe unsophisticated," as Lee Scott later said of the *Dateline* experience, it had not been arrogant. It was that kind of ambivalence toward *Dateline* that characterized the debate at the senior levels during the early 1990s.

CHANGING LANDSCAPE

The moderates read the changing landscape and understood that a company the size of Wal-Mart, so powerful and so influential, could not expect the media to remain docile. They wanted Wal-Mart to take the task of public relations more seriously, to worry less about how to avoid future ambushes and concentrate more on getting all the positive aspects of Wal-Mart into every major story. These same voices advocated a renewed effort to whip the stores into shape and make sure that employees were properly treated. The moderates understood, certainly far better than the extremists, that the media would write negatively about Wal-Mart only if legitimate complaints from employees or customers surfaced and if those complaints appeared to affect large numbers. "We started to ask," said Scott, "is what others are saying true? How do we make sure it's not true?"

For three years after the *Dateline* program, all of these issues bubbled up to the surface as a grand debate of sorts occurred, focused on some of the toughest and most significant questions the company had ever asked itself.

Do we simply continue our policy of being very cool to the media?

Should we become proactive and actively promote ourselves to the media?

If we decide to be more active, what changes in the organization would that entail?

The debate within the Wal-Mart board of directors lasted a long time, not only because some board members remained in shock over the *Dateline* experience but also because for some board members, becoming proactive toward the media represented a veritable revolution in their minds. For the disciples of Sam Walton, which included some board members, the power of his thinking on the media still held sway.

Ultimately, the balance was tipped in favor of giving Wal-Mart's public relations effort a professional feel, giving those in charge of p.r. a mandate to become far more proactive toward the media. The board feared that the company would be caught flat-footed again, as it had been in December 1992.

★ ★ ★

In the mid 1990s, as the company had grown to become one of the most visible and recognized brands in the United States, Wal-Mart senior management decided to add depth and professional resources in the corporate affairs area, which included corporate communications (news media relations), government relations, and the Wal-Mart Foundation (community relations). At the time senior management was particularly concerned with the interaction between Wal-Mart and the news media, but it also realized that all three of these areas needed to be improved in order to better support the company's growth.

In 1995 the company hired Jay Allen to head and further develop the corporate affairs area for Wal-Mart. He had studied journalism at the University of Texas and wanted to become a sportswriter, but he has spent his career on the public relations side of the business. Thus he came to Wal-Mart with a strong background in corporate and agency communications: eight years in public relations and community relations work at Southwestern Bell and then another eight years at the public relations firm of Fleishman-Hillard. He inherited a staff that included fifteen professional managers. By 2002, with new corporate affairs initiatives, added expertise in the government relations area, and improved capabilities in corporate communications and the Wal-Mart Foundation, Allen had, reluctantly, increased the size of his division more than double since 1995. He did make the point that it remained small compared with similar departments in many other major companies.

"When I joined corporate affairs in 1995, I saw a relatively small group of people working as hard as they could in a difficult environment," Allen said. "It was so clear that we had to get better and that we had to get there fast."

In the past Wal-Mart's public-relations staff understood that its main function was to keep Wal-Mart out of the news. Jay Allen and his team took a different, more proactive approach. From now on, the company would attempt to deal head-on and professionally with the hundreds of reporters who called Wal-Mart every week, providing information and messages that did a better job of portraying Wal-Mart as a leading retailer, good employer, and responsible corporate citizen. The company became much more opportunistic in placing positive stories about Wal-Mart. In short, rather than allowing others to define Wal-Mart, Allen was given marching orders to make sure that Wal-Mart was the one that defined what the company stood for.

NOT AN OPEN BOOK

In the spring of 2002, members of Wal-Mart's public-relations team understood that with Wal-Mart getting a lot of media attention, the wisest course was to be as helpful and credible as possible. To be sure, Wal-Mart had not become an open book. Its leaders still had a natural inclination to avoid publicity, unless the publicity produced a clear benefit to the business. "The company never seeks out publicity on behalf of its senior leaders. That would never work at Wal-Mart," said Tom Williams, senior manager, U.S. media relations. For example, for two years CNBC made repeated requests to interview Lee Scott. Finally, the timing felt right, and he agreed to sit down for an interview with CNBC's Maria Bartiromo in Bentonville in early 2002. The interview aired in March of that year. The company wanted as much of the story as possible to focus on the Wal-Mart culture rather than Scott. The visit was timed so that Bartiromo could attend one of the legendary Saturday morning meetings.

However, the company was still chary with financial disclosure beyond its obligations as a public company, believing that vagueness was a virtue. The less their competitors knew about the specific operations of the company, the better, in Wal-Mart's view. The company accordingly publishes very few figures. It will not divulge how much money hourly employees make (except to say that they are paid the minimum wage in all cases and that wages are competitive in their individual communities). In conversation its public relations staff will note that some of its Supercenters can bring in over $100 million a year and that the manager of a successful Wal-Mart store can earn in excess of $100,000 a year. But none of these figures appear in print in any official form.

But unlike the period before the mid-1990s, it was now possible to talk to public relations managers and get answers on a wide variety of issues affecting Wal-Mart. That had not always been the case. Among the 600 to 800 queries that the p.r. staff receives each week, it might answer a question on how Wal-Mart handles forged checks or what the company's policy is on current 401(k) legislation. When a deer ran loose in a Wal-Mart in the spring of 2002, journalists were eager to know every detail the p.r. staff could supply. And the staff obliged, even volunteering that the deer had not tried to make any purchases.

The company also began to give out stories proactively on a variety of topics, particularly at the local level.

★ ★ ★

Just as the attitude toward public relations was changing, becoming more proactive and more open, so too was there a loosening-up of Wal-Mart's long-standing resistance to proactive government relations. Setting the tone and the policy of noninvolvement in government relations, Sam Walton saw little reason to cultivate government officials in order to improve Wal-Mart's situation. He established friendships with politicians, especially Bill Clinton and George Bush the elder.

It took Wal-Mart some time before it decided that it needed a stepped-up lobbying effort.

One reason for the turnabout was a growing sense within Wal-Mart that regulatory agencies were increasingly eager to take on the retail giant, if only because of its size and influence. Plagued with limited enforcement budgets, and too few lawyers, the agencies were increasingly casting an eye on Wal-Mart because, at least in the view of the company's legal staff, it was the most practical, sensible way for the agency to behave. To make a legal point on some employment issue, did it make more sense to go after the largest employer in the country or one of the smaller ones? The answer was obvious. To succeed against the largest employer meant that smaller employers would most likely fall in line. Wal-Mart had accordingly watched with growing concern as regulatory agencies at the federal and state level became more aggressive toward the company.

With interest groups, including the unions, seeking legislation to weaken Wal-Mart, the need for a greater lobbying effort on Wal-Mart's part grew increasingly obvious. Turning to the politicians, these groups sought "big box" legislation that would specifically bar Wal-Mart from putting a Supercenter in a community. Most of these efforts failed, including a proposed state law in California that would have barred Supercenters from the state. But a few such laws have passed.

The need for lobbying efforts at the state level was made clear as well when protest groups sought to restrict Wal-Mart's power through legislation. In October 2002, a law was passed in California barring Wal-Mart from acquiring an industrial bank. Wal-Mart had hoped to acquire the bank so that it could process its own credit-card transactions, thus driving costs down and passing the savings on to the customer.

After Walton's death, Wal-Mart did step up its activities in Washington, D.C., at first getting its point of view across through various trade associations then, in 1999, opening its first government-relations office in the nation's capital. (The office grew to four people by December 2002. Another twelve in Bentonville handle state and local government issues.) "We've reached a point," said Jay Allen, "where we have to be more active in Washington, D.C., and at all levels of government. And so we have become much more involved on matters that affect our business and our associates."

Wal-Mart's policy is not to get involved in trying to affect legislation unless it has a direct impact on customers and employees. It will try to stop only legislation that would cause the company to raise its prices, since that would harm its ability to maintain everyday low prices. It would also rally against certain kinds of health-care or tax legislation, because such legislation would make it more expensive to run its operation. Lee Scott summed up the new policies in Washington: "Our efforts in government are to do no harm. We ask only, does [the legislation] affect our customers or our associates?"

★ ★ ★

All the railing against Wal-Mart for allegedly causing harm to small communities eventually led the company to take a careful look at its community relations efforts through the Wal-Mart Foundation. The management certainly believed that Wal-Marts were not harmful to small communities; indeed, it felt strongly that Wal-Mart was raising the standard of living for millions of consumers through its everyday low prices. But the management also wondered whether there were things that Wal-Mart could be doing better to demonstrate that when it entered communities it could be counted on to be a good corporate citizen.

Sam Walton encouraged his stores and store managers to be involved in their communities. It became clear in the mid-1990s that such involvement needed to have even higher priority.

ACTIVATING THE STORE MANAGERS

It had been conventional wisdom at Wal-Mart that while store managers had very demanding jobs—working twelve-hour days, sometimes more—many did not see themselves or their stores as community leaders. The truth was, however, that Wal-Mart stores and store managers were thought of as very important in their communities; often store managers were the most important business figures in that town.

The communities were eager for Wal-Mart store managers to participate in community affairs, to give to local charities, to serve on local chambers of commerce, to take turns running merchant organizations. But to many of the store managers, that kind of participation seemed countercultural: Wal-Mart's culture had taught them to be humble, to keep their heads down, to do their work and focus on their store and their employees. And yet, the local Wal-Mart was often the largest employer in the community, leading community leaders to believe that the managers had a responsibility to share some of their business acumen and profits with the community.

Starting in the mid-1990s a beefed-up Wal-Mart community-affairs operation began to take a serious look at how to improve the relationship between the stores and the community. "We told the stores that community involvement was important to do because it was the right thing to do," said Jay Allen. Wal-Mart had another motive for strengthening store-community ties: The most profitable stores were those most strongly engaged in the community. In short, community involvement was good business.

The Wal-Mart Foundation staff, numbering eighteen in 2002, labored hard to get the stores involved in community affairs with considerable success. Members of the senior management noted that by the fall of 2002, every store was participating satisfactorily in the communities, and the company was routinely recognized as a leader in such endeavors. All of this was brought home to me on my very first day of touring Wal-Mart stores in the spring of 2002: It seemed that everyone I met at Wal-Mart was involved in some kind of community effort or another. Sharon Weber, a communications manager in the public-relations department, was a leader in a missing-child program, a problem Wal-Mart has, what with so many stores and so many parents taking kids to the stores. Weber took me to the Morgan Nick Foundation, where I met Colleen Nick, whose daughter Morgan disappeared five years ago. The Morgan Nick Foundation was a Wal-Mart project.

★ ★ ★

In the same way that Wal-Mart was organizing its public-relations and community-relations operations differently, it was taking a whole new look at its legal effort. Just as much a part of the public relations problems that Wal-Mart experienced in the nineties was the storm of litigation thrown its way day after day.

Power, influence, and especially bigness had brought with it a whole new set of problems that put Wal-Mart in constant legal disputes. As long as the company kept getting larger and the number of customers visiting its stores increased, the number of lawsuits filed against the company was likely to increase. Indeed, in the early 1990s there were from 2,000 to 2,500 lawsuits pending against the company; that figure had grown to 8,000 by October 2002.

No matter how carefully the company operated its stores, some people were going to slip on the floors. Boxes were going to be accidentally dropped on customers. Employees would feel discriminated against—whether on the basis of pay, gender, or work conditions.

With a hundred million people visiting Wal-Mart stores every week, with more than 1.3 million employees in over 4,000 stores, the opportunity for legal disputes and lawsuits grew and grew. The ever-expanding Wal-Mart was carrying more and more goods and providing more services in its stores. Lawsuits filed against Wal-Mart by customers slipping and falling as a result of spilled French fries or soft drinks were unheard of in earlier days, but with Wal-Mart opening floor space to fast-food franchises, yet another source of litigation had developed.

The number of class-action suits, the most dangerous kind for Wal-Mart, had grown from only one in 1998 to more than ninety in October 2002. The explosion in these class-action suits was a relatively new phenomenon and has become a priority for the Wal-Mart legal staff, because if a class is certified within Wal-Mart, tens of thousands of people would become part of the case.

Disgruntled customers and employees have become so litigious that legal analysts believe that other than the U.S. government, no

American entity is sued more than Wal-Mart. Whether that statement is true, it was reported that the company was sued nearly once every two hours, every day of the year. Juries were deciding cases in which Wal-Mart was a defendant six times every business day.

All of those lawsuits could not help but harm the company's reputation. Worsening its reputation was Wal-Mart's tactic to admit only rarely that it was wrong. Judges and lawyers grew increasingly frustrated with a company that seemed to suggest that it could do almost no wrong and appeared to use a variety of aggressive tactics, all of them perfectly legal, to minimize its chances of losing in the courts.

Wal-Mart developed a reputation within the legal system that once it made up its mind not to settle a lawsuit, nothing could budge it. That reputation was not entirely true, but the view of Wal-Mart was of a company that said: "By God, when we're right, we'll fight." This perception was so widely believed that one circuit court stated that it would not set up settlement conferences, since it understood that Wal-Mart would never settle. A veritable cottage industry has arisen among lawyers who specialize in suing Wal-Mart, using the Internet to share documents and other material.

ONLY PART OF THE BATTLE

Winning in court was only part of the battle. The other was winning on the public relations front. Here Wal-Mart was losing ground. That explains why the old attitudes that Wal-Mart had been employing in the courtroom were by the turn of the twenty-first century giving away to a far less rigid view. Without announcing any change of policy, Wal-Mart adopted a more open view of the lawsuits that had been piling up over the years and helping to define the company's reputation.

The old tactics, especially rarely admitting to being wrong, ran counter to the way that most American companies handled lawsuits. They would often settle the suits, preferring not to go to trial, even if their opponents had weak cases. Wal-Mart's tactics were aimed at protecting the company's reputation—and maintaining its privacy. Company papers were kept private. When it entered into a settlement, Wal-Mart sought a confidentiality agreement to keep the amount paid to the plaintiff a secret.

★ ★ ★

Of the roughly 8,000 cases pending against Wal-Mart, some 5,100 were injury related. In October 2002 a Wal-Mart driver settled into the driver's seat of a company truck, introduced himself, and pointed out a few cars nearby: "They would like nothing better than to have an accident with a Wal-Mart truck. They think they can clean up that way."

Thousands of the lawsuits against Wal-Mart were fairly ordinary—people allegedly falling on slippery floors or icy parking lots. Some were unpleasant, among them claims made by the survivors of an Alabama woman whose husband killed her after he allegedly purchased a rifle illegally at a Wal-Mart. There were employment-discrimination suits, such as the one filed in San Francisco in June 2001 by six women who were or had been Wal-Mart employees. In three cases filed in federal and state courts in Colorado, judges agreed to give class status to Wal-Mart pharmacists who alleged that the company had not paid them overtime, thus violating the Fair Labor Standards Act. When bargain-hunters rushed to a Wal-Mart just before Christmas in 1998 to purchase the much-sought-after Furby toys, those who were injured when shoppers stampeded through the store filed suit. At least six female plaintiffs argued that they were injured when hundreds of shoppers pushed for a good position at Wal-Mart stores in Pennsylvania, Tennessee, and Georgia to try to buy the few furry, owl-like dolls that were huge sellers that holiday season.

Wal-Mart once fought such suits with unbridled tenacity, earning it a bad reputation in the court system. Illustrating that tenacity was a case in Ohio where a company forklift operator died of injuries sustained when a truck he was loading prematurely pulled away from the dock. Although on-the-job injuries are ordinarily handled as workers' compensation claims, the employee's family filed a wrongful death suit against the company seeking additional damages. The suit and another filed by the family against Wal-Mart dragged on for years before they were settled. After numerous trials, large jury awards, and appeals—all unfavorable to Wal-Mart—the company finally settled the case in 2002 for an undisclosed sum. Similarly, Wal-Mart vigorously defended a number of defamation and malicious prosecution lawsuits filed in the mid-1990s by former employees who had been accused of stealing tools and other company property. In several of these suits, the local prosecutor refused to press charges, and Wal-Mart was unable to produce clear ownership records for the property or to refute testimony that the employees had received permission to borrow or keep the items in question. The first trial resulted in a jury verdict against Wal-Mart for $1.6 million and was settled after the state court of appeals affirmed the verdict against the company. Wal-Mart settled the related cases in 2002 under terms that remain confidential.

But the old attitude—of fighting cases with unbridled tenacity—was changing. A new attitude of flexibility was developing.

The change was especially apparent in late July 2002 when Wal-Mart settled a suit that was brought by Robert McClung, whose wife had been abducted from a parking lot in Memphis, Tennessee, and murdered. Wal-Mart shared the parking lot with other stores. For a decade Wal-Mart fought McClung vigorously. Then in May 2002 Wal-Mart proposed mediation. His lawyer, Bruce Kramer, was "more than skeptical." However, a few months later Kramer acknowledged that Wal-Mart had indeed settled the highly publicized case through voluntary mediation.

ENDING A CONFLICT OF INTEREST

No one at Wal-Mart acknowledged to the outside world that the legal department was becoming more open. But it was certainly felt inside the home office. One of the first inside changes occurred when a new policy was invoked that a Wal-Mart official named as a defendant in a suit against Wal-Mart would no longer be invited to take part in high-level strategy meetings on how to defend that suit. It had been common practice for individuals and departments named in a suit as defendants to take part in the decision making that helped determine how Wal-Mart would defend the suit. Having an accused Wal-Mart official participate in those high-level strategy meetings had a subtle detrimental effect on the decision making, in the view of the new legal management. To the new legal management, the participation of Wal-Mart defendants in those strategy meetings was a conflict of interest and the practice was stopped.

Another policy was shaped inside the legal department, a less specific one but equally important. Shedding its past policy of fighting nearly every lawsuit, the legal department would take a careful look at each piece of litigation against Wal-Mart and do some objective soul-searching to try to determine what a judge and jury might think and decide about the case. In effect, Wal-Mart's legal staff would force itself to take off its partisan hat and act as if it were a third party. By adopting this new policy of dispassionately assessing its chances of winning litigation, Wal-Mart sought to send a credible message that it was in fact a reasonable litigant.

Facilitating the communication of the message was the company's decision to bring in a great many new lawyers with deep litigation experience into the litigation group. In the past Wal-Mart had engaged lawyers lacking such experience. The Wal-Mart legal department grew from only thirty lawyers as late as the year 2000 to ninety in the fall of 2002. Merely having so many new people with litigation experience automatically resulted in far more dispassionate analysis. With a fresh team that had substantial litigation experience, the legal team was ready to work on a fresh approach toward settling lawsuits.

Why the more open legal attitude? Most likely it had to do with a number of court losses in the late 1990s—described as both embarrassing and expensive for Wal-Mart—and with the continuing negative publicity it was receiving for its tough stance against lawsuits.

But perhaps most important was the appointment of Lee Scott as Wal-Mart's CEO in January 2000. He had clearly signaled to the legal department that he welcomed the changes. That was all that Tom Hyde and Tom Mars needed to know. These were the two men, both hired after Scott became CEO, who spearheaded the legal changes.

The 52-year-old Hyde had been senior vice president and general counsel of the defense contractor Raytheon since 1992. He was hired in June 2001 to the newly created position of executive vice president for legal and corporate affairs. Hyde had charge of the legal operation, which meant that Robert Rhoads, general counsel for seventeen years, now reported to Hyde instead of to another senior Wal-Mart official. In May 2002 Rhoads retired and was replaced by Tom Mars, who had served as head of the Arkansas State Police from 1998 to 2001. Before that Mars had acquired a reputation in Arkansas for bringing a number of successful class-action lawsuits against large companies. That kind of experience would serve him well since Wal-Mart faced a growing number of class-action suits.

One of the main reasons Hyde was hired was the recognition that Wal-Mart was losing cases it should have won and being publicly criticized in the process.

Built into the new legal culture was a fresh attitude that the company's lawyers were there to represent the company, to do what was in the best interest of the company and its shareholders, not to protect management.

There was a sense of caution among Wal-Mart litigators as these new policies, decreed from the top, were implemented. Announcing them slowly, the litigators recognized that the policies would take time to gain traction. The last thing they wanted was to announce a policy shift only to have the courts, sensing that nothing had really changed, fall back on its old perceptions of Wal-Mart.

By October 2002 the legal department believed it was still too early to assess how the changes were being perceived within the legal community. But its opponents in courtrooms had already sensed a change and were talking to the media about it.

In view of Hyde's responsibility to reshape Wal-Mart's image, he could have easily been given the title of executive vice president for Wal-Mart's reputation.

★ ★ ★

Deeply engrained in the Wal-Mart culture was the view that anyone working for the company had to be able to show that his or her labors contributed directly to the customers, to getting the customers to come back to the stores time after time. The company's legal department was working hard to gear its efforts toward the customer. The best example was the manner in which the Wal-Mart legal staff adopted a new approach toward store-related injury lawsuits. In the past, Wal-Mart's lawyers sought only to win these lawsuits, but under the new legal team, that was too narrow a view of their role: Wal-Mart's lawyers were now expected to understand why store accidents occurred in order to reduce or eliminate them.

Clearly there was a reason to fix what was wrong. Wal-Mart had no desire to have a reputation that its stores or parking lots were unsafe or that items might fall on a customer in a store, because all these unpleasant events influenced whether a customer returned to the store or not. No one expected Wal-Mart to have an unblemished record when it came to store accidents, but equally no one would tolerate the same accident happening over and over again. That could cause terrible harm to Wal-Mart's reputation.

Previously Wal-Mart's lawyers contended that the company was not responsible for some of the accidents. Now they acknowledged that what mattered was not whether Wal-Mart was responsible but whether it was doing everything within reason to prevent their recurrence.

With so many lawsuits pending, meaningful statistical data now existed that enabled someone at Wal-Mart to figure out to the penny what a slip and fall in a Wal-Mart store was likely to cost. When the new legal management team told management: This is costing you money here, this is coming right out of your margins, driving the price up to the customer, the management listened—and acted.

Wal-Mart's lawyers were pleased to discover that their ability to identify patterns in injuries could prove very helpful indeed.

Here were lawyers, usually considered so important to a company that they never had to justify what they did on a day-to-day basis, now making a serious attempt to show that they were functioning well not only as lawyers but as proactive celebrants of the culture, watching out for costs by reducing store accidents. Nothing would have made Sam Walton as pleased as the double-edged mission that these lawyers were carving out for themselves.

By taking a more open attitude toward lawsuits, by trying to help reduce store accidents, the lawyers were playing a major role in recasting Wal-Mart's reputation. It would probably take time for the new attitude to reach the courts and the media, but a start had been made.

★ ★ ★

What was new about Wal-Mart's attitude toward the growing controversy surrounding the company's reputation was the way the nineties' management team handled the problem. It could have relied on its old policies and attitudes. But Wal-Mart's leaders sensed that new attitudes and new strategies were needed. They had looked at the criticism of the company and decided that too many people with hostile intent were defining, or trying to define, Wal-Mart. So they decided to develop a higher degree of sophistication in their public relations, legal, and community affairs departments. All of these areas in 2002 were projecting a new attitude of engagement, of openness, of trying to understand what the roots of the criticism were, of making quick assessments on whether the criticism was valid, and, if valid, fixing the problem.

In an interview in October 2002, Lee Scott noted that he was spending a good deal more time on the issue of Wal-Mart's reputation than David Glass had. He believed that the effort was paying off. "I've been critical that we've let someone else define our reputation. We are doing a much more thorough and sophisticated job of understanding what our reputation is with the people that matter the most.

What are those issues that we are creating for ourselves that we need to resolve?

"So we've taken a much more sophisticated stance. We are now more likely to ask: What does it mean to us? What do we have to do? We've taken a very healthy attitude. Take the *New York Times*. When they write something critical of Wal-Mart, instead of throwing the article in the trash and saying simply that it's inaccurate, we now say, is it possible that this is true? Is there something we're not doing that we're not admitting to ourselves that we need to face up to? We want to stop being so defensive toward external criticism. After all, we're not defensive when a customer says your store is dirty and I got rude treatment. We get it fixed. But when the media attacks us, some find it easy to assume it's because they are biased and there's some agenda that they have. I don't think that's particularly healthy for us. We have to read the article and see if it's true."

★ ★ ★

Even as a new degree of sophistication was showing up in Wal-Mart's relationships with the external world, the company still felt that it needed more research, more data, more understanding of how important audiences viewed the company. That determination to learn more about what people felt about the company reflected Wal-Mart's new willingness to engage in in-depth self-examination and to become proactive in improving its reputation.

For the first time, the company undertook a comprehensive reputation research strategy. It was launched early in 2002. Initially the strategy aimed at five key audiences: 1) customers; 2) local community leaders, including city council members, newspaper editors and members of chambers of commerce; 3) Wal-Mart employees; 4) suppliers; and 5) the financial community. Each group would be asked how it felt about Wal-Mart's reputation as a retailer, as a valued local business and citizen, and as an employer. Not included in the survey were inquiries about how frequently people shopped at a Wal-Mart or which products they preferred. The purpose of the survey was to gauge the company's reputation, nothing else.

By August 2002 most of the research on the first three audiences had been completed. Jay Allen, who was in charge of the reputation survey, offered a preliminary finding on the results thus far, noting that on the whole "we are seeing that our reputation is very good." But the research did reveal certain important facts: One was that people who did not respect Wal-Mart in general also had little respect for the company's jobs. They were filled with misperceptions about Wal-Mart employees: that a majority were part time (not true: two-thirds of Wal-Mart's jobs are full time); that the pay was the minimum wage (not true: It is above minimum wage in all cases and competitive in the local market); that employees do not receive benefits (not true: They do); that there was nowhere to go in a Wal-Mart job (not true: 70 percent of Wal-Mart managers started as hourly employees, including many people in senior positions with the company in 2002).

Learning that those misperceptions existed could prove vital for Wal-Mart as it searched for ways to improve its reputation. The misperceptions certainly suggested that Wal-Mart had to find ways to inform the public more successfully about the company, particularly with regard to its employees and their jobs.

The survey also revealed that the people who did not respect Wal-Mart also did not respect Wal-Mart as a good neighbor, defined as anything from charitable involvement in the communities to maintaining the cleanliness of the stores inside and outside.

"The board and senior management have become extremely interested in this research and our overall reputation," said Jay Allen. "They see the lawsuits and the other negative stories instigated by our opponents. Their concern is appropriate. The world changed for Wal-Mart after Sam Walton passed away. When you reach the size and success level that we have, the rules are going to change, and many are going to use your good name to focus attention on their respective agendas. There are agendas associated with labor unions, antigrowth agendas; there are all kinds of agendas out there. One way to get your story in the paper is to include Wal-Mart in it.

"However, we also have to balance this with the fact that there are people and communities with sincere concerns and even misconceptions about Wal-Mart. We have to be sure that we listen in these cases and that we do our best to answer and respond to their concerns."

"The research shows us that we have a very good reputation. That tells us we're doing OK; it's not like we have a bad reputation. In fact, we have a great opportunity to tell our good story, given all the interest in us and the fact that we are entering new communities all the time. It's perfectly fair for the public and for local city councils to question us as a company and expect us to be a good citizen in our communities. It is clear that we need to do a better job of explaining that we provide jobs that pay competitively and offer unlimited career opportunities.

"We received definite feedback that some of our stores weren't being kept up, and this hurt us in communities as showing a lack of respect. We need to do better to maintain stores, whether landscaping or too many trailers in the back or a dirty parking lot. And we need to do better at helping people understand the positive economic benefit we represent in communities, from jobs and taxes paid to raising the standard of living through lower prices."

★ ★ ★

A new attitude was beginning to surface in the top management at Wal-Mart. It had to do with turning the controversy and the negative criticism on its head. Rather than show disdain for the negativism, a feeling was growing that there was a virtue in having the media and community activists monitoring Wal-Mart. If not for such vigilance, Wal-Mart might not have a complete sense of what needed to be fixed in its stores. The new attitude embraced the idea that discovering faults need not be embarrassing. Wal-Mart was a huge operation with many moving parts; no one could possibly expect perfect behavior 100 percent of the time.

In keeping with this new openness was a growing belief that Wal-Mart's leaders should have some media exposure. The pain and suffering caused by the *Dateline* program was clearly receding. This did not mean that Rob Walton would start granting interviews, but it did mean that Lee Scott would appear more in public. It might not take a year or two before a television network could interview Scott, nor would it be out of the question for an author to gain access to the upper echelons of the company.

Scott was fully conscious that he was leading the largest company in the world in terms of revenue. He was all too aware that the media wanted to hear from him on a continuing basis. No longer did a Wal-Mart leader have to fear that he would divulge information that a rival might feast on. Scott knew what to say and, more importantly, what not to say. He was confident that whatever questions he might be asked, he could deal with. He doubted there would be any more ambushes.

★ ★ ★

That Wal-Mart had the time and energy to devote so many resources to sprucing up its reputation was perhaps as much a sign of the company's financial success as anything else. As the year 2002 was coming to a close, Wal-Mart was poised to set new records and to maintain its position as the largest company in the world in terms of revenue. Few believed that the growth engine would slow down. Within Wal-Mart the leadership exuded cautious optimism in public; in private it believed that the company had a chance to get even closer to the stars.

PART SIX

WHITHER WAL-MART?

CHAPTER 14

WHERE THE FUTURE
WILL TAKE WAL-MART

Wal-Mart's leadership remained confident in the winter of 2002 that the company had plenty more room to grow.

Still moving into American suburbs, still building Wal-Marts in small American towns and medium-sized cities, Wal-Mart continued to shy away from the large cities. "We've never felt compelled," said Scott, "to put a store in downtown New York City."

CEO Lee Scott believes that Wal-Mart has a great deal more opportunity to grow. "When you think about our market share (7.9 percent in the United States) there are a lot of companies that have achieved 35 to 40 percent in specific categories like food; Tesco has 25 percent of food sales in the United Kingdom. When you think of those numbers, the truth is we could be twice or four times the size we are. On an international basis we hardly register in retail stores internationally. We are not in France, Italy, Spain, or Turkey. Just go through the list.

"In the big population centers, we think it could be a little more difficult. Real estate is difficult. It's a big step when you get into rents and costs. We think getting into the cities is a great opportunity, but it is not one we have to step into in a significant way today. We have all those opportunities in those suburbs around major population centers. You'll see us sprinkle a store here or there that will give us a base of understanding so when we decide to be more aggressive we would be equipped to answer questions about that (urban market) strategy."

★ ★ ★

The future continues to look rosy for Wal-Mart.

One indication of how well Wal-Mart was doing came on November 29, 2002, the day after Thanksgiving, when it reported record one-day sales of $1.4 billion at its American stores. That represented the largest single-day sales figure for Wal-Mart ever, higher than its day-after Thanksgiving Day sales of $1.25 billion in 2001.

Sales for the nine months that ended October 31, 2002, were $173 billion, an increase of 12.9 percent over the same period a year before. Profit for the same nine months jumped 22.9 percent to a record $5.5 billion or $1.24 per share, up from $4.5 billion or $1.00 per share.

The international division was on course for another record-breaking year as well: The division's sales for the first thirty-nine weeks of 2002 were $29 billion, up 10.9 percent over the $26 billion in the similar period a year ago.

★ ★ ★

If Wal-Mart's leaders worried about any one area of growth as the year 2002 was ending, it was staffing the managerial positions in stores fast enough to keep up with planned expansion. Michael Duke, the executive vice president for administration, insisted that "we will not build stores when we feel we can't put the right leaders in the stores. We could open more Supercenters this year and next year, but what we want to make sure is that we can manage them effectively. That has to do with how quickly you train managers. We can train a manager quickly, but you can't develop a leader quickly."

To cope with the challenge, Lee Scott asked Coleman Peterson, the head of the people division, to organize a series of two-week training programs, known as the Business Leadership Series, for Wal-Mart personnel deemed to have managerial potential.

The series began in October 2001. All the sessions are taught by

David Glass, Lee Scott, and those executives who report directly to Scott. The sessions are split into five days in the spring and five days in the fall. Besides a series of lectures from the senior Wal-Mart leadership team there is an action learning component, in which a cross-functional group from each class dissects a Wal-Mart or Sam's Club business case and offers recommendations to Scott and his direct reports. David Glass and Michael Duke teach a course on seasoned judgment, which includes a discussion on how to say no. Tom Coughlin teaches Driving Execution; Lee Scott, Transformational Leadership; Tom Schoewe, Financial Acumen (Cash Is King); Coleman Peterson, Attracting and Selecting Talent; Tom Hyde, People and Compliance; and John Menzer, Strategic Planning and Global Marketplace. The program is held at the University of Arkansas in Fayetteville. With new managers and leaders being trained all the time, Wal-Mart felt comfortable announcing ambitious plans to expand for 2003.

In the United States, Wal-Mart plans to open 45 to 55 new discount stores and 200 to 210 new Supercenters; 40 to 45 Sam's Clubs and 20 to 25 Neighborhood Markets. Wal-Mart international planned to open 120 to 130 units in existing markets. All of these additions will represent some 48 million square feet of new retail space, an 8 percent increase over the previous year. Another three regional general merchandise distribution centers and six new food distribution centers would be built, adding nearly 8.7 million square feet in distribution space.

With such ambitious plans for expansion, Wal-Mart will most likely require 800,000 more employees in the United States through 2008. Wal-Mart and Sam's Club expect to hire 6,500 new managers for their American stores and clubs in 2003.

★ ★ ★

As each day passed, the new generation of Wal-Mart leaders applied Sam Walton's business philosophy and culture through its thousands of stores, still believing that Walton's business wisdom continued to have profound relevance for the running of the stores in the twenty-first century. At the same time, Lee Scott and his leadership team were starting to come to grips with the new Wal-Mart, one that had become far more complex, visible, and controversial.

Some of the issues that had propelled the controversies still remained, though some had disappeared. The false advertising charge that NBC's *Dateline* tried to pin on Wal-Mart had become a distant memory. The Wal-Mart Buy America campaign ended in the mid-1990s: The company, becoming more globalized, sought to encourage the purchase of local products in the various countries it served. The so-called sweatshop issue, replete with charges that Wal-Mart had employed illegal child labor in Bangladesh, cropped up now and again. Wal-Mart's leadership made clear that it was keeping a close eye on the overseas factories where Wal-Mart merchandise was made. To make sure that those factories were not employing anyone illegally, Wal-Mart organized a steady stream of inspections. In 2002 a new global procurement organization in Wal-Mart had responsibility for the inspection program.

★ ★ ★

On January 30, 2003, Wal-Mart kicked off its annual opening meeting for ten thousand store managers. The venue was the Kansas City, Missouri, Convention Center. As with all Wal-Mart mass gatherings, the celebrities stopped by: ex-NFL star quarterback John Elway, New York Yankee shortstop Derek Jeter, former Baltimore Orioles shortstop Cal Ripkin, country and western singer Tracy Atkins, and poet Maya Angelou. They were there to motivate, entertain, and, in some cases, promote products that store managers are then supposed to highlight in their stores. The audience loved seeing them. But there was more to the meeting than the cameo appearances of celebrities.

The rock and roll music that warmed up the crowd, the enthusiastic screaming of the audience, and the Wal-Mart cheer that opened the session lent the proceedings the same celebratory air as the June 2002 shareholder meeting. And, as at the shareholder gathering, there was much for Wal-Mart to celebrate.

Not a single speaker mentioned that Wal-Mart would likely be the number-one company in the world in terms of revenue for the second year in a row. But since the company's revenues were due to increase by at least $25 billion in 2002—up from $219.8 billion in 2001—it was all but inevitable that Wal-Mart would head the *Fortune* 500 list once again.

There was no mention of the heady statistic because the senior leadership knew all too well how uncertain the future of retailing was, given the harsh economic landscape that seemed likely to prevail for much of 2003. And so the main themes for store managers to absorb on this cold Thursday morning in Kansas City were execution and ownership. Speaker after speaker urged the crowd to execute better—specifically, to improve customer service by keeping shelves stocked and reducing the wait in checkout lines, among other things.

The secret of execution was making sure that employees felt a sense of ownership over the segment of the store under their sway. To instill the sense of ownership, senior executives rolled out a brand-new message for employees: It's My Wal-Mart!

"Whose Wal-Mart is it?" various division managers yelled out to the audience over and over.

And each time ten thousand store managers responded, "It's *my* Wal-Mart."

Senior executives congratulated the audience for another sparkling year as sales and earnings soared once again into double-digit territory. But always there were voices attempting to keep the store managers' focus on the need to avoid coasting. CFO Tom Schoewe warned that store managers had to pay greater attention to asset management in order to help Wal-Mart realize its ambitious growth plans. To get the audience's attention, he walked in between a pair of jugglers, who were tossing flaming batons back and forth.

Wal-Mart's leadership zealously imparted the message: Don't rest on your laurels. There are still mountains to conquer. To that end, Schoewe acknowledged that Wal-Mart's share of overall retail sales in the United States had increased from 6 percent in 1998 to 7.9 percent in 2002. But he threw out the statistic only to point out that there was another 92.1 percent of possible retail share for Wal-Mart to pursue.

★ ★ ★

If the future held out the opportunity for even greater prospects of growth for Wal-Mart, the same future also had senior executives worrying about the company's reputation. That reputation had been damaged in 2002 in part by allegations against a handful of store managers accused of forcing employees to work "off the clock" in order to keep costs in line. As noted in Chapter 13, executives were tackling the reputation issue head on, but until now they had kept a relatively low profile on their efforts to improve the company's reputation, at least with the store managers.

And so, Lee Scott spoke at length that morning in Kansas City of the urgent need for Wal-Mart employees to comply with the company's rules. He did not raise the issue right away. Instead he spoke of the likely pressures on American consumers in 2003—higher oil prices, further unemployment, etc.—and suggested that as consumers accordingly tightened their belts, they would be prone to shop at low-priced Wal-Marts. This preference for Wal-Mart represented an opportunity he hoped the store managers would make the most of in 2003.

Scott segued neatly into the reputation issue by noting how many retail buyers had been guests of suppliers at the recent NFL Super Bowl in San Diego. "We don't do that at Wal-Mart. Our customer is not paying a penny more so our buyers can go to the Super Bowl."

Then, as part of the list of things he worried about in 2003, Scott included "those class action lawsuits." Scott was referring to several recent and well-publicized lawsuits against Wal-Mart alleging that some company managers, in order to control payroll expenses, encouraged or instructed hourly associates to perform unpaid work. Otherwise known as working off the clock, this practice violates Wal-Mart policy. Addressing the store managers directly, he asked:

"How could you believe that it would be OK to ask someone to work off the clock so you weren't in trouble with the district manager? You can't understand the company if you're willing to do that."

Proudly noting that Wal-Mart escaped mention within the media in the corporate corruption scandals of 2001 and 2002, Scott suggested it was "because we follow the law. We do the right thing." Pausing, he told the store managers: "You have to do the right thing."

Observing that the world had changed and people want to define a company like Wal-Mart "by our exceptions," he suggested it was no longer possible to escape scrutiny if 95 percent of your employees were obeying the rules—"100 percent of us must do the right thing every day . . . Can you do that?" he shouted. "Do you understand it is life threatening to the company? This goes to the very being of Wal-Mart and our ability to exist."

★ ★ ★

February 18, 2003 was a day for the Wal-Mart history books. For it was on that day that *Fortune* magazine announced that Wal-Mart ranked number one on its 2003 Most Admired List of American companies, marking the first time that the giant retailer had headed that list (Wal-Mart had been number three in 2002). With Wal-Mart's ranking number one on the 2002 *Fortune* list of American corporations, it was also the first time that one company headed both lists at the same time. And on that same February 18, 2003, Wal-Mart announced record revenue and earnings for 2002: Revenue was up just over 12 percent to $244.5 billion from $219.8 billion the year before; and earnings rose to $7.8 billion, a healthy increase from the previous year's nearly $7 billion. And on that same day, an article appeared in *Fortune,* exalting Wal-Mart for capturing the top spot on its Most Admired List, suggesting that Lee Scott was running what was arguably the world's most powerful company and one that was playing an important role in raising the standards of living for millions of consumers. As evidence of its power, the article noted that Wal-Mart had become the largest customer for many of the mightiest companies in the United States, including Procter & Gamble,

Kraft, and Revlon. It also suggested that Wal-Mart had become the largest single revenue producer for Hollywood. Indeed, February 18, 2003 had been quite a day for Wal-Mart.

★ ★ ★

In case anyone had had any doubts, it was now clear to all Wal-Mart managers that the company had become fully engaged in a broader mission. In addition to being the best retailer in the world, Wal-Mart now felt it must be equally dedicated to becoming the best possible employer and best possible local citizen. Wal-Mart officials believed that heading the *Fortune* Most Admired List was an important step toward achieving that broader mission. With the battle still not won, Wal-Mart knew that it could not afford to grow complacent, not even when it was the largest and most admired company.

ACKNOWLEDGMENTS

When Adrian Zackheim, the publisher of Penguin Putnam's Portfolio, raised the idea of my writing a book on Wal-Mart in its post-Sam Walton years, I was only mildly conscious of the company's achievements. I instantly recalled Jack Welch, the former chairman and CEO of General Electric, telling me what great affection he had for Sam Walton and how much he admired Wal-Mart's "quick market intelligence," its system of gathering data from senior executives on a weekly basis after their three-or four-day visits to Wal-Mart stores. Looking into Wal-Mart, I quickly realized Wal-Mart was one of the most powerful and influential companies in America. And indeed, within a month of my conversation with Adrian, Wal-Mart, for the first time, topped the *Fortune* 500 list of American companies in terms of revenue, with $219.8 billion. It took little time or effort for me to conclude that a book on Wal-Mart at this juncture would be both timely and (hopefully) significant.

As I began the research for *The Wal-Mart Triumph: Inside the World's #1 Company*, I approached Wal-Mart's public relations department to let them know that I was under contract to Portfolio to do a book on Wal-Mart. I hoped that I would be able to interview senior officials and make the rounds of Wal-Mart stores. At this juncture, I had no real grasp of how media- and author-shy Wal-Mart had been over the years. I knew of course that Sam Walton had written his memoirs, *Sam Walton: Made in America*. I knew also that a number of books, some of them quite negative, had been written about Walton and Wal-Mart during the 1990s. What I did not know was that Wal-Mart had never cooperated with an author.

I made my first visit to Wal-Mart's home office in early May 2002, where I met Tom Williams, Wal-Mart's senior manager for U.S. Media Relations. He arranged for me to visit some Wal-Mart stores, permitted me to interview store managers, and sat down with me for some lengthy interviews. He then invited me to return on June 7 for the annual shareholder meeting. Although it was still six weeks before the gathering, everyone I met at the home office talked excitedly about it. I couldn't quite understand why people would get pumped up over a shareholder meeting, an event that normally makes most people yawn. I looked forward to returning to Bentonville not only to attend the meeting but also to get some indication if I would be able to interview the senior leaders of Wal-Mart.

Upon my returning to Bentonville that first week of June, Tom Williams informed me that a meeting had been scheduled two days after at which I would get to meet Tom Hyde, the executive vice president for legal and corporate affairs, and Jay Allen, the senior vice president for corporate affairs. I was told that the purpose of the meeting was for them to meet me, not for me to interview them. I realized how important this get-together was for the future of my project.

The meeting began on a friendly note, and lots of questions were put to me about the kind of book that I planned to write. But while I had broached the question of my interviewing senior officials, no one had given me the green light. Then Tom Hyde exited without explaining why; a few minutes later, he returned and announced that he had brought a special guest. I looked at the door. There was Lee Scott, Wal-Mart's CEO. A few minutes earlier I was concerned over whether I would get a chance to interview senior executives, now here was Lee Scott, sitting down for our first chat. He knew that I had just finished a book called *Eye of the Storm: How John Chambers Steered Cisco Through the Technology Collapse.* John Chambers, the president and CEO of Cisco Systems, is a member of the Wal-Mart board. That was an interesting coincidence, I thought.

It didn't take very long for Scott to indicate that I could go forward with interviews of Wal-Mart executives and that I would be able to continue my visits to Wal-Mart stores.

Two days later, I attended the shareholder meeting at the Bud Walton Arena in Fayetteville, a thirty-minute drive south from Wal-

Mart's Home Office in Bentonville. By the time I entered the arena at 6 A.M., many of the twenty thousand people who showed up that morning were already in their seats, cheering, shouting, having a great time. There was no yawning at this event. The shareholder meeting was crucial to my research for a number of reasons. It gave me a chance to listen for the first time to most of the company's senior executives as they gave brief talks during the morning. It gave me a rare opportunity to hear Rob Walton, Sam's eldest son and Wal-Mart's chairman for the past decade, as he conducted the meeting. (I eventually interviewed both Rob and his brother John, who like Rob served on the Wal-Mart board.) Sitting in the arena that day, I gained appreciation for the excitement and enthusiasm that is part and parcel of the Wal-Mart culture, and it helped me get a sense of how far the company had come in the past decade, the decade when Sam Walton's successors ruled the roost and took the company to its Number One perch.

Throughout the rest of my research, I made a point of visiting as many Wal-Mart stores as I could, not only to interview various Wal-Mart staffers but also to soak up the culture and the atmosphere of the company. I learned quickly that the culture Sam Walton created and his successors are still applying exists in the stores but has much less application to Wal-Mart's corporate organization. It was crucial to walk the aisles and watch employees and customers interact, to watch the greeters at the front door in action, to talk to store managers. I visited stores in many places: Bentonville and Alma, Arkansas; Newport News, Virginia; Queensbury, New York; Los Angeles, California; and Shenzhen, China. It occurred to me that I could not write about Wal-Mart's international operations without getting to see at least one of those overseas efforts. I chose China for reasons that I set out in the chapter on my visit there. The visit added enormously to my understanding of the complexity and the achievements of the company.

Getting the chance to roam far and wide, to talk with numerous Wal-Mart executives, to soak up the atmosphere of the stores—none of this could have come about without some exceptionally professional people at Wal-Mart, who helped me get to know the place as much as an outsider can in the time allotted to my research.

A number of people in the corporate affairs/public relations section of Wal-Mart were enormously helpful, and I want to give them special thanks: First and foremost, I want to express my gratitude to Tom Hyde, executive vice president, legal and corporate affairs; Jay Allen, the senior vice president for corporate affairs; and the other public-relations professionals who were there to guide me through Wal-Mart, to answer my many questions, and to help me understand the company. I want to express special thanks to Jay. When we met he told me that he wanted to do everything he could to help the project. He fulfilled that promise in many ways, in numerous phone and in-person conversations and lots of E-mails.

Besides them, there was Mona Williams, vice president for communications; Tom Williams, senior manager of communications; and Sharon Weber, Karen Burk, and Cynthia Illick, all communications managers. I am also extremely appreciative of the help that James Lee, vice president for corporate affairs, legal, and administration for Wal-Mart China, provided me during my visit to China. Thanks also to May Huang, government relations manager for Wal-Mart China.

I also wish to thank those who granted me interviews: Celia Clancy, Cassian Cheung, Ed Clifford, Tom Coughlin, Doug Degn, Trevor Drinkwater, Michael Duke, Irene Du, David Ferguson, Al Galvan, David Glass, Don Harris, Joe Hatfield, Deborah Lee, Jorge López, Bob Martin, Kent Martz, John Menzer, Claudia Mobley, Noam Meppen, Emily Nelson, Jeff Necessary, Frank Paris, Angel Pérez, Coleman Peterson, Gary Raines, Elizabeth Sanders, Jack Shewmaker, Tom Schoewe, Jeff Slater, Don Soderquist, Jason Sotkin, Steven Sotkin, Sonny Sue, Alisa Swire, Kevin Turner, Wes Waddell, John Walton, Rob Walton, Deborah Weinswig, Wesley C. Wright, and George Zhao.

I've been very fortunate to have both a loving and caring wife and a professional editor, all in the same person: Elinor Slater. While carrying on with her own full-time job as a university administrator and keeping our home and family in good working order, she managed to edit this book with great care and toughness. I am deeply grateful for the time and effort she made.

It's been a pleasure working closely once again with Adrian Zackheim, who came up with the idea of this book and who had faith from the beginning that I would be able to tackle the subject successfully. Knowing that he was there day in and day out and had a great sense of how this book should be shaped and executed has given me great comfort. Just as important, he is a good friend. An author cannot do better than that.

I thank also Will Weisser, marketing director at Portfolio, for his deep interest in the book and all the hard work he has put in to make this book a success.

I dedicate this book to the three most veteran shoppers in my immediate family, who could never have guessed that one day I would write a book about a chain of retail stores: my late mother, Gertrude Slater; my sister, Roslyn Winick; and my sister-in-law, Bea Slater.

Robert Slater
January 2003

NOTES

CHAPTER 1 CELEBRATING IN A BASKETBALL ARENA

"The betting in dozens. . . ." *Time*, "The Two Sides of the Sam Walton Legacy," April 20, 2002.

"We thought it was crucial. . . ." John Walton, interview with author, October 30, 2002. All John Walton quotes are from that interview.

"There's no feeling . . ." Rob Walton, interview with author, August 5, 2002. All Rob Walton quotes are from that interview unless otherwise stated.

CHAPTER 2 THE MAN FROM KINGFISHER

"No one better personified . . ." *Time*, "Sam Walton," December 7, 1998.

"I lack the ability. . . ." *Sam Walton: Made in America, My Story*. New York: Bantam Books (paperback), June 1993 pp. 4–5. (Doubleday hardcover published June 1992.)

"sad-looking country town." Helen Walton, quoted in *Sam Walton: Made in America*, p. 41.

"Say I bought. . . ." ibid., pp. 32–33.

"I have always been a maverick. . . ." ibid., p. 61.

"he could have owned. . . ." David Glass, interview with author, August 8, 2002. All David Glass quotes are from my interviews with him on August 8, 2002, and October 3, 2002, unless otherwise stated.

"I have occasionally heard myself compared . . ." *Sam Walton: Made in America*, pp. 100–101.

In the spring of 1987. *Time*, "Make That Sale, Mr. Sam." May 18, 1987.

"Sam never went. . . ." Helen Walton, quoted in *Sam Walton: Made in America*, p. 91.

"Sam Walton had more wealth. . . ." *Fortune*, "David Glass Won't Crack Under Fire," February 8, 1993.

"folksy, frugal retailing dynamo." *Time*, Milestones, April 20, 1992.

CHAPTER 3 GIVE ME A SQUIGGLY: SAM WALTON'S CULTURE

"just over one million people. . . ." *Fortune*, "Sam Walton Made Us a Promise," March 18, 2002.

"I wasn't on the front row. . . ." Lee Scott, interview with CNBC, March 18, 2002.

Walton's Ten Rules of Business appear in *Sam Walton: Made in America*, pp. 314–17.

"Find some humor in your failures." ibid., p. 316.

"Go the other way." ibid., p. 317.

"Outfitted like a bus station, complete with plastic seats." "Make That Sale, Mr. Sam," ibid.

"Dad always said. . . ." Jim Walton, quoted in *Sam Walton: Made in America*, p. 89.

"was that we can always do. . . ." Kevin Turner, interview with author, August 6, 2002.

CHAPTER 4 AVOID THE LAYERS, AVOID THE FRILLS

"He didn't want us to become. . . ." Don Soderquist, interview with author, August 5, 2002. All Don Soderquist quotes are from that interview unless otherwise stated.

"We were rarely thought. . . ." Jack Shewmaker, interview with author, October 15, 2002.

"We gave up something. . . ." Bob Martin, interview with author, October 4, 2002. All other Bob Martin quotes are from that interview.

"Sam had no use . . . ," Lee Scott, interview with author, August 8, 2002. All other Lee Scott quotes are from that interview or another one with the author on October 3, 2002, unless otherwise stated.

"As companies get larger. . . ." *Sam Walton: Made in America*, p. 137.

"He would tell us. . . ." Wesley Wright, interview with author, October 5, 2002. All Wesley Wright quotes are from that interview.

"I've taken fourteen media. . . ." interview with author, September 30, 2002. The official asked not to be identified.

"We never did. . . ." *Sam Walton: Made in America*, p. xi.

"When you go public. . . ." Helen Walton, quoted in *Sam Walton: Made in America*, p. 127

"we were just a bunch. . . ." *Sam Walton: Made in America*, p. 3.

"as a really cheap. . . ." ibid., p. 3.

CHAPTER 5 A NEW MANAGEMENT TEAM FOLLOWS MR. SAM

"He was such an icon." Kent Marts, interview with author, August 15, 2002.

"We don't need the money." *Sam Walton: Made in America*, p. 9.

"We're not made up of celebrities." Lee Scott, quoted by Reuters, December 18, 2002.

"an unmatched feat. . . ." *Fortune*, "Can Wal-Mart Get Back the Magic?" April 29, 1996.

CHAPTER 6 A STRATEGY OF GROWTH

"It was the retail equivalent. . . ." *Sam Walton: Made in America*, p. 152.

"I always wanted to be. . . ." ibid., p. 276–77.

"itch." ibid., p. 44.

"quite a stretch." David Glass, quoted in the 1997 Wal-Mart Annual Report, p. 3.

"you constantly have. . . ." *Sam Walton: Made in America*, p. 135.

"When I came to Wal-Mart. . . ." David Glass, the 2000 Wal-Mart Annual Report, p. 4.

At least 650,000. . . . Jay Allen told me this in an E-mail dated November 27, 2002. This was the number of employees who participate in the Wal-Mart profit-sharing plan; the actual number of employees who own stock could be higher, as other employees may have bought the stock on their own.

"To say they were a struggle. . . ." Don Harris, interview with author, August 15, 2002. All Don Harris quotes in this chapter are from that interview.

"When Wal-Mart Mart strides into a new market," *Newsweek*, "Wal-Mart World," April 20, 2002.

CHAPTER 7 THE MORE COMPLEX WAL-MART TODAY

"We do everything we can. . . ." Tom Coughlin, interview with author, October 3, 2002. All Tom Coughlin quotes are from my interviews with him on August 29, 2002, and October 3, 2002.

"When I came here . . ." Coleman Peterson, interview with author, August 13, 2002. All Coleman Peterson quotes are from that interview unless otherwise stated.

"There was an underlying. . . ." interview with author, October 3, 2002. The official asked not to be identified.

"We're a bunch of suits to them." Tom Hyde, interview with author, October 3, 2002.

CHAPTER 8 APPLYING THE CULTURE A STORE AT A TIME

"If you treat. . . ." Gary Raines, interview with author, May 2, 2002.

David Glass's anecdote of his tour of Wal-Mart stores is in *Fortune*, "David Glass Won't Crack Under Fire," February 8, 1993.

CHAPTER 9 BEYOND THE SEAS: A NEW OUTLET FOR GROWTH

"Over the years many. . . ." Don Soderquist, quoted in the 1999 Wal-Mart Annual Report, p. 5.

"The company's distribution system is regarded. . . ." "The Retail Revolution," *McLean's*, March 1, 1999.

"The international division was very. . . ." John Menzer, interview with author, August 6, 2002. All John Menzer quotes are from that interview.

"We got confused. . . ." Lee Scott, CNBC, March 18, 2002.

"We'll be successful because. . . ." ibid.

"They had a great management team. . . ." Rob Walton, quoted in the 2000 Wal-Mart Annual Report, p. 3.

CHAPTER 10 LIVE SNAKES AND TURTLE RACES: WAL-MART IN CHINA

"Probably the biggest issue. . . ." Joe Hatfield, interview with author, November 7, 2002. All Joe Hatfield quotes are from that interview.

"If an employee made a mistake. . . ." George Zhao, interview with author, November 8, 2002.

"We have had to get. . . ." Cassian Cheung, interview with author, November 7, 2002.

"If you are not performing. . . ." Irene Du, interview with author, November 8, 2002.

CHAPTER 11 MR. LOGISTICS TAKES OVER

"I may not be the smartest person. . . ." Lee Scott, quoted in *Fortune*, "Sam Would be Proud," April 17, 2000.

"If it's right for the company, let's do that." Scott, quoted in *Business Week*, "Someday, Lee, This May All Be Yours," November 15, 1999.

"Although this was an acceptable year. . . ." David Glass quoted in letter to shareholders in the 1996 Wal-Mart Annual Report, p. 2.

"This is a company. . . ." *Fortune*, "Can Wal-Mart Get Back the Magic?"

"David [Glass] and Lee talked. . . ." Jay Allen, interview with author, August 5, 2002. All Jay Allen quotes are from my interviews with him on June 7, 2002; August 5, 2002; November 13 and 27, 2002; and December 17, 2002.

CHAPTER 12 A MATTER OF REPUTATION: TAKING THE GLOVES OFF

"The more successful you become. . . ." *Sam Walton: Made in America,* p. 227.

CHAPTER 13 A STRATEGY FOR THE TWENTY-FIRST CENTURY: THE NEW OPENNESS

"The company never seeks out. . . ." Tom Williams, interview with author, September 30, 2002. All Tom Williams quotes are from my interviews with him on May 2, 2002; August 5, 2002; and September 30, 2002.

CHAPTER 14 WHERE THE FUTURE WILL TAKE WAL-MART

"we will not build stores. . . ." Michael Duke, interview with author, August 15, 2002.

INDEX